PRACTICE – ASSESS – DIAGNOSE

180 Days of MATH for Second Grade

Developed by
Jodene Smith

Shell Education

Publishing Credits

Dona Herweck Rice, *Editor-in-Chief*; Lee Aucoin, *Creative Director*;
Don Tran, *Print Production Manager;* Timothy J. Bradley, *Illustration Manager*;
Chris McIntyre, M.A.Ed., *Editorial Director*; Sara Johnson, M.S.Ed., *Senior Editor*;
Aubrie Nielsen, M.S.Ed., *Associate Education Editor*; Juan Chavolla, *Cover/Interior Layout Designer;*
Robin Erickson, *Production Artist;* Karen Lowe, *Illustrator;* Corinne Burton, M.A.Ed., *Publisher*

Shell Education
5482 Argosy Avenue
Huntington Beach, CA 92649-1030
www.tcmpub.com/shell-education

ISBN 978-1-4258-0805-1

Printed by: 51497
Printed in: China

TABLE OF CONTENTS

INTRODUCTION AND RESEARCH

The Need for Practice

In order to be successful in today's mathematics classroom, students must deeply understand both concepts and procedures so that they can discuss and demonstrate their understanding. Demonstrating understanding is a process that must be continually practiced in order for students to be successful. According to Marzano (2010, 83), "practice has always been, and will always be, a necessary ingredient to learning procedural knowledge at a level at which students execute it independently." Practice is especially important to help students apply their concrete, conceptual understanding to a particular procedural skill.

Understanding Assessment

In addition to providing opportunities for frequent practice, teachers must be able to assess students' understanding of mathematical procedures, terms, concepts, and reasoning (Kilpatrick, Swafford, and Findell 2001). This is important so that teachers can adequately address students' misconceptions, build on their current understanding, and challenge them appropriately.

Assessment is a long-term process that often involves careful analysis of student responses from a lesson discussion, project, practice sheet, or test. When analyzing the data, it is important for teachers to reflect on how their teaching practices may have influenced students' responses and to identify those areas where additional instruction may be required. In short, the data gathered from assessments should be used to inform instruction: slow down, speed up, or reteach. This type of assessment is called *formative assessment* and is used to provide a seamless connection between instruction and assessment (McIntosh 1997).

HOW TO USE THIS BOOK

180 Days of Math for Second Grade offers teachers and parents a full page of daily mathematics practice activities for each day of the school year.

Easy to Use and Standards-Based

These activities reinforce grade-level skills across a variety of mathematical concepts. The questions are provided as a full practice page, making them easy to prepare and implement as part of a classroom morning routine, at the beginning of each mathematics lesson, or as homework.

Every second-grade practice page provides 8 questions, each tied to a specific mathematical concept. Students are given the opportunity for regular practice in each mathematical concept, allowing them to build confidence through these quick standards-based activities.

Question	Mathematics Concept	NCTM Standard
1	**Number Sense**	Understands numbers, ways of representing numbers, relationships among numbers, and number systems
2	**Addition**	Understands meanings of operations and how they relate to one another; Computes fluently and makes reasonable estimates
3	**Subtraction**	
4	**Algebraic Thinking**	Understands patterns, relations, and functions; Represents and analyzes mathematical situations and structures using algebraic symbols
5	**Geometry**	Analyzes characteristics and properties of two-dimensional and three-dimensional geometric shapes and develops mathematical arguments about geometric relationships
6	**Measurement**	Understands measurable attributes of objects and the units, systems, and processes of measurement; Applies appropriate techniques, tools, and formulas to determine measurements
7	**Data Analysis**	Formulates questions that can be addressed with data and collects, organizes, and displays relevant data to answer them; Selects and uses appropriate statistical methods to analyze data
8	**Word Problem/Logic Problem or Mathematical Reasoning**	Builds new mathematical knowledge through problem solving; Solves problems that arise in mathematics and in other contexts

Standards are listed with the permission of the National Council of Teachers of Mathematics (NCTM). NCTM does not endorse the content or validity of these alignments.

HOW TO USE THIS BOOK *(cont.)*

Using the Practice Pages

As outlined on page 4, every question is aligned to a mathematics concept and standard.

Practice pages provide instruction and assessment opportunities for each day of the school year.

Each question ties student practice to a specific mathematics concept.

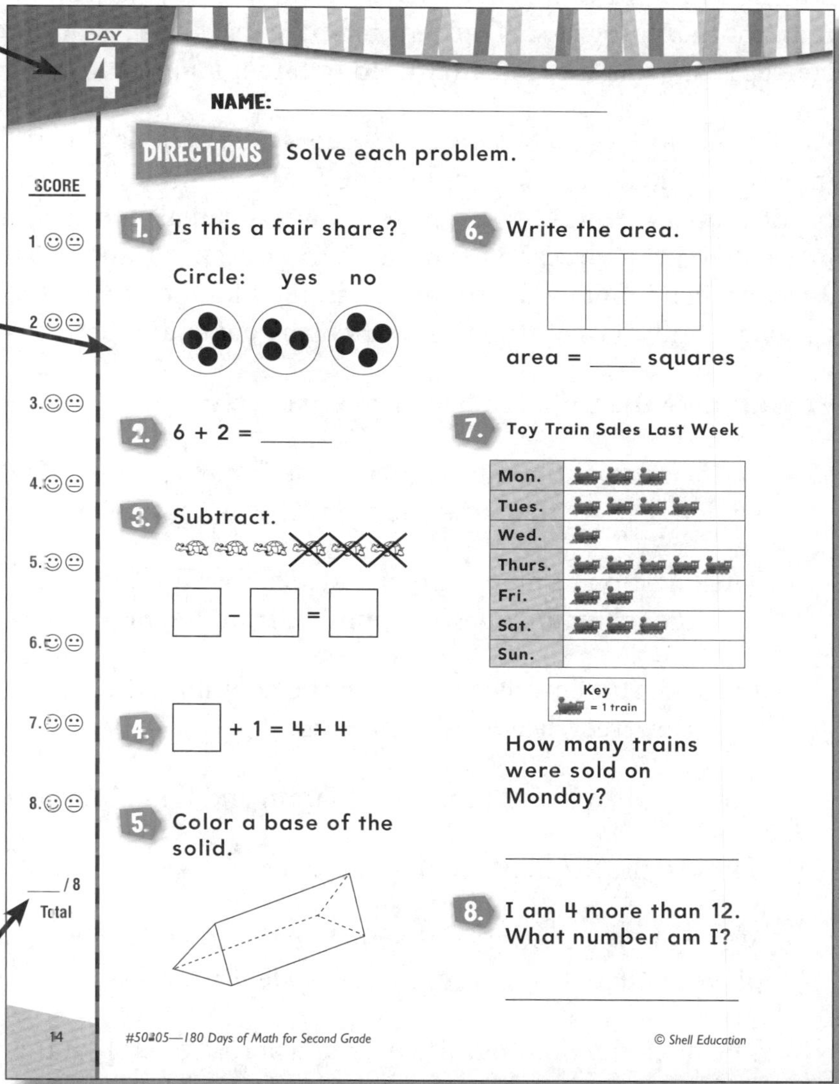
DAY 4

NAME: ____________

DIRECTIONS Solve each problem.

SCORE

1. Is this a fair share?

Circle: yes no

2. 6 + 2 = _____

3. Subtract.

☐ − ☐ = ☐

4. ☐ + 1 = 4 + 4

5. Color a base of the solid.

6. Write the area.

area = _____ squares

7. Toy Train Sales Last Week

Mon.	🚂🚂🚂
Tues.	🚂🚂🚂🚂
Wed.	🚂
Thurs.	🚂🚂🚂🚂🚂
Fri.	🚂🚂
Sat.	🚂🚂🚂
Sun.	

Key 🚂 = 1 train

How many trains were sold on Monday?

8. I am 4 more than 12. What number am I?

___ / 8 Total

14 #50805—180 Days of Math for Second Grade © Shell Education

Using the Scoring Guide

Use the scoring guide along the side of each practice page to check answers and see at a glance which skills may need more reinforcement.

Fill in the appropriate circle for each problem to indicate correct (☺) or incorrect (😐) responses. You might wish to indicate only incorrect responses to focus on those skills. (For example, if students consistently miss numbers 2 and 6, they may need additional help with those concepts as outlined in the table on page 4.) Use the answer key at the back of the book to score the problems, or you may call out answers to have students self-score or peer-score their work.

HOW TO USE THIS BOOK *(cont.)*

Diagnostic Assessment

Teachers can use the practice pages as diagnostic assessments. The data analysis tools included with the book enable teachers or parents to quickly score students' work and monitor their progress. Teachers and parents can see at a glance which mathematics concepts or skills students may need to target in order to develop proficiency.

After students complete a practice page, grade each page using the answer key (pages 191–205). Then, complete the *Practice Page Item Analysis* (page 7) for the whole class, or the *Student Item Analysis* (page 8) for individual students. These charts are also provided in the digital resources (filenames: G2_practicepage_analysis.pdf, G2_student_analysis.pdf). Teachers can input data into the electronic files directly on the computer, or they can print the pages and analyze students' work using paper and pencil.

To complete the Practice Page Item Analysis:

- Write or type students' names in the far-left column. Depending on the number of students, more than one copy of the form may be needed or you may need to add rows.
- The question numbers are included across the top of the chart. Each item correlates with the matching question number from the practice page.
- For each student, record an *X* in the column if the student has the item incorrect. If the item is correct, leave the item blank.
- Count the *X*s in each row and column and fill in the correct boxes.

To complete the Student Item Analysis:

- Write or type the student's name on the top row. This form tracks the ongoing progress of each student, so one copy per student is necessary.
- The question numbers are included across the top of the chart. Each item correlates with the matching question number from the practice page.
- For each day, record an *X* in the column if the student has the item incorrect. If the item is correct, leave the item blank.
- Count the *X*s in each row and column and fill in the correct boxes.

Practice Page Item Analysis

Directions: Record an *X* in cells to indicate where students have missed questions. Add up the totals. You can view: (1) which questions/concepts were missed per student; (2) the total correct score per student; and (3) the total number of students who missed each question.

Day: ________	Question #	1	2	3	4	5	6	7	8	# Correct
Student Name										
Sample Student			X			X	X			5/8
# of Students Missing Each Question										

HOW TO USE THIS BOOK *(cont.)*

Student Item Analysis

Directions: Record an *X* in cells to indicate where the student has missed questions. Add up the totals. You can view: (1) which questions/concepts the student missed; (2) the total correct score per day; and (3) the total number of times each question/concept was missed.

Student Name: Sample Student									
Question	**1**	**2**	**3**	**4**	**5**	**6**	**7**	**8**	**# Correct**
Day									
1		X			X	X			5/8

HOW TO USE THIS BOOK *(cont.)*

Using the Results to Differentiate Instruction

Once results are gathered and analyzed, teachers can use the results to inform the way they differentiate instruction. The data can help determine which concepts are the most difficult for students and which need additional instructional support and continued practice. Depending on how often the practice pages are scored, results can be considered for instructional support on a daily or weekly basis.

Whole-Class Support

The results of the diagnostic analysis may show that the entire class is struggling with a particular concept or group of concepts. If these concepts have been taught in the past, this indicates that further instruction or reteaching is necessary. If these concepts have not been taught in the past, this data is a great pre-assessment and demonstrates that students do not have a working knowledge of the concepts. Thus, careful planning for the length of the unit(s) or lesson(s) must be considered, and extra frontloading may be required.

Small-Group or Individual Support

The results of the diagnostic analysis may show that an individual or small group of students is struggling with a particular concept or group of concepts. If these concepts have been taught in the past, this indicates that further instruction or reteaching is necessary. Consider pulling aside these students while others are working independently to instruct further on the concept(s). Teachers can also use the results to help identify individuals or groups of proficient students who are ready for enrichment or above-grade level instruction. These students may benefit from independent learning contracts or more challenging activities. Students may also benefit from extra practice using games or computer-based resources.

Digital Resources

Reference page 207 for information about accessing the digital resources and an overview of the contents.

HOW TO USE THIS BOOK *(cont.)*

NCTM Standards

The lessons in this book are aligned to the National Council of Teachers of Mathematics (NCTM) standards. The standards listed on page 4 support the concepts and skills that are consistently presented on each of the practice pages.

Standards Correlations

Shell Education is committed to producing educational materials that are research and standards based. In this effort, we have correlated all of our products to the academic standards of all 50 states, the District of Columbia, and the Department of Defense Dependent Schools, as well as to the college and career readiness standards.

How to Find Standards Correlations

To print a customized correlation report of this product for your state, visit our website at **www.tcmpub.com/shell-education** and follow the on-screen directions. If you require assistance in printing correlation reports, please contact Customer Service at 1-877-777-3450.

Purpose and Intent of Standards

The No Child Left Behind legislation mandates that all states adopt academic standards that identify the skills students will learn in kindergarten through grade twelve. While many states had already adopted academic standards prior to NCLB, the legislation set requirements to ensure the standards were detailed and comprehensive.

Standards are designed to focus instruction and guide adoption of curricula. Standards are statements that describe the criteria necessary for students to meet specific academic goals. They define the knowledge, skills, and content students should acquire at each level. Standards are also used to develop standardized tests to evaluate students' academic progress.

Teachers are required to demonstrate how their lessons meet state standards. State standards are used in development of all of our products, so educators can be assured they meet the academic requirements of each state.

NAME: ____________________

DIRECTIONS Solve each problem.

SCORE

1. Write the numeral. Each bundle has 10 sticks.

____

2. Add.

☐ + ☐ = ☐

3. Subtract.

☐ − ☐ = ☐

4. Write the missing number.

10	12	14	16	

5. Name the solid.

____

6. How many days are in a week?

____

7. Record the data in the chart.

- Marcia likes carrots.
- Trish likes broccoli.
- Gail likes corn.
- Tammy likes peas.
- Terri likes corn.

Favorite Vegetables

Gail	
Tammy	
Marcia	
Trish	
Terri	

8. There are 9 birds sitting on a roof. Two more come. How many birds are on the roof now?

____

1.
2.
3.
4.
5.
6.
7.
8.

____ / 8 Total

DAY 2

NAME: ______________________

DIRECTIONS Solve each problem.

SCORE

1. ☺ 😐
2. ☺ 😐
3. ☺ 😐
4. ☺ 😐
5. ☺ 😐
6. ☺ 😐
7. ☺ 😐
8. ☺ 😐

____ / 8
Total

1. Circle the smaller number.

110　　100

2.

$$\begin{array}{r} 4 \\ +\ 5 \\ \hline \end{array}$$

3. 10 – 7 = ______

4. ☐ – 0 = 10

5. Name the shape.

____

6. Circle the tool you use to measure time.

ruler　　scale　　clock

7.

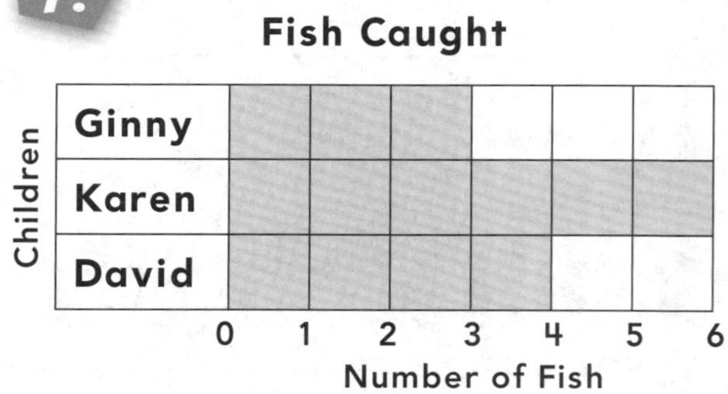

How many fish did Karen catch?

____

8. Write a related subtraction problem.

8 + 9 = 17

____

NAME: ____________________

DIRECTIONS Solve each problem.

1. Name the shaded fraction.

____

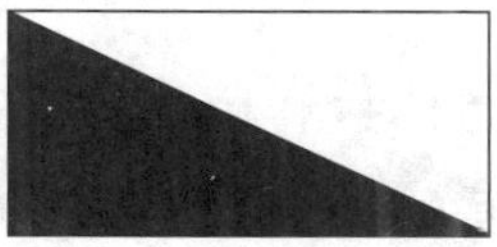

2. Add.

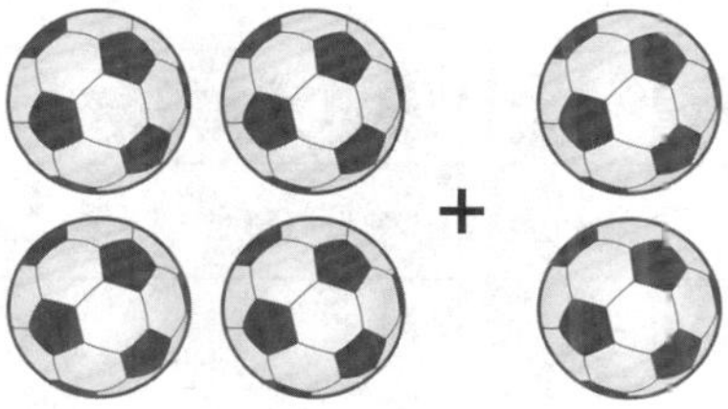

☐ + ☐ = ☐

3. Find the difference between 8 and 6.

____

4. 10 – 1 = 9 – ☐

5. Complete.

Shape	Number of Sides	Number of Angles
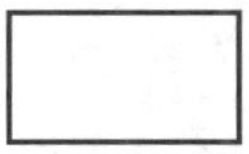		

6. True or false? Length is the distance between two points.

____

7.

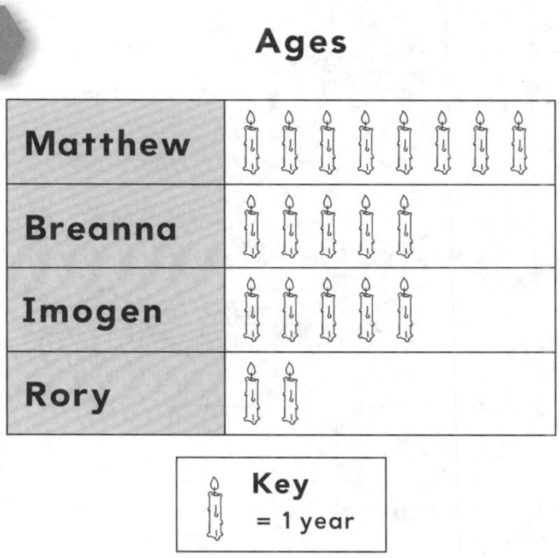

Is Matthew older than Rory?

Circle: yes no

8. Olivia's family is going on vacation in the last month of the year. In what month will they take a vacation?

____

SCORE

1. ☺ 😐

2. ☺ 😐

3. ☺ 😐

4. ☺ 😐

5. ☺ 😐

6. ☺ 😐

7. ☺ 😐

8. ☺ 😐

___ / 8 Total

DAY 4

NAME: ______________________

DIRECTIONS Solve each problem.

SCORE
1. ☺ 😐
2. ☺ 😐
3. ☺ 😐
4. ☺ 😐
5. ☺ 😐
6. ☺ 😐
7. ☺ 😐
8. ☺ 😐
____ / 8 Total

1. Is this a fair share?

Circle: yes no

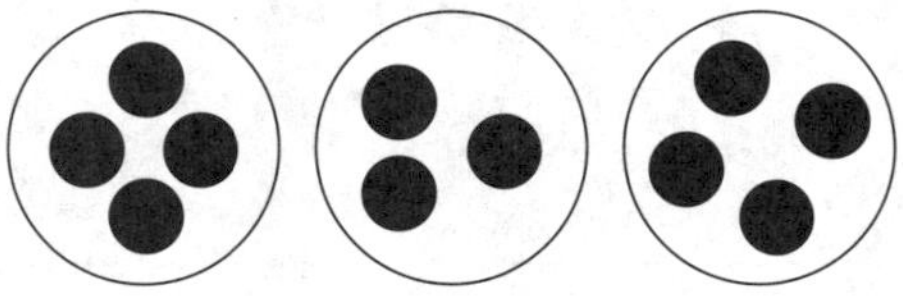

2. 6 + 2 = ______

3. Subtract.

☐ – ☐ = ☐

4. ☐ + 1 = 4 + 4

5. Color a base of the solid.

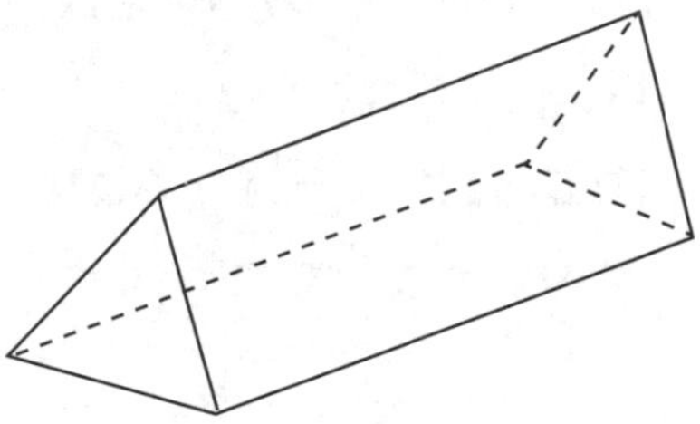

6. Write the area.

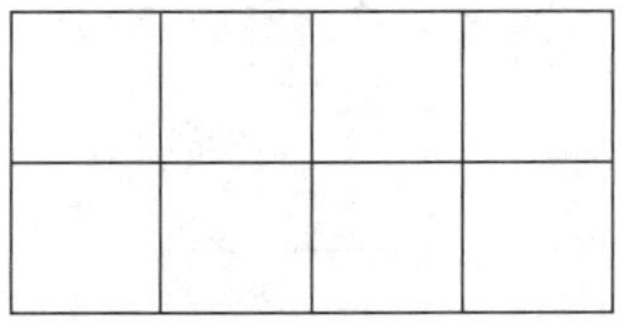

area = ____ squares

7. Toy Train Sales Last Week

Mon.	
Tues.	
Wed.	
Thurs.	
Fri.	
Sat.	
Sun.	

Key

 = 1 train

How many trains were sold on Monday?

____

8. I am 4 more than 12. What number am I?

____

DAY 5

NAME: ______________________________

DIRECTIONS Solve each problem.

1. Write the missing number.

23	24	25	26	

2. Add.

☐ + ☐ = ☐

3.

$$\begin{array}{r} 6 \\ -\ 1 \\ \hline \end{array}$$

4. Continue the pattern.

A B A B A ___

5. Draw a line of symmetry.

6. Write the time shown.

______ o'clock

7. How many tally marks are there?

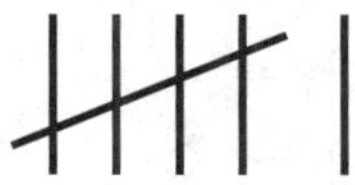

____

8. Jackie eats a carrot every day. How many carrots does she eat in two weeks?

____

SCORE

1.
2.
3.
4.
5.
6.
7.
8.

___ / 8
Total

DAY 6

NAME: ______________________________

DIRECTIONS Solve each problem.

SCORE

1. ☺ 😐
2. ☺ 😐
3. ☺ 😐
4. ☺ 😐
5. ☺ 😐
6. ☺ 😐
7. ☺ 😐
8. ☺ 😐

____ / 8
Total

1. Write the numeral.

6	tens	7	ones

____

2.

$$\begin{array}{r} 8 \\ +\ 1 \\ \hline \end{array}$$

3. 5 – 4 = ______

4. 8 + 6 = 14

14 – ☐ = 8

5. How many vertices on a square?

________ vertices

6. Write the month that comes next.

January, __________

7.

Favorite Pets

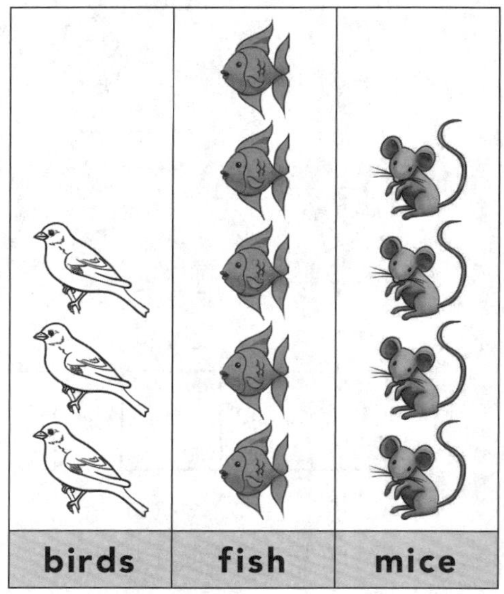

Which pet is the favorite?

____

8. Would you most likely use a ruler or a yardstick to measure the height of a person?

____

DAY 7

NAME: ______________________

DIRECTIONS Solve each problem.

1. Order the numbers from smallest to largest.

34 17 22 9

____, ____, ____, ____

2. Add.

☐ + ☐ = ☐

3. 9 – 8 = ______

4. 4 ☐ 1 = 3

5. Color the shape with 4 sides.

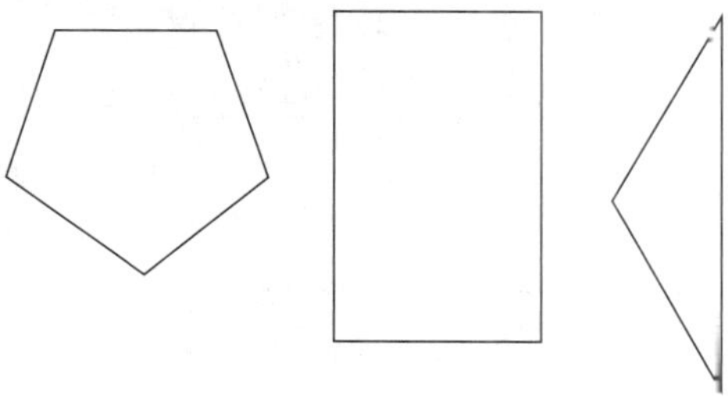

6. Circle the solid that takes up more space.

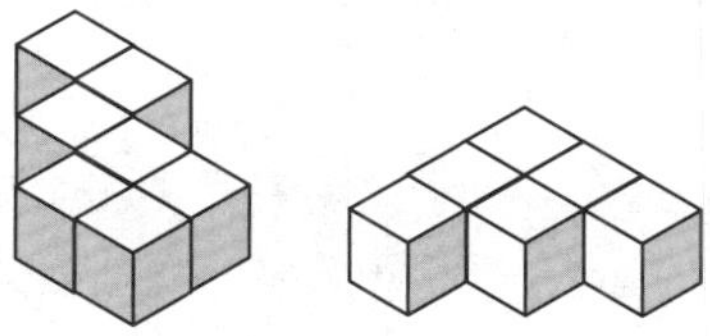

7. Car Colors

Red	卌 卌 |||
Blue	卌 卌 卌 卌 |
Yellow	卌 ||||
Green	卌 卌 卌 ||

How many cars are yellow?

____

8. How many legs are on 3 spiders?

____

SCORE

1. ☺ 😐
2. ☺ 😐
3. ☺ 😐
4. ☺ 😐
5. ☺ 😐
6. ☺ 😐
7. ☺ 😐
8. ☺ 😐

____ / 8 Total

DAY 8

NAME: ______________________

DIRECTIONS Solve each problem.

SCORE

1. ☺ 😐
2. ☺ 😐
3. ☺ 😐
4. ☺ 😐
5. ☺ 😐
6. ☺ 😐
7. ☺ 😐
8. ☺ 😐

___ / 8
Total

1. Circle half.

2. 10 plus 4 is

______________________.

3. Subtract.

☐ – ☐ = ☐

4. ☐ – 1 = 9 – 2

5. Circle the object that can roll.

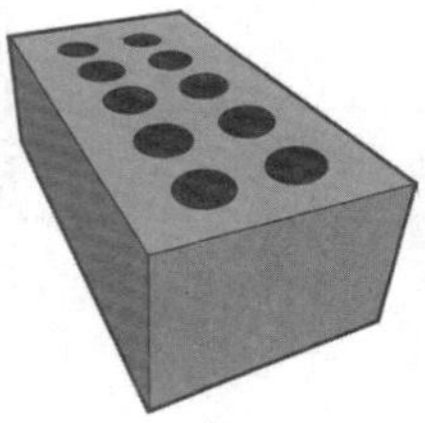

6. Circle the best estimate for the height.

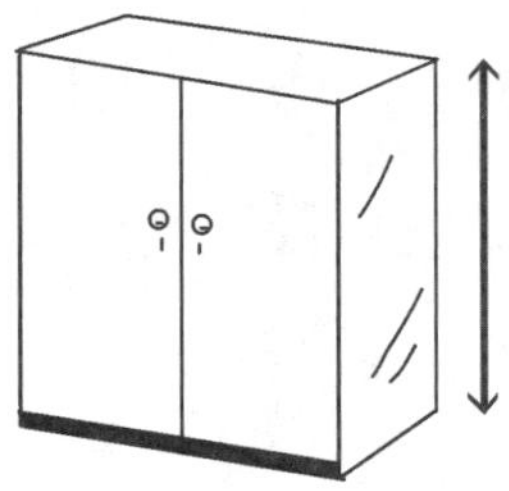

2 m   6 cm

7. Sports Played

	Soccer	Swimming	Baseball
Mark	X		X
Tracy		X	
Mike		X	X

How many children swim?

____

8. Write the number sentence.

Ten plus eight equals eighteen.

____

DAY 9

NAME: ____________________

DIRECTIONS Solve each problem.

1. Write the numeral thirty-nine.

____

2. Add.

 + 

☐ + ☐ = ☐

3.

$$\begin{array}{r} 7 \\ -\ 6 \\ \hline \end{array}$$

4. 2 + ☐ = 5 + 0

5. True or false?
A solid shape is a three-dimensional object.

____

6. Circle the object with less mass.

7. Flower Shop Orders

Rose	16
Daisy	23
Tulip	15
Iris	25

Which type of flower had the largest order?

____

8. What is the smallest 3-digit number you can make with the numbers 4, 6, and 8?

____

SCORE

1. ☺ 😐

2. ☺ 😐

3. ☺ 😐

4. ☺ 😐

5. ☺ 😐

6. ☺ 😐

7. ☺ 😐

8. ☺ 😐

____ / 8
Total

DAY
10

NAME: ____________________________

DIRECTIONS Solve each problem.

SCORE

1. 🙂 😐
2. 🙂 😐
3. 🙂 😐
4. 🙂 😐
5. 🙂 😐
6. 🙂 😐
7. 🙂 😐
8. 🙂 😐

____ / 8
Total

1. Circle about how many children are in your classroom.

25 100

2. 5 + 6 = ______

3. 1 less than 5 is

____________________.

4. Count by tens and color each number counted.

1	2	3	4	5	6	7	8	9	10
11	12	13	14	15	16	17	18	19	20
21	22	23	24	25	26	27	28	29	30
31	32	33	34	35	36	37	38	39	40
41	42	43	44	45	46	47	48	49	50

5. Draw the front view of the solid.

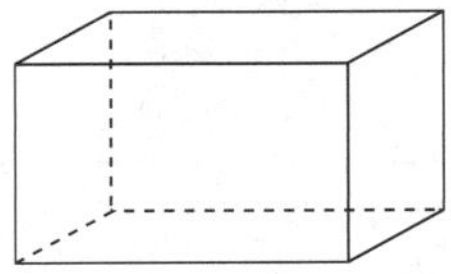

6. Circle the sphere that takes up the most space.

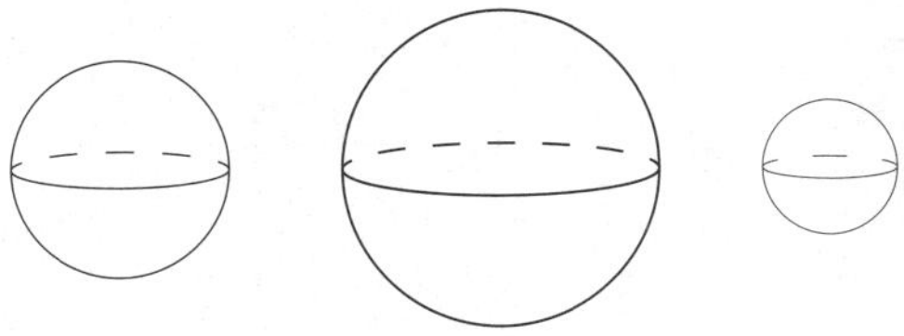

7. Make 9 tally marks.

8. The Sluggers scored 9 runs in a baseball game. The Tigers scored 7 runs. How many more runs did the Sluggers score than the Tigers?

____

NAME: ______________________________

DIRECTIONS Solve each problem.

1. Write the numeral.

____

2. Add.

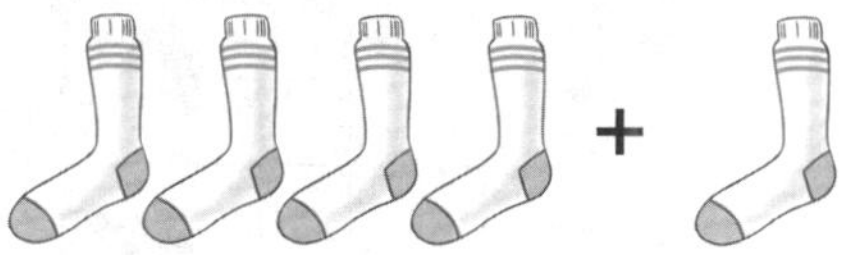

☐ + ☐ = ☐

3.

$$\begin{array}{r} 9 \\ -\ 6 \\ \hline \end{array}$$

4. Write the missing number.

20	30	40	50	

5. Color one face on the solid.

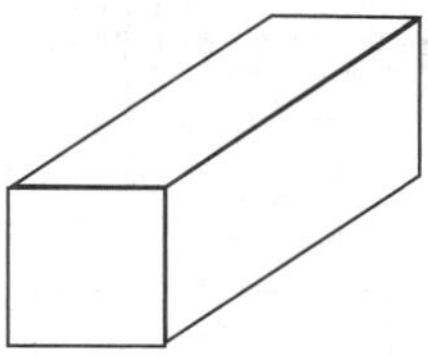

6. Write the time.

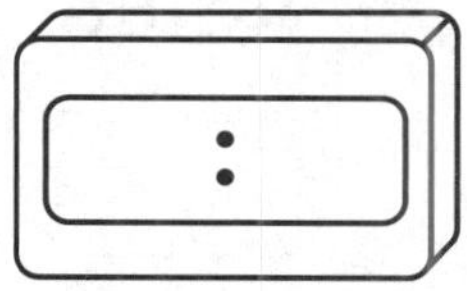

7. Make tally marks to record the data in the chart.

- Thirteen people like to go to the movies.
- Nine people like to go to a restaurant.
- Twelve people like to go to a park.

Favorite Activity

Movies	
Restaurant	
Park	

8. Mom is cooking breakfast for the family. She needs 16 eggs. How many dozens of eggs should she buy?

____

SCORE

1. ☺ 😐
2. ☺ 😐
3. ☺ 😐
4. ☺ 😐
5. ☺ 😐
6. ☺ 😐
7. ☺ 😐
8. ☺ 😐

____ / 8
Total

DAY 12

NAME: ____________________

DIRECTIONS Solve each problem.

SCORE

1. ☺ 😐
2. ☺ 😐
3. ☺ 😐
4. ☺ 😐
5. ☺ 😐
6. ☺ 😐
7. ☺ 😐
8. ☺ 😐

____ / 8 Total

1. What is the place value of 6 in 64?

____

2. 9 more than 3 is

____

3. Subtract.

[ ] – [ ] = [ ]

4. 10 – [ ] = 5

5. Circle the hexagon.

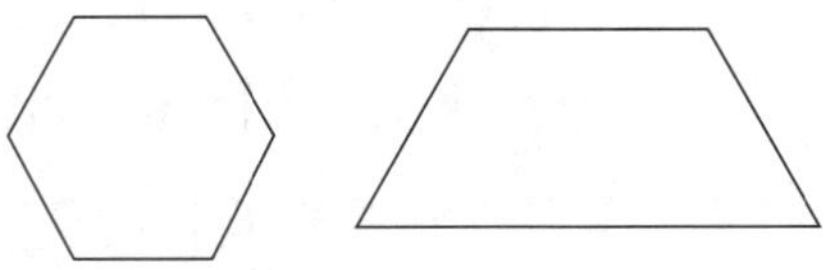

6. Circle the longer row.

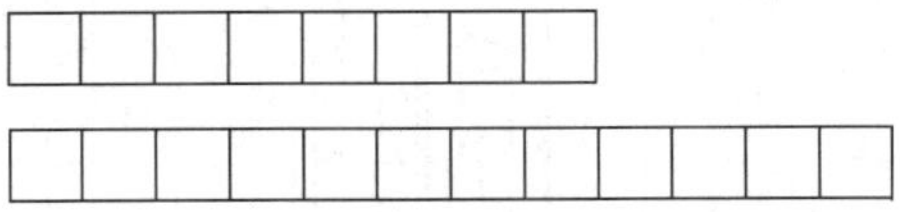

7. **Miles Run**

Max	
Cheryl	
Brandon	

Key
 = 10 miles

Who ran the most miles?

____

8. Write the number that is 4 more tens and 6 more ones than the number 41.

____

NAME: ______________________

DIRECTIONS Solve each problem.

1. Name the shaded fraction.

____

2. Add.

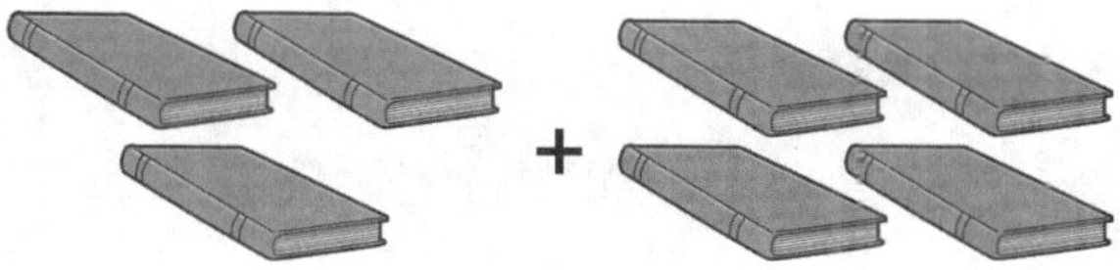

☐ + ☐ = ☐

3. 7 – 2 = ______

4. 6 – ☐ = 4 – 1

5. True or false? A solid can have one or more faces.

____

6. Write the length.

__________ inches

7. Use an X to record the data in the chart.

- Mary has a hamster and a fish.
- Julia does not have a fish, but has the other pets.
- Evan has every animals with 4 feet.

Pets

	Hamster	Dog	Fish	Cat
Mary				
Julia				
Evan				

8. Kwan has 26¢. He has 2 coins. What coins does Kwan have?

____

____

SCORE

1. ☺ 😐
2. ☺ 😐
3. ☺ 😐
4. ☺ 😐
5. ☺ 😐
6. ☺ 😐
7. ☺ 😐
8. ☺ 😐

____ / 8
Total

NAME: ____________________

DIRECTIONS Solve each problem.

SCORE

1. ☺ 😐
2. ☺ 😐
3. ☺ 😐
4. ☺ 😐
5. ☺ 😐
6. ☺ 😐
7. ☺ 😐
8. ☺ 😐

____ / 8
Total

1. Is this a fair share?
Circle: yes no

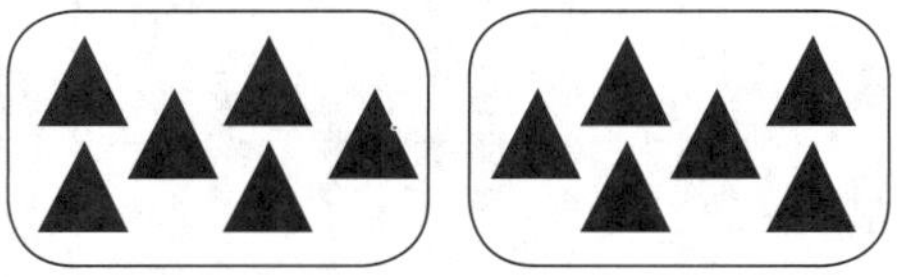

2. 7 + 4 = ______

3. 5 – 5 = ______

4. 6 + 2 = ☐ + 1

5. Circle the cylinder.

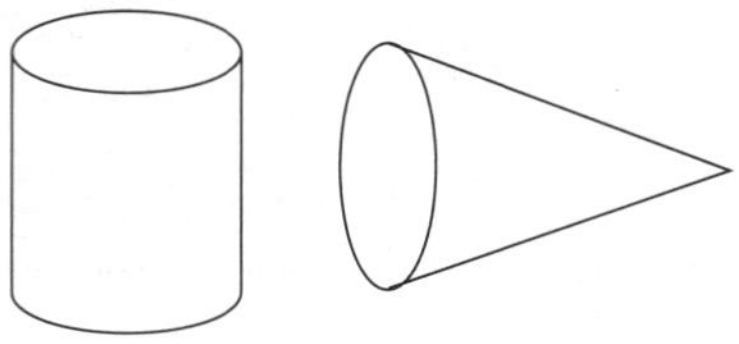

6. Record the area.

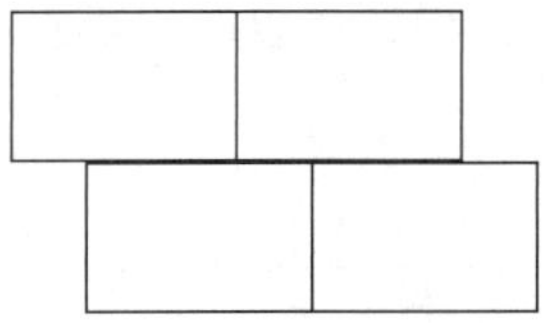

area =
______ rectangles

7. How much did Kiko save?

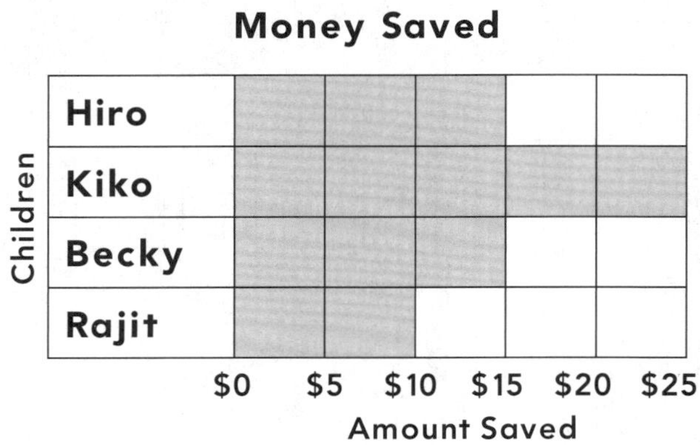

____

8. A banana costs 19¢, an apple costs 26¢, and a pear costs 35¢. Simon has 45¢. Which two pieces of fruit can he buy?

____

NAME: ______________________

DIRECTIONS Solve each problem.

1. Write the missing number.

37	38	39	40	

2. Add.

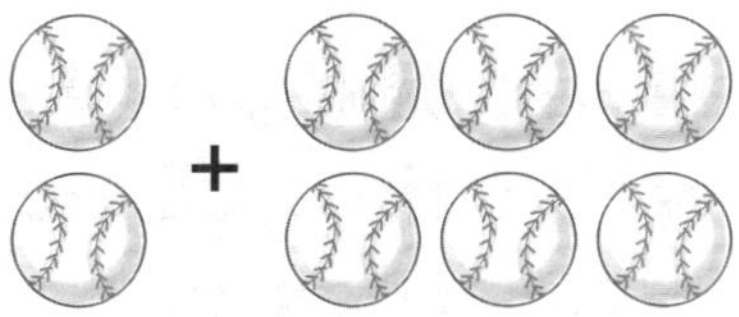

☐ + ☐ = ☐

3. 10 – 1 = ______

4. Continue the pattern.

1 1 2 1 1 ____ ____

5. Draw all lines of symmetry.

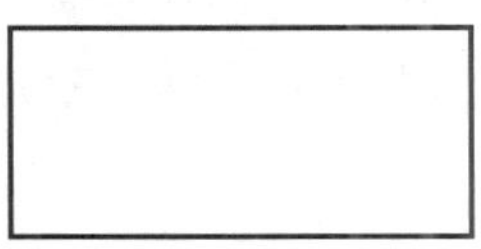

6. Show 5 o'clock.

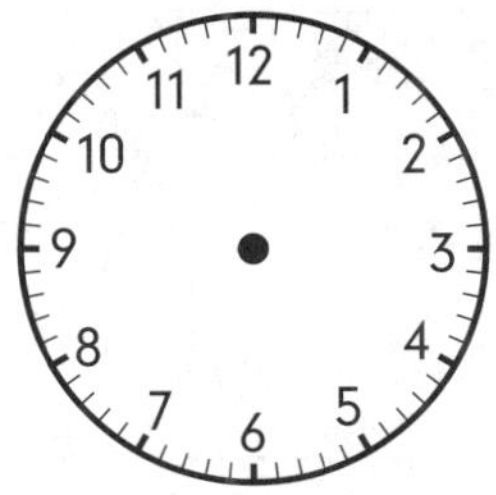

7. Teeth Lost

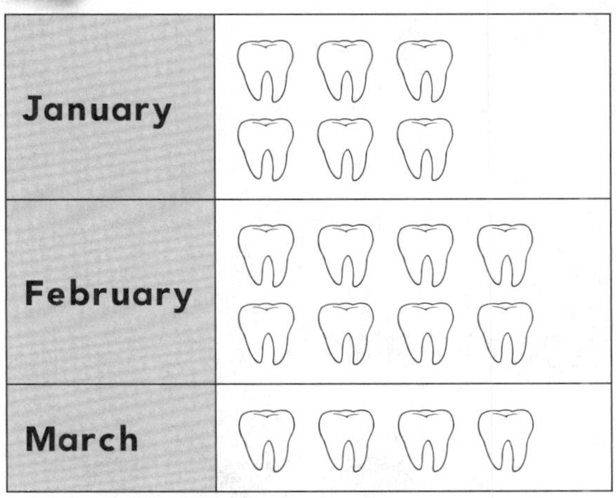

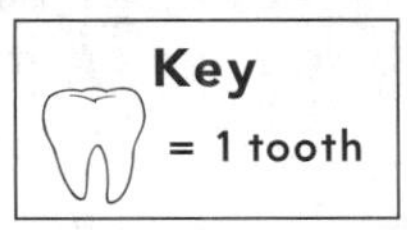

In which month were the most teeth lost?

____

8. Which solid has two flat circle bases and a curved surface?

____

SCORE

1. ☺ ☹
2. ☺ ☹
3. ☺ ☹
4. ☺ ☹
5. ☺ ☹
6. ☺ ☹
7. ☺ ☹
8. ☺ ☹

____ / 8 Total

DAY 16

NAME: ______________________

DIRECTIONS Solve each problem.

SCORE

1. ☺ 😐
2. ☺ 😐
3. ☺ 😐
4. ☺ 😐
5. ☺ 😐
6. ☺ 😐
7. ☺ 😐
8. ☺ 😐

____ /8 Total

1. Write the numeral.

3	Tens	9	Ones

____

2.

$$\begin{array}{r} 7 \\ +\ 9 \\ \hline \end{array}$$

3. Subtract.

☐ − ☐ = ☐

4. 14 − 8 = 6

6 + ☐ = 14

5. How many vertices?

______ vertices

6. Write the day of the week that comes after Tuesday.

____

7.

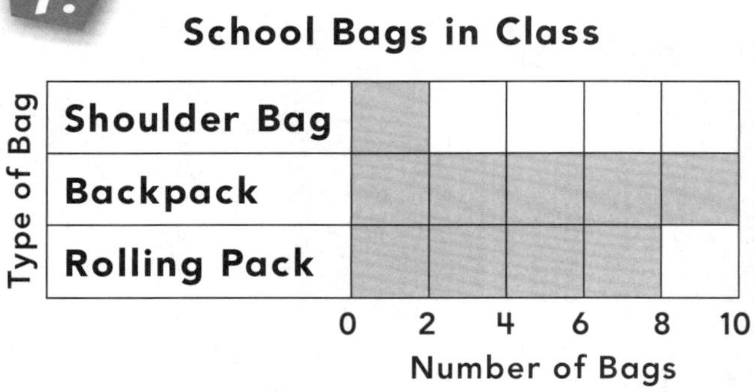

How many kids have rolling packs?

____

8. Edward can jump about 1 yard. About how many feet can Edward jump?

____

NAME: ______________________________

DIRECTIONS Solve each problem.

1. Use >, <, or =.

17 ◯ 37

2. Add.

☐ + ☐ = ☐

3.

$$\begin{array}{r} 8 \\ -\ 7 \\ \hline \end{array}$$

4. ☐ − 5 = 3

5. Color the shapes that have vertices.

6. What is the volume?

______ blocks

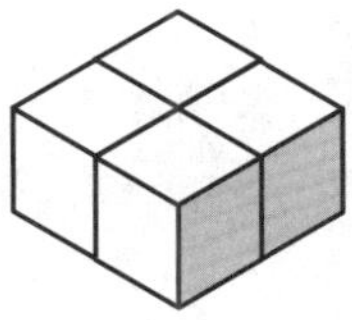

7.

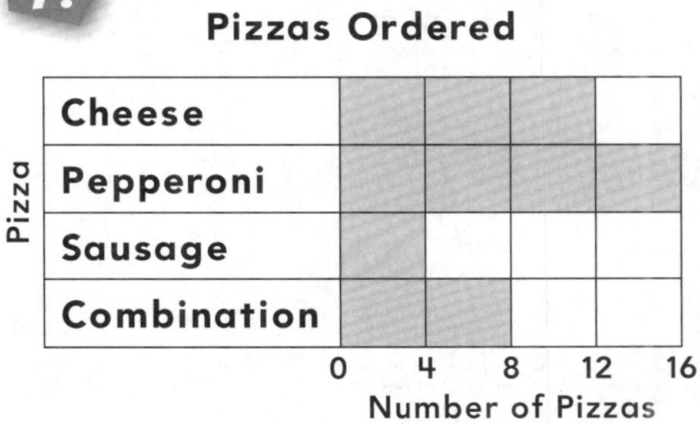

Which type of pizza was ordered most often?

____

8. Melissa's hair is 12 inches long. She lets it grow out 3 more inches and then she cuts 4 inches off. How long is her hair now?

____

SCORE

1. ☺ ☹
2. ☺ ☹
3. ☺ ☹
4. ☺ ☹
5. ☺ ☹
6. ☺ ☹
7. ☺ ☹
8. ☺ ☹

___ / 8

Total

DAY 18

NAME: ______________________________

DIRECTIONS Solve each problem.

SCORE

1. ☺ 😐
2. ☺ 😐
3. ☺ 😐
4. ☺ 😐
5. ☺ 😐
6. ☺ 😐
7. ☺ 😐
8. ☺ 😐

___ / 8
Total

1. Circle half.

2. 5 + 3 = ______

3. Subtract 3 from 6 to find the difference.

____

4. 4 – 0 = ☐ – 4

5. Circle the object that can stack.

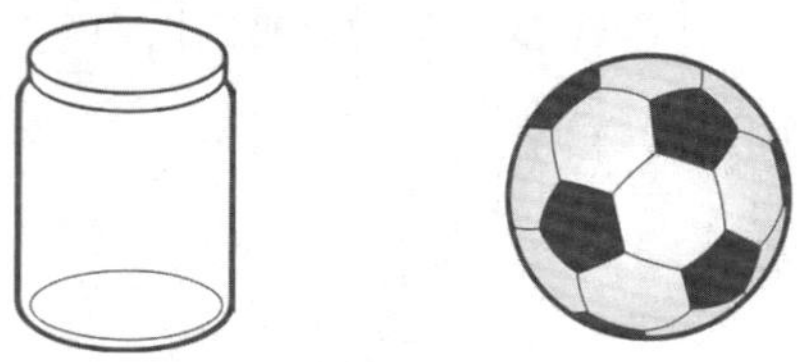

6. Circle the object that would be taller than 1 meter.

7. Library Books Checked Out

	Week 1	Week 2	Week 3
Jody	4	5	5
Emily	4	4	4
Brenda	5	7	6
Alison	6	3	6

How many library books did Alison check out the first week?

____

8. Six friends are at a party. Ten more come. How many are at the party now?

____

NAME: ____________________

DIRECTIONS Solve each problem.

1. Write the numeral sixty-seven.

____

2. Complete.

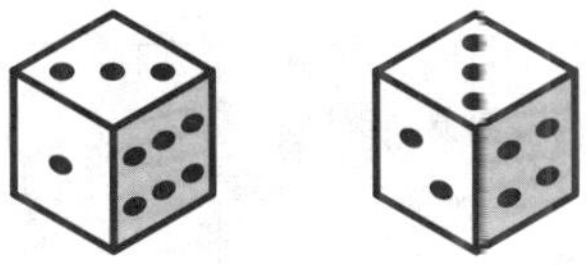

Double 3 = ______

3.

$$\begin{array}{r} 4 \\ -\ 4 \\ \hline \end{array}$$

4. 1 + 1 = 2 + ☐

5. Color the correct cross-section.

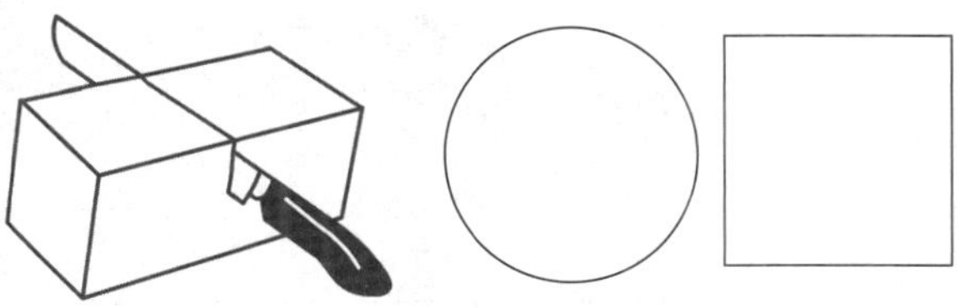

6. True or false? You can eat dinner in less than 1 minute.

____

7. Record the data in the chart. Use numbers.

Soccer Games Played

	April	May
Sue		
Toni		

- Sue played 13 soccer games in April and 16 in May.
- Toni played 14 soccer games in April and 12 in May.

8. Write an addition number sentence using the numbers 6, 4, and 10.

____

SCORE

1. ☺ 😐
2. ☺ 😐
3. ☺ 😐
4. ☺ 😐
5. ☺ 😐
6. ☺ 😐
7. ☺ 😐
8. ☺ 😐

____ / 8
Total

NAME: ____________________

DIRECTIONS Solve each problem.

SCORE

1. ☺ 😐
2. ☺ 😐
3. ☺ 😐
4. ☺ 😐
5. ☺ 😐
6. ☺ 😐
7. ☺ 😐
8. ☺ 😐

____ / 8 Total

1. Circle about how many marbles you can hold in your hand.

10   300

2. Four plus five equals

____________________.

3. Subtract.

☐ – ☐ = ☐

4. Sue eats 2 oranges every day. How many oranges does she eat in 4 days?

____

Day 1	Day 2	Day 3	Day 4
2	4	6	

5. Color the solid.

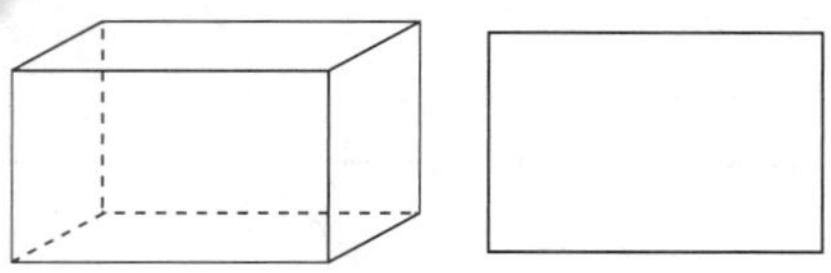

6. Circle the heavier object.

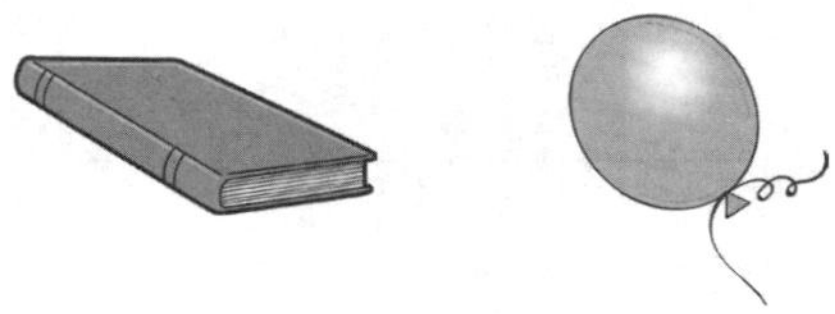

7.

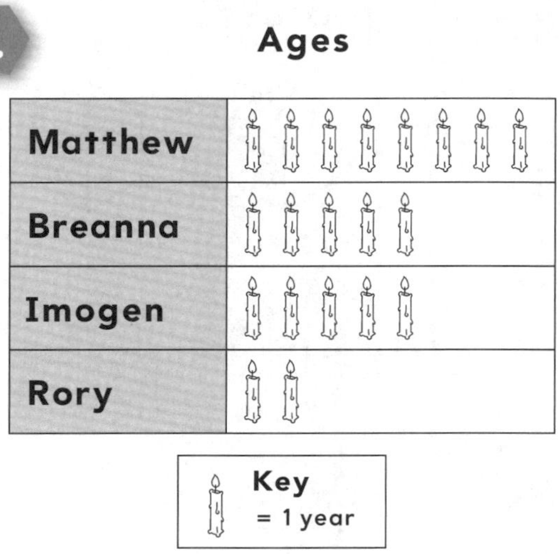

How old is Matthew?

____

8. Lalani's family wants to go to a movie when they get up in the morning. Would they see the movie that starts at 11:00 A.M. or 3:00 P.M.?

____

NAME: ____________________________

DIRECTIONS Solve each problem.

1. Write the numeral.

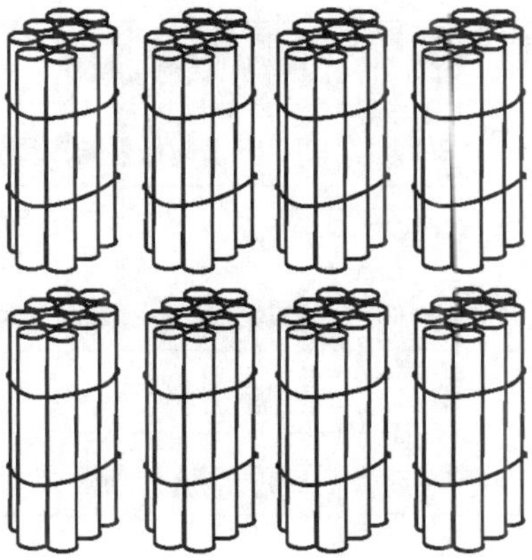

____

2.

$$\begin{array}{r} 7 \\ +\ 10 \\ \hline \end{array}$$

3. 10 – 0 = ______

4. Write the missing number.

24	26	28	30	

5. Circle the object that looks like the solid.

6. How many days are in June?

____

7.

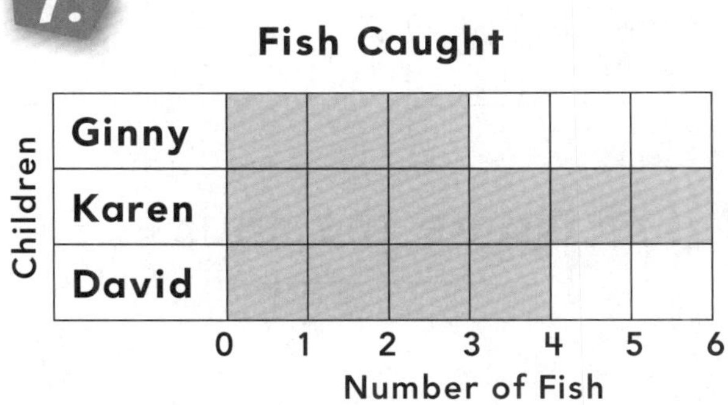

Who caught the most fish?

____

8. I am 9 less than 18. What number am I?

____

SCORE

1. ☺ 😐

2. ☺ 😐

3. ☺ 😐

4. ☺ 😐

5. ☺ 😐

6. ☺ 😐

7. ☺ 😐

8. ☺ 😐

____ / 8 Total

DAY 22

NAME: ____________________

DIRECTIONS Solve each problem.

SCORE

1. 🙂 😐
2. 🙂 😐
3. 🙂 😐
4. 🙂 😐
5. 🙂 😐
6. 🙂 😐
7. 🙂 😐
8. 🙂 😐

____ / 8 Total

1. Circle the larger number.

87 81

2. 6 + 9 = ______

3. 4 less than 8 is

____________________.

4. 5 ☐ 2 = 3

5. Name the shape.

☐

____

6. Circle how long it would take to fill a pool with water.

more than 1 hour

less than 1 hour

7. Toy Train Sales Last Week

Mon.	
Tues.	
Wed.	
Thurs.	
Fri.	
Sat.	
Sun.	

Key
 = 1 train

How many trains were sold on Wednesday?

____

8. Greg runs 3 miles every day. How many miles does Greg run in 3 days?

____

NAME: ____________________

DIRECTIONS Solve each problem.

1. Name the shaded fraction.

____

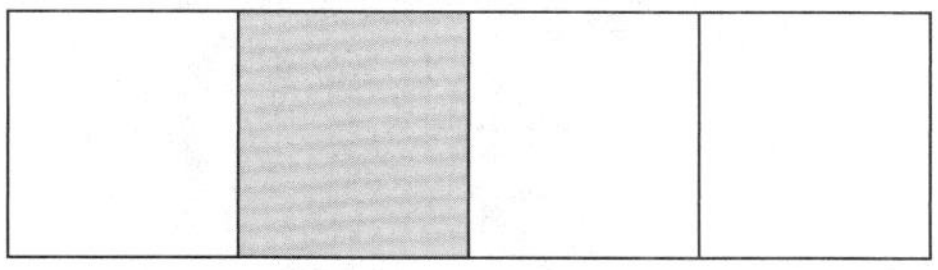

2. 4 more than 4 is

____________________.

3.
$$\begin{array}{r} 6 \\ -\ 5 \\ \hline \end{array}$$

4. 2 − 1 = 9 − ☐

5. True or false? There is symmetry when one half of a shape is a mirror image of the other half.

____

6. Write the length.

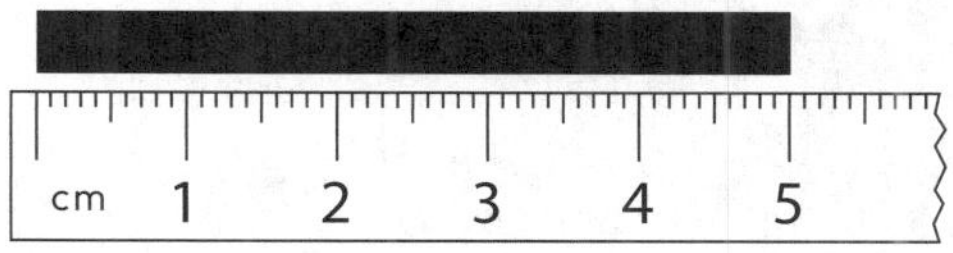

______ centimeters

7. How many tally marks?

____

8. Rank from lightest to heaviest.

_____ a car
_____ a shoe
_____ a paperclip

SCORE

1. ☺ 😐
2. ☺ 😐
3. ☺ 😐
4. ☺ 😐
5. ☺ 😐
6. ☺ 😐
7. ☺ 😐
8. ☺ 😐

____ / 8 Total

DAY 24

NAME: ______________________________

DIRECTIONS Solve each problem.

SCORE

1. ☺ 😐
2. ☺ 😐
3. ☺ 😐
4. ☺ 😐
5. ☺ 😐
6. ☺ 😐
7. ☺ 😐
8. ☺ 😐

____ / 8
Total

1. Is this a fair share?

Circle: yes no

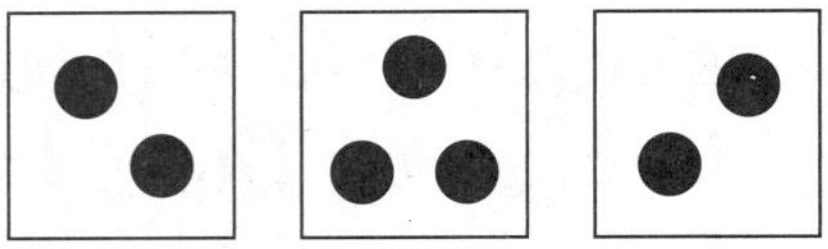

2. 9 + 0 = ______

3. Subtract.

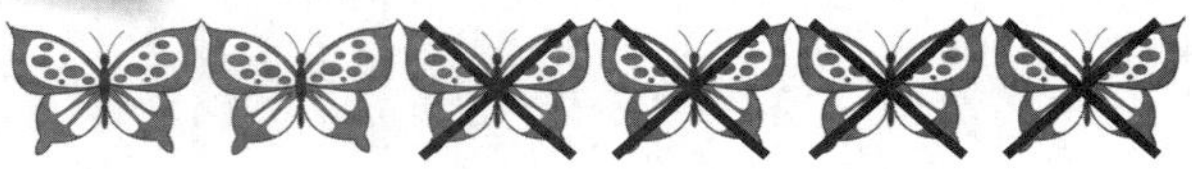

☐ – ☐ = ☐

4. ☐ + 5 = 9 + 3

5. Circle the cone.

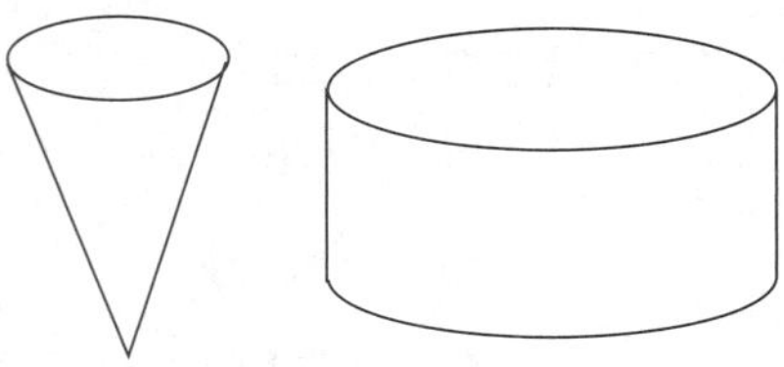

6. Color the larger area.

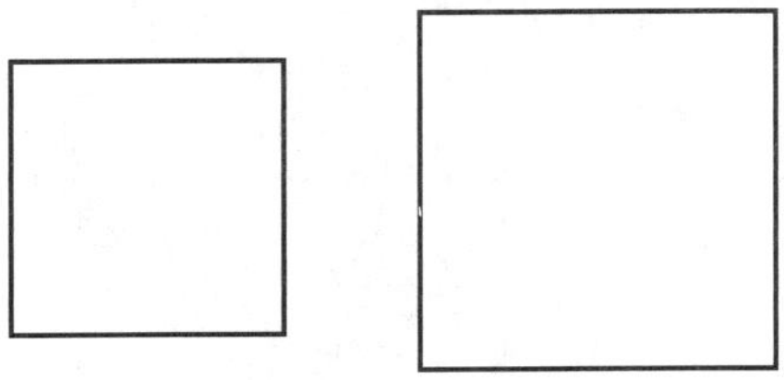

7.

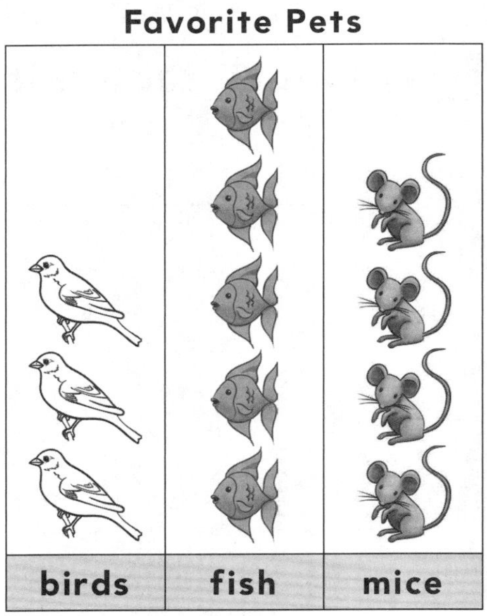

How many of the pets are fish?

____

8. There are 10 shoes on a group of kids. How many kids are there?

____

NAME: ______________________________

DIRECTIONS Solve each problem.

1. Write the missing number.

62	63		65	66

2.

$$\begin{array}{r} 4 \\ +\ 2 \\ \hline \end{array}$$

3. 4 – 1 = ______

4. Continue the pattern.

red, blue, red,

blue, red, ______

5. Draw all lines of symmetry.

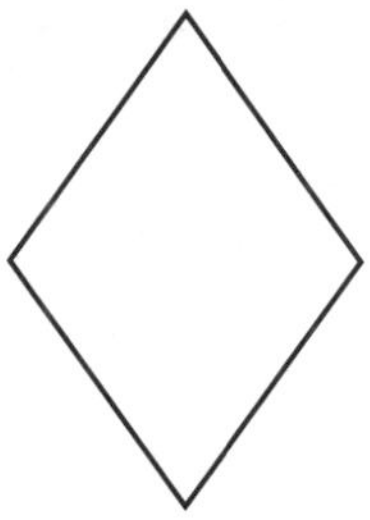

6. Write the time.

______ o'clock

7. Car Colors

Red	卌 卌 |||
Blue	卌 卌 卌 卌 |
Yellow	卌 ||||
Green	卌 卌 卌 ||

Are there more red cars or blue cars?

____

8. Write the number that has 8 in the tens place and 9 in the ones place.

____

SCORE

1. ☺ 😐

2. ☺ 😐

3. ☺ 😐

4. ☺ 😐

5. ☺ 😐

6. ☺ 😐

7. ☺ 😐

8. ☺ 😐

____ / 8

Total

DAY 26

NAME: ____________________

DIRECTIONS Solve each problem.

SCORE

1. ☺ ☹
2. ☺ ☹
3. ☺ ☹
4. ☺ ☹
5. ☺ ☹
6. ☺ ☹
7. ☺ ☹
8. ☺ ☹

___ / 8

Total

1. Write the numeral.

4	Tens	2	Ones

____

2. 8 + 6 = ______

3.

$$\begin{array}{r} 9 \\ -\ 7 \\ \hline \end{array}$$

4. ☐ – 9 = 7

5. How many vertices does a trapezoid have?

____

6. Write the month that comes after September.

____

7. Sports Played

	Soccer	Swimming	Baseball
Mark	X		X
Tracy		X	
Mike		X	X

Which sports does Mike play?

____

____

8. What is the largest 3-digit number you can make with the numbers 6, 7, and 9?

____

DAY 27

NAME: ______________________

DIRECTIONS Solve each problem.

1. Order the numbers from least to greatest.

75 61 36 19

____, ____, ____, ____

2. One plus four more is

______________________.

3. 7 – 5 = ______

4. 9 – ☐ = 2

5. How many sides does the shape have?

__________ sides

6. What is the volume?

______ cubes

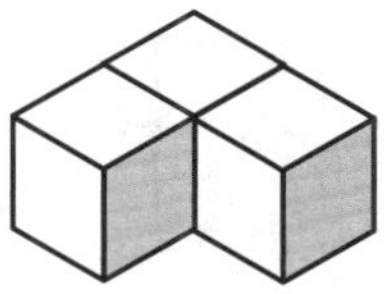

7. Flower Shop Orders

Rose	16
Daisy	23
Tulip	15
Iris	25

How many roses were ordered?

____

8. It takes Julian 14 minutes to walk to school. It takes Michelle 8 minutes to walk to school. How much longer does it take Julian than Michelle to walk to school?

____

SCORE

1. ☺ ☹
2. ☺ ☹
3. ☺ ☹
4. ☺ ☹
5. ☺ ☹
6. ☺ ☹
7. ☺ ☹
8. ☺ ☹

____ / 8 Total

NAME: ____________________

DIRECTIONS Solve each problem.

SCORE

1. ☺ 😐
2. ☺ 😐
3. ☺ 😐
4. ☺ 😐
5. ☺ 😐
6. ☺ 😐
7. ☺ 😐
8. ☺ 😐

____ / 8 Total

1. Color half.

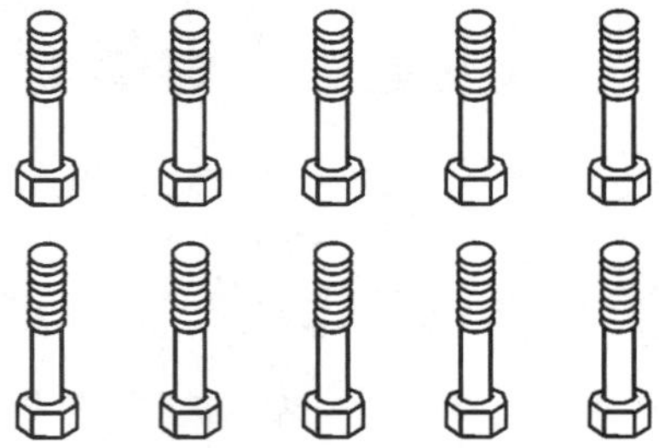

2.

$$\begin{array}{r} 10 \\ +\ \ 5 \\ \hline \end{array}$$

3. Subtract.

☐ − ☐ = ☐

4. ☐ − 5 = 7 − 3

5. Can the object stack?

Circle: yes no

6. Circle the object that would be shorter than 1 meter.

7. Make 14 tally marks.

8. Grandma is having 13 people over for breakfast. She wants to buy enough muffins for everyone. Muffins come in packs of 6. How many packs of muffins should she buy?

____

NAME: ____________________

DIRECTIONS Solve each problem.

1. Write the numeral for ninety-three.

____

2.

$$\begin{array}{r} 6 \\ +\ 6 \\ \hline \end{array}$$

3. 5 – 2 = ______

4. 4 + ☐ = 6 + 3

5. Draw the top view of the solid.

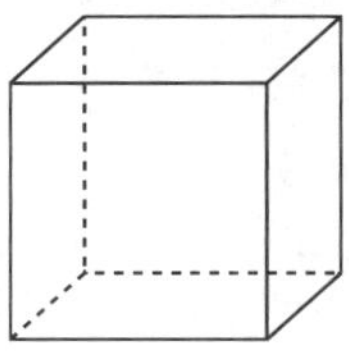

6. Show the time on the clock.

7. Favorite Activity

Movies	卌 卌 |||
Restaurant	卌 ||||
Park	卌 卌 ||
Stay Home	卌 |||

Which activity did most of the people like the best?

____

8. Write the number that is 7 more tens and 2 more ones than the number 12.

____

SCORE

1. ☺ 😐
2. ☺ 😐
3. ☺ 😐
4. ☺ 😐
5. ☺ 😐
6. ☺ 😐
7. ☺ 😐
8. ☺ 😐

____ / 8 Total

DAY 30

NAME: ______________________

DIRECTIONS Solve each problem.

SCORE

1. ☺ 😐
2. ☺ 😐
3. ☺ 😐
4. ☺ 😐
5. ☺ 😐
6. ☺ 😐
7. ☺ 😐
8. ☺ 😐

____ / 8 Total

1. Circle about how many blocks would fit in your hand.

5 100

2.

$$\begin{array}{r} 7 \\ +\ 8 \\ \hline \end{array}$$

3. 2 less than 8 is

______________________.

4. Count by fives and color each number counted.

1	2	3	4	5	6	7	8	9	10
11	12	13	14	15	16	17	18	19	20
21	22	23	24	25	26	27	28	29	30
31	32	33	34	35	36	37	38	39	40
41	42	43	44	45	46	47	48	49	50

5. Color the rectangle.

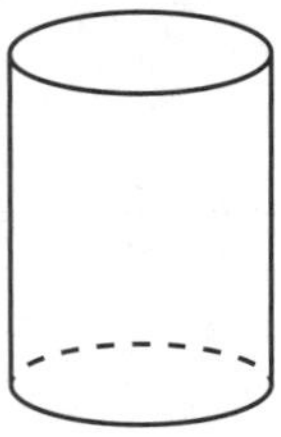

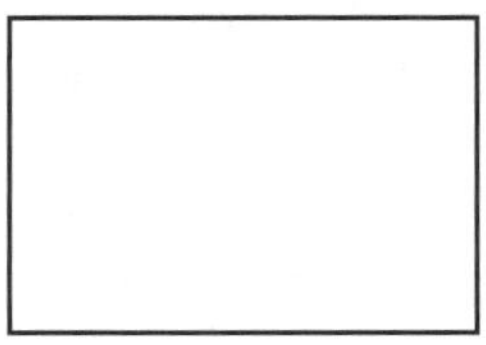

6. Circle the object that weighs less.

7.

How many miles did Max run?

____

8. Match the fruit to the child who likes it. Tim does not like bananas. Kayla likes apples. Rachel does not like oranges.

Kayla Tim Rachel

NAME: ____________________

DIRECTIONS Solve each problem.

1. Write the numeral.

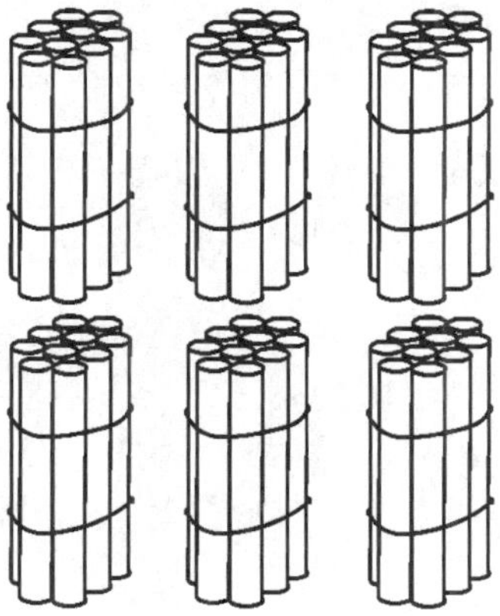

____

2. The sum of 9 and 9 is

____________________.

3. 4 – 0 = ______

4. Write the missing number.

90	80		60	50

5. Color the solid.

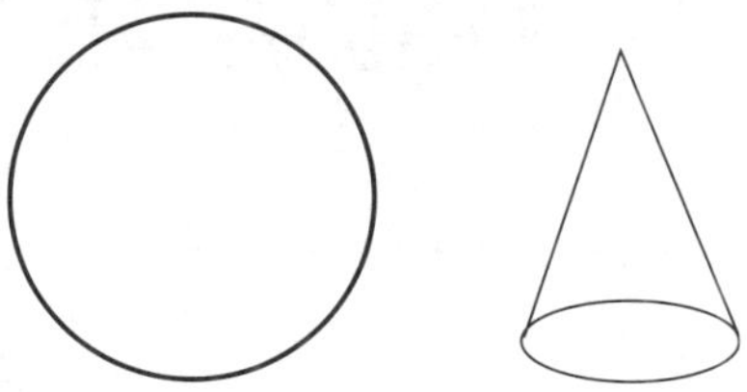

6. Write the time.

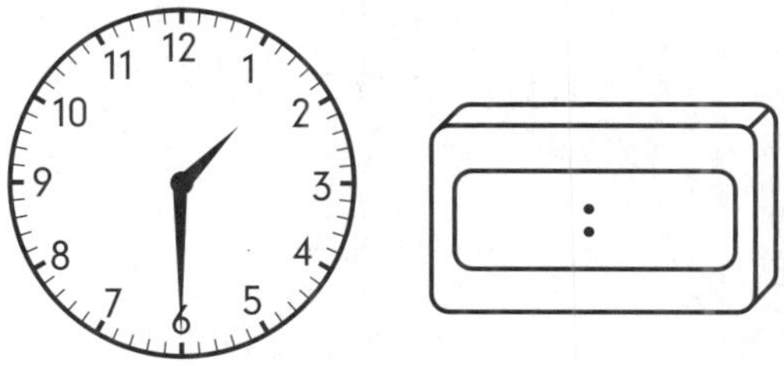

7.

Pets

	Hamster	Dog	Fish	Cat
Mary	X		X	X
Julia	X	X		X
Evan	X	X		X

Which pets does Evan have?

____

8. Tia has 23¢. She finds a quarter, a dime, and two nickels. Now how much money does she have?

____

SCORE

1.

2.

3.

4.

5.

6.

7.

8.

____ / 8
Total

NAME: ______________________________

DIRECTIONS Solve each problem.

SCORE

1. ☺ 😐

2. ☺ 😐

3. ☺ 😐

4. ☺ 😐

5. ☺ 😐

6. ☺ 😐

7. ☺ 😐

8. ☺ 😐

___ / 8 Total

1. What is the place value of 7 in the number 37?

____

2. 5 + 8 = ______

3. Subtract.

☐ – ☐ = ☐

4. ☐ – 6 = 3

5. True or false? Squares have a right angle at each vertex.

____

6. Circle the longer snake.

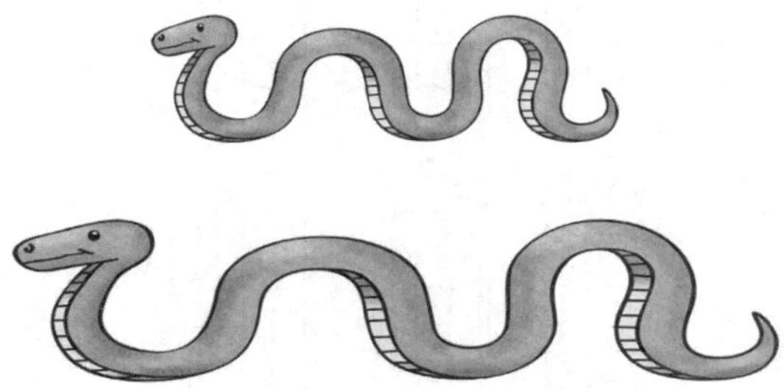

7.

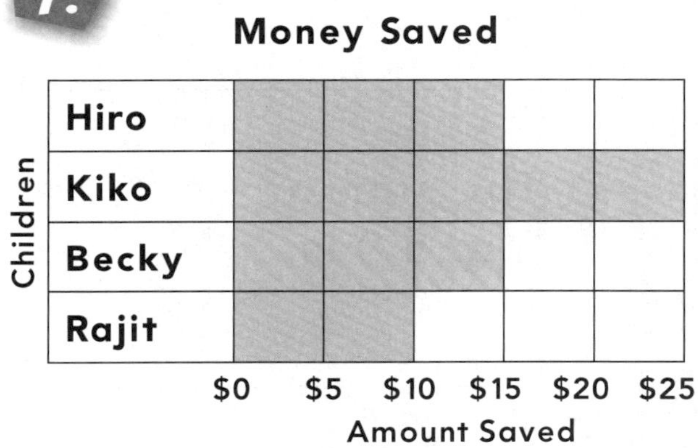

Who saved the most money?

____

8. Yon has 4 nickels. How much money does she have?

____

NAME: ______________________________

DIRECTIONS Solve each problem.

1. Name the shaded fraction.

____

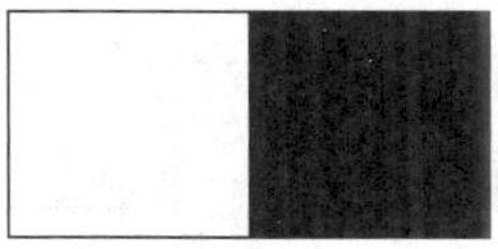

2. 9 more than 7 is

______________________.

3.

$$\begin{array}{r} 7 \\ -\ 7 \\ \hline \end{array}$$

4. 7 – ☐ = 8 – 7

5. True or false? This shape is a prism.

____

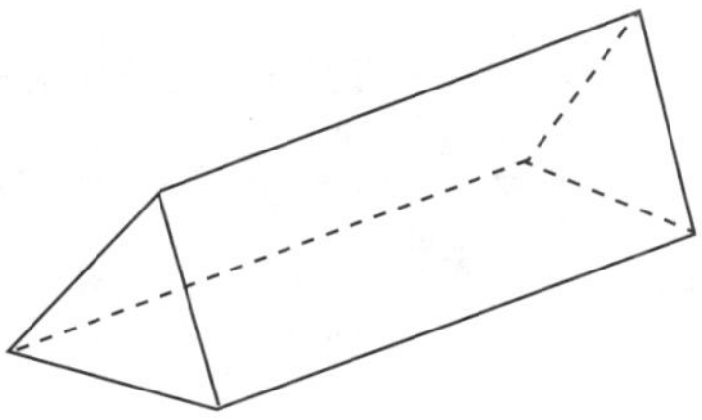

6. Write the length.

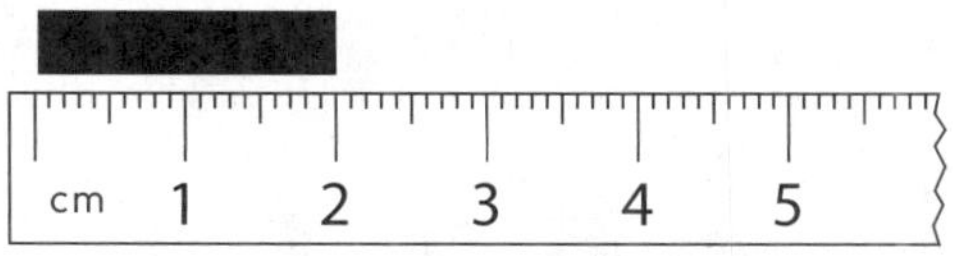

______ centimeters

7. Teeth Lost

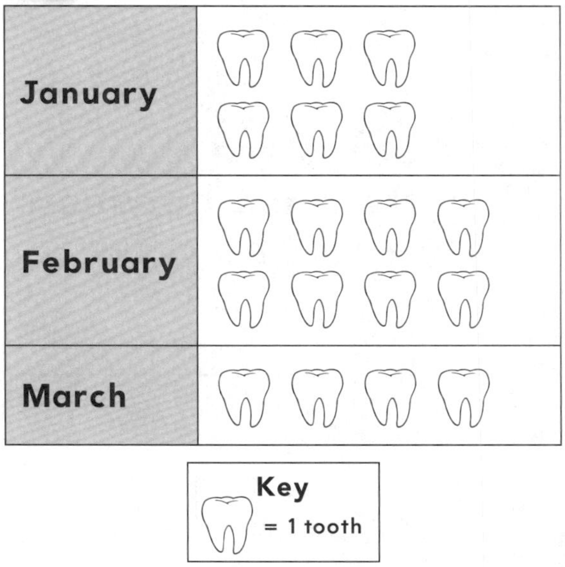

How many teeth were lost in January?

____

8. How many nickels do you need to make 65¢?

____

SCORE

1.

2.

3.

4.

5.

6.

7.

8.

____ / 8

Total

DAY 34

NAME: ____________________

DIRECTIONS Solve each problem.

SCORE

1. ___
2. ___
3. ___
4. ___
5. ___
6. ___
7. ___
8. ___

___ / 8 Total

1. Is this a fair share?

Circle: yes no

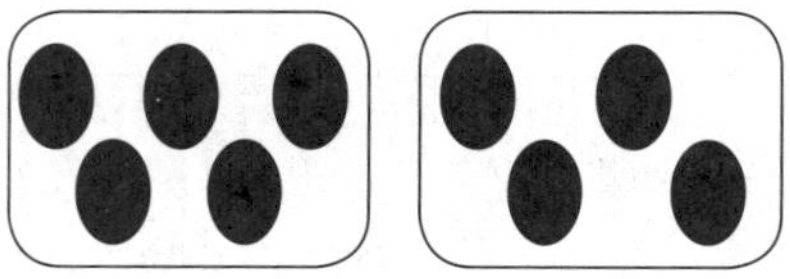

2. 6 + 4 = ______

3. What is the difference between 10 and 8?

____

4. 8 + 7 = ☐ + 9

5. Color the base of the solid.

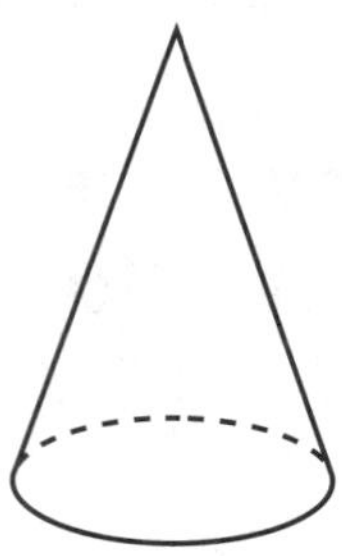

6. Write the area.

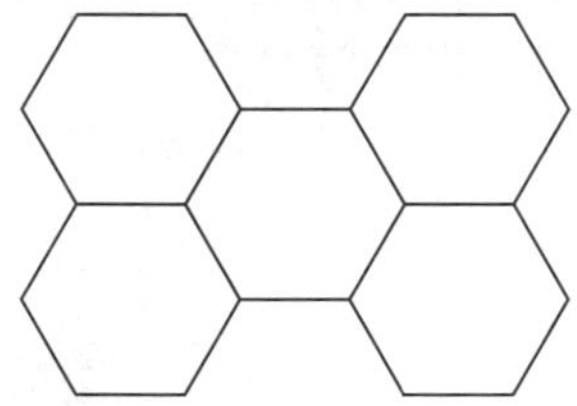

area = ______ hexagons

7.

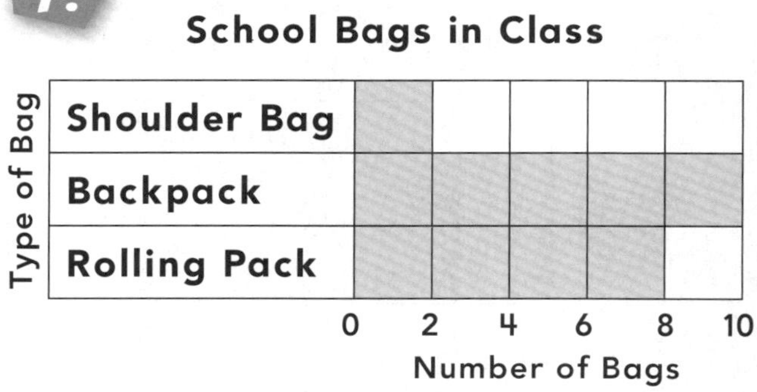

Which kind of school bag did the fewest kids have?

____

8. Molly's bag of chips had 15 chips in it. She gave 6 to her friend Mike and 4 to her friend Sally. How many chips were left for Molly to eat?

____

NAME: ______________________

DIRECTIONS Solve each problem.

1. Write the missing number.

69		71	72	73

2.
$$\begin{array}{r} 4 \\ +\ 8 \\ \hline \end{array}$$

3. 6 – 4 = ______

4. Continue the pattern.

A A B B A

______ ______ ______

5. Draw a line of symmetry.

6. Show 10 o'clock.

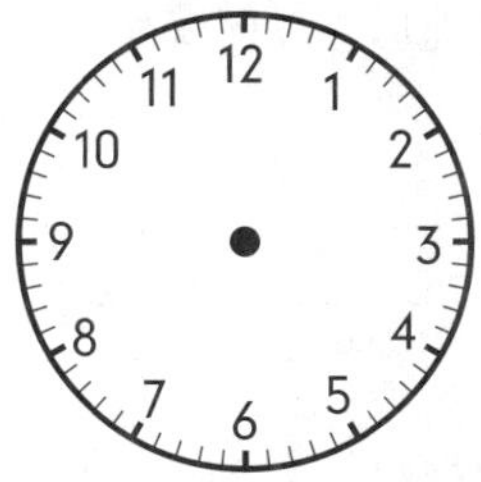

7.

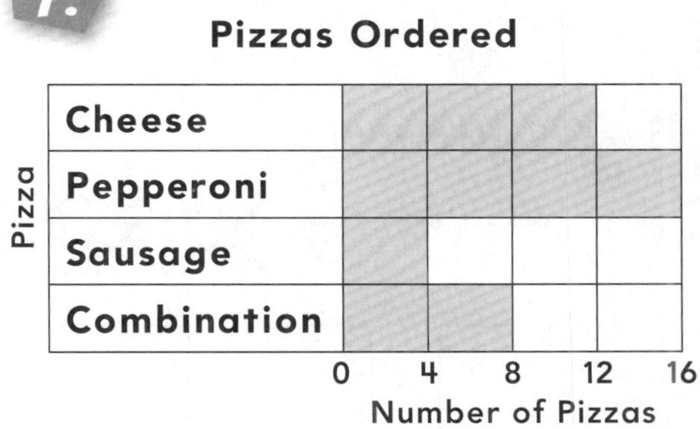

How many pepperoni pizzas were ordered?

____

8. Six frogs are on a log. Two hop off the log. How many frogs are still on the log?

____

SCORE

1. ☺ 😐
2. ☺ 😐
3. ☺ 😐
4. ☺ 😐
5. ☺ 😐
6. ☺ 😐
7. ☺ 😐
8. ☺ 😐

____ / 8
Total

NAME: ______________________

DIRECTIONS Solve each problem.

SCORE

1. ☺ ☹
2. ☺ ☹
3. ☺ ☹
4. ☺ ☹
5. ☺ ☹
6. ☺ ☹
7. ☺ ☹
8. ☺ ☹

____ / 8 Total

1. Write the numeral.

7	Tens	6	Ones

____

2. Seven plus six equals

______________________.

3. Subtract.

☐ – ☐ = ☐

4. 9 + ☐ = 17

5. How many vertices are there?

______ vertices

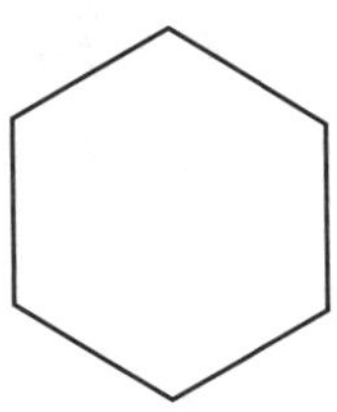

6. Write the day of the week that comes after Sunday.

____

7. Library Books Checked Out

	Week 1	Week 2	Week 3
Jody	4	5	5
Emily	4	4	4
Brenda	5	7	6
Alison	6	3	6

In which week did Brenda check out the most books?

____

8. Write the related addition problem.

23 – 8 = 15

____

NAME: ____________________

DIRECTIONS Solve each problem.

1. Use >, <, or =.

72 ◯ 42

2.

$$\begin{array}{r} 7 \\ +\ 1 \\ \hline \end{array}$$

3. 9 – 3 = ______

4. 10 ☐ 6 = 4

5. Color the shape with 4 sides.

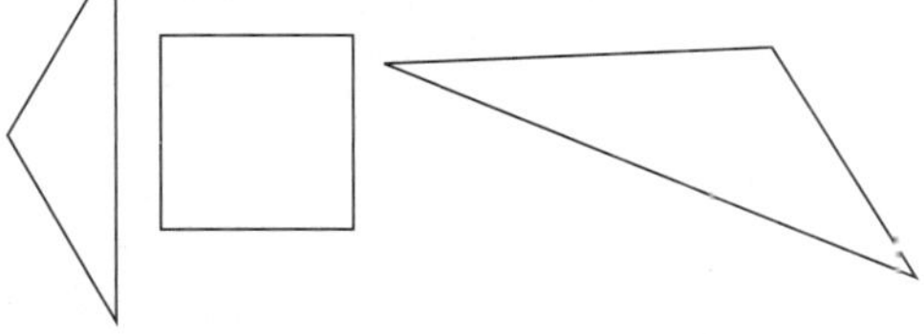

6. What is the volume?

______ cubes

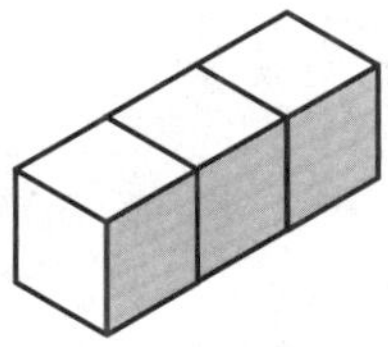

7. Record the data in the chart.

- Dawn scored 4 goals.
- Carrie scored 2 goals.
- Tom scored 5 goals.

8. Daniel practices piano every day. How many days a week does he practice?

____

SCORE

1.

2.

3.

4.

5.

6.

7.

8.

____ / 8 Total

DAY 38

NAME: ______________________

DIRECTIONS Solve each problem.

SCORE

1.

2.

3.

4.

5.

6.

7.

8.

____/8 Total

1. Color half.

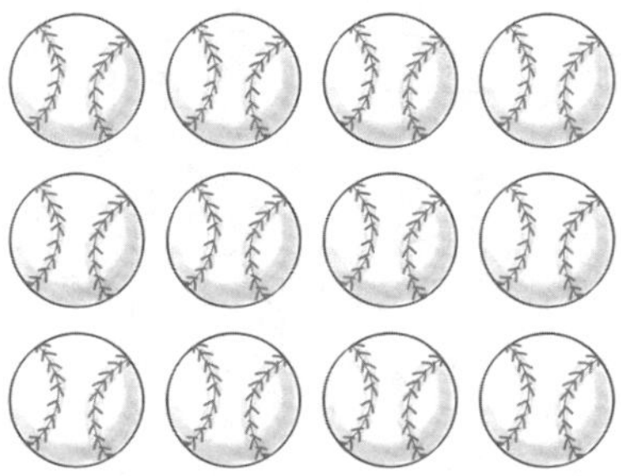

2. 5 + 1 = ______

3. 7 – 4 = ______

4. 5 – 3 = ☐ – 6

5. Circle the object that can roll.

6. Circle the best estimate.

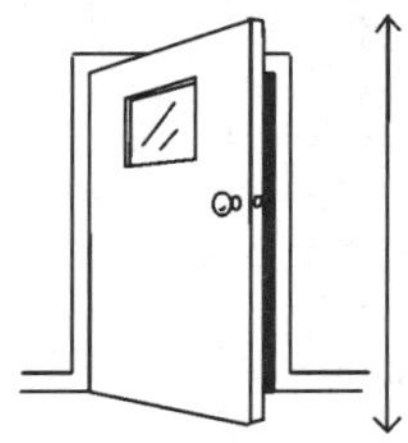

5 m 2 m

7. Ages

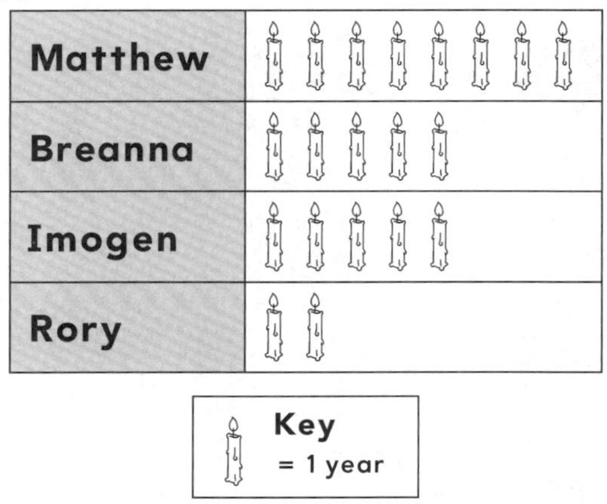

Is Matthew older than Imogen?

Circle: yes no

8. I am 6 more than 13. What number am I?

____

DAY **39**

NAME: ____________________

DIRECTIONS Solve each problem.

1. Write the numeral for eighty-six.

____

2.

$$\begin{array}{r} 8 \\ +\ 3 \\ \hline \end{array}$$

3. 5 – 3 = ______

4. 10 + 3 = 7 + ☐

5. Draw the front view of the solid.

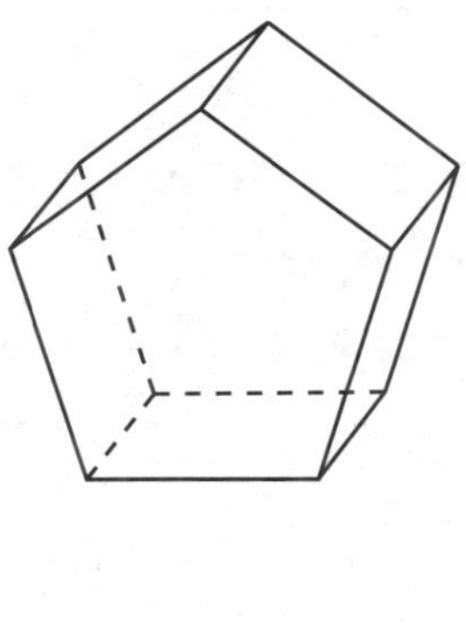

6. Is a door taller or shorter than a yard?

____

7.

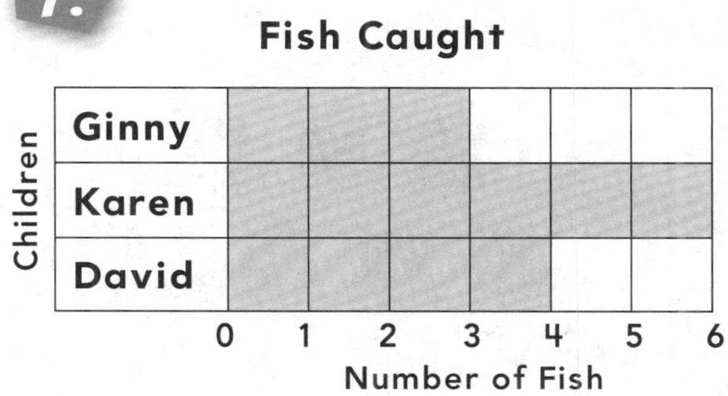

How many fish did David catch?

____

8. Three families went out for pizza. Each family ordered 2 medium pizzas. What was the total number of pizzas ordered?

____

SCORE

1. ☺ 😐
2. ☺ 😐
3. ☺ 😐
4. ☺ 😐
5. ☺ 😐
6. ☺ 😐
7. ☺ 😐
8. ☺ 😐

____ / 8
Total

NAME: ____________________________

DIRECTIONS Solve each problem.

SCORE

1. ☺ 😐
2. ☺ 😐
3. ☺ 😐
4. ☺ 😐
5. ☺ 😐
6. ☺ 😐
7. ☺ 😐
8. ☺ 😐

___ / 8
Total

1. Circle about how many times a week you take a bath.

7 60

2. 6 + 10 = ______

3. Subtract.

☐ – ☐ = ☐

4. Eunice has 5 soccer games every month. How many games does she have after 4 months?

____

1 Month	2 Months	3 Months	4 Months
5	10	15	

5. Color the solid.

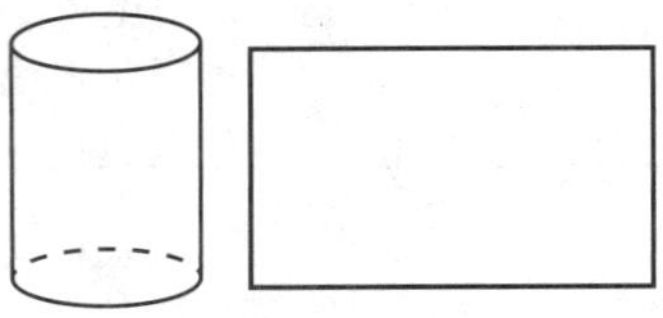

6. Circle the container that holds the least.

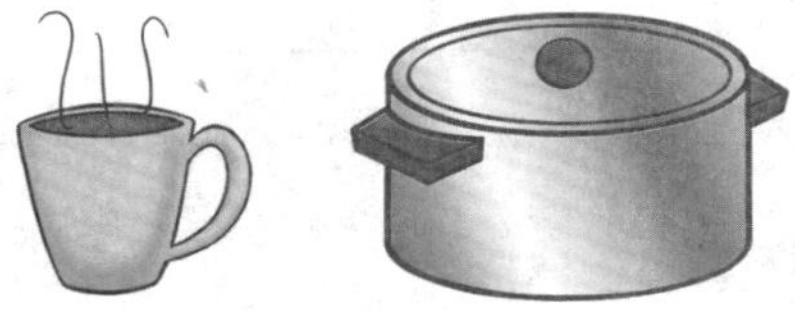

7. Toy Train Sales Last Week

Mon.	
Tues.	
Wed.	
Thurs.	
Fri.	
Sat.	
Sun.	

Key
 = 1 train

On which day were the most trains sold?

____

8. Is a book about 12 yards, 12 feet, or 12 inches tall?

____

NAME: ______________________

DIRECTIONS Solve each problem.

SCORE

1. Write the numeral.

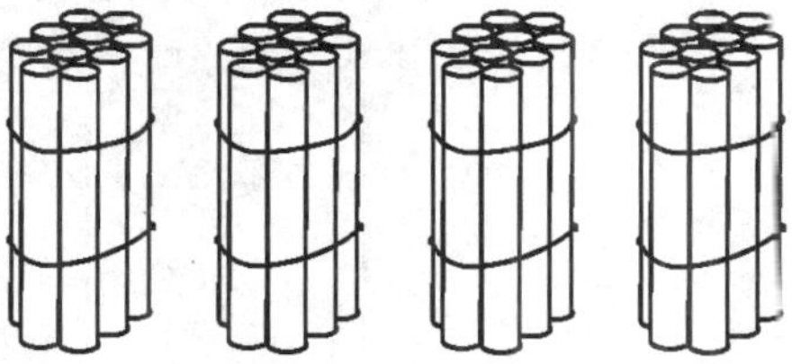

____

2. 4 + 8 = ______

3.
$$\begin{array}{r} 10 \\ -\ 4 \\ \hline \end{array}$$

4. Write the missing number.

15	20	25	30	

5. Circle the object that looks like the solid.

6. Jamal begins to watch TV at 4:00 P.M. and stops at 5:00 P.M. For how long does he watch TV?

____

7. How many tally marks are there?

____

8. Would a hot day be about 19°F, 49°F, or 89°F?

____

1. ☺ ☹
2. ☺ ☹
3. ☺ ☹
4. ☺ ☹
5. ☺ ☹
6. ☺ ☹
7. ☺ ☹
8. ☺ ☹

___ / 8
Total

NAME: ____________________

DIRECTIONS Solve each problem.

SCORE

1.

2.

3.

4.

5.

6.

7.

8.

____ / 8 Total

1. Circle the smaller number.

139   193

2.

$$\begin{array}{r} 5 \\ +\ 7 \\ \hline \end{array}$$

3. 2 less than 4 is

____________________.

4. 8 – ☐ = 6

5. Circle the triangle.

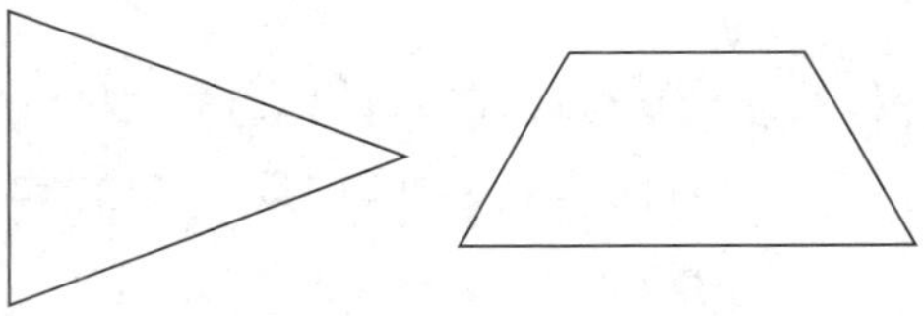

6. Circle how long it takes to brush your teeth.

more than 1 hour

less than 1 hour

7.

Favorite Pets

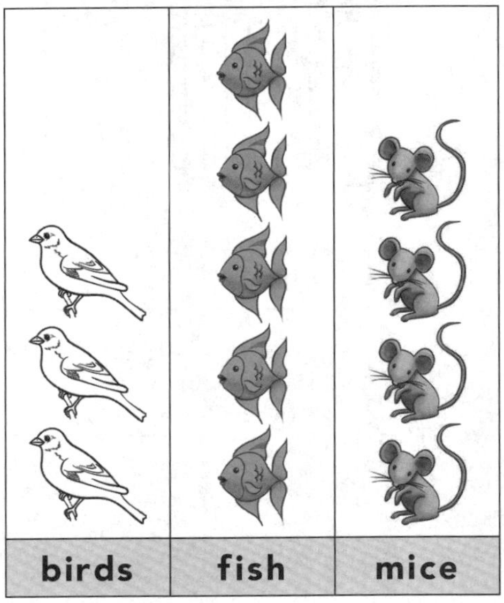

How many people like birds best?

____

8. How many wheels are on 5 cars?

____

NAME: ____________________

DIRECTIONS Solve each problem.

1. Name the shaded fraction.

____

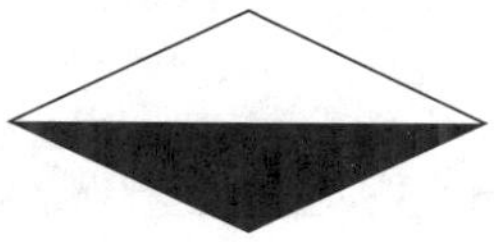

2. 9 + 6 = ______

3.

$$\begin{array}{r} 9 \\ -\ 5 \\ \hline \end{array}$$

4. 3 − 0 = 9 − ☐

5. True or false? Shapes with four sides can have more than four angles.

____

6. Circle the season that matches the months below.

winter spring
summer fall

December
January
February

7. Car Colors

<table>
<tr><td>Red</td><td>𝍸 𝍸 |||</td></tr>
<tr><td>Blue</td><td>𝍸 𝍸 𝍸 𝍸 |</td></tr>
<tr><td>Yellow</td><td>𝍸 ||||</td></tr>
<tr><td>Green</td><td>𝍸 𝍸 𝍸 ||</td></tr>
</table>

Are there more yellow cars or green cars?

____

8. Write the number that has 3 in the ones place and 7 in the tens place.

____

SCORE

1. ☺ 😐
2. ☺ 😐
3. ☺ 😐
4. ☺ 😐
5. ☺ 😐
6. ☺ 😐
7. ☺ 😐
8. ☺ 😐

___ / 8
Total

NAME: ______________________

DIRECTIONS Solve each problem.

SCORE

1. ☺ 😐
2. ☺ 😐
3. ☺ 😐
4. ☺ 😐
5. ☺ 😐
6. ☺ 😐
7. ☺ 😐
8. ☺ 😐

____ / 8 Total

1. Is this a fair share?

Circle: yes no

2.

$$\begin{array}{r} 5 \\ +\ 2 \\ \hline \end{array}$$

3. Subtract.

☐ – ☐ = ☐

4. ☐ + 8 = 7 + 7

5. Draw all lines of symmetry.

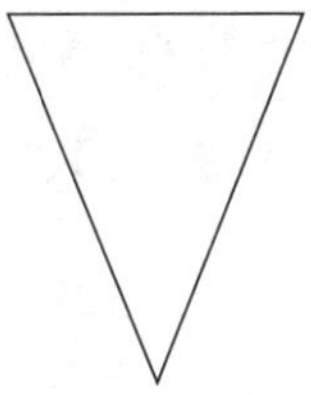

6. Write the area.

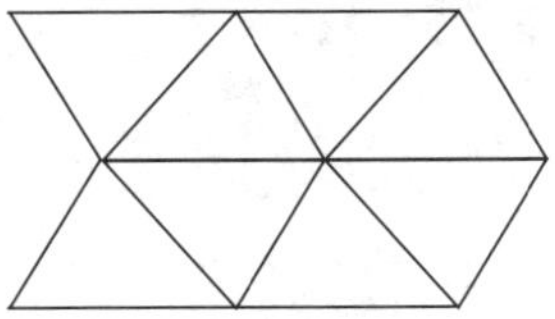

area = ______ triangles

7. Sports Played

	Soccer	Swimming	Baseball
Mark	X		X
Tracy		X	
Mike		X	X

Which two children play baseball?

____

8. Write all the 1-digit and 2-digit numbers you can make using the digits 4 and 6 once per number.

____

NAME: ____________________

DIRECTIONS Solve each problem.

1. Write the missing number.

87	88	89		91

2. 4 + 6 = ______

3. 7 – 3 = ______

4. Continue the pattern.

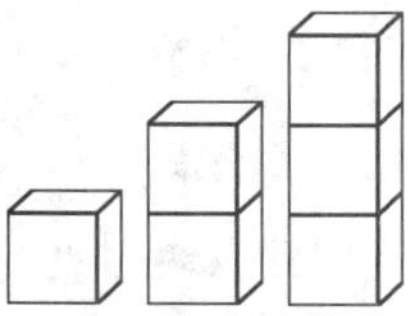

______ ______

5. Circle the cylinder.

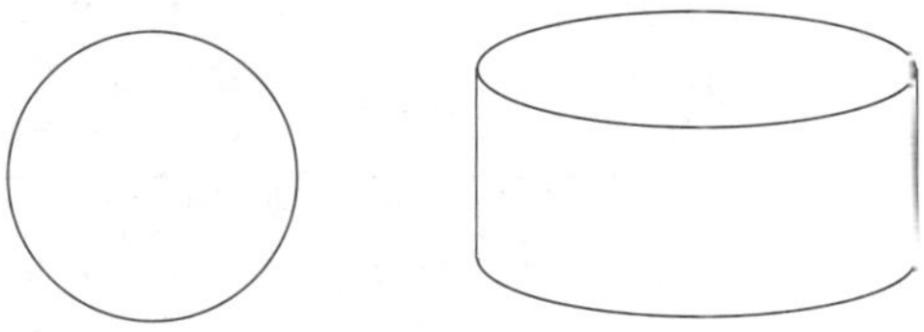

6. Show 7 o'clock.

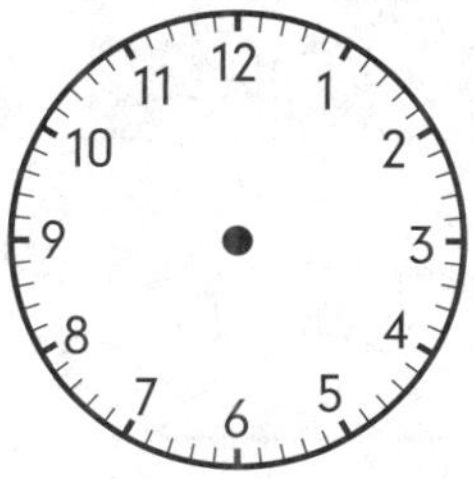

7. Flower Shop Orders

Rose	16
Daisy	23
Tulip	15
Iris	25

How many daisies and tulips were ordered?

____

8. There are 16 children on a soccer team. 13 show up to practice on Thursday. How many did not show up for practice?

____

SCORE

1. ☺ 😐
2. ☺ 😐
3. ☺ 😐
4. ☺ 😐
5. ☺ 😐
6. ☺ 😐
7. ☺ 😐
8. ☺ 😐

____ / 8
Total

NAME: ____________________

DIRECTIONS Solve each problem.

SCORE

1. ☺ 😐
2. ☺ 😐
3. ☺ 😐
4. ☺ 😐
5. ☺ 😐
6. ☺ 😐
7. ☺ 😐
8. ☺ 😐

____ / 8 Total

1. Write the numeral.

8	Tens	4	Ones

____

2. 6 more than 8 is

____________________.

3.

$$\begin{array}{r} 5 \\ -\ 3 \\ \hline \end{array}$$

4. 10 − ☐ = 4

5. Count the vertices.

______ vertices

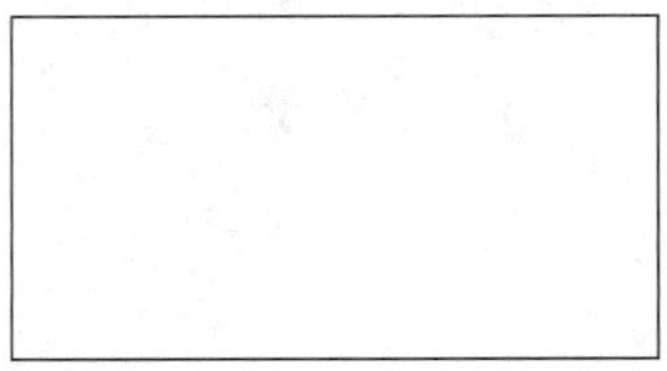

6. Write the day of the week that comes after Friday.

____

7. Make 23 tally marks.

8. Mrs. Mitchell wants to give one red pen to each of the 24 children in her class. Pens come in packs of 10. How many packs of pens should she buy?

____

NAME: ______________________________

DIRECTIONS Solve each problem.

1. Order the numbers from smallest to largest.

43 82 39 99

____

2. 8 + 2 = ______

3. Subtract 2 from 6 to find the difference.

____

4. ☐ − 1 = 4

5. How many sides does the shape have?

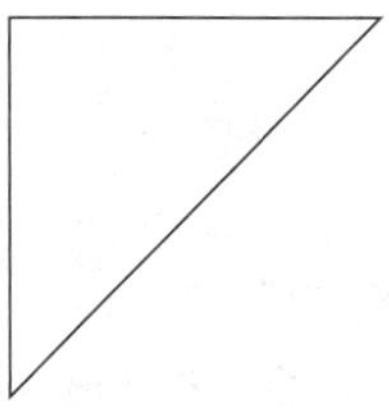

________ sides

6. What is the volume?

______ cubes

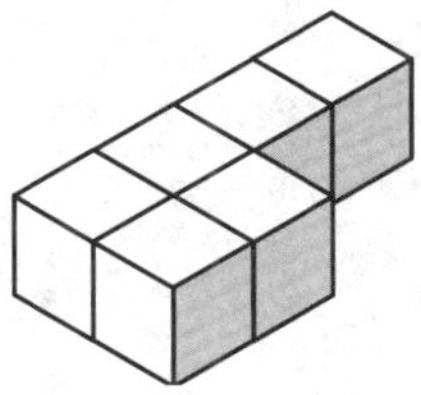

7. **Favorite Activity**

Movies	𝍸 𝍸 |||
Restaurant	𝍸 ||||
Park	𝍸 𝍸 ||
Stay Home	𝍸 |||

How many people like to go to the movies?

____

8. Write the number that is 5 more tens and 7 more ones than the number 32.

____

SCORE

1. ☺ 😐

2. ☺ 😐

3. ☺ 😐

4. ☺ 😐

5. ☺ 😐

6. ☺ 😐

7. ☺ 😐

8. ☺ 😐

____ / 8 Total

NAME: ____________________

DIRECTIONS Solve each problem.

SCORE

1. ☺ 😐

2. ☺ 😐

3. ☺ 😐

4. ☺ 😐

5. ☺ 😐

6. ☺ 😐

7. ☺ 😐

8. ☺ 😐

____ / 8

Total

1. Color half.

2. Two plus seven is

____________________.

3. Subtract.

☐ – ☐ = ☐

4. ☐ – 4 = 8 – 2

5. Circle the object that can stack.

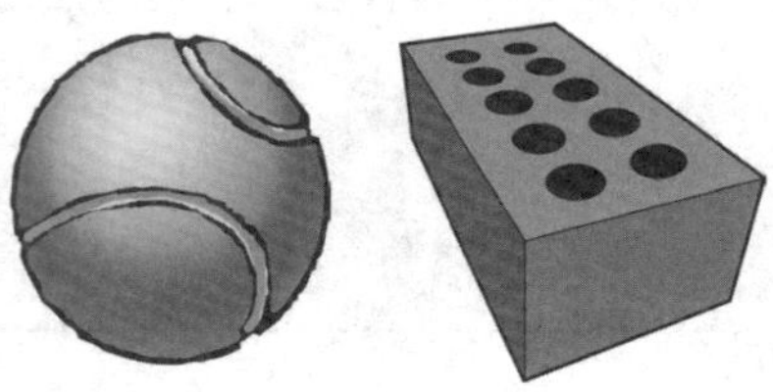

6. Is the object less than 1 meter, about 1 meter, or more than 1 meter tall?

____

7.

Who ran the fewest miles?

____

8. What is 12¢ less than 2 quarters?

____

NAME: ____________________

DIRECTIONS Solve each problem.

1. Write the numeral for seventy-four.

____

2.

$$\begin{array}{r} 7 \\ +\ 5 \\ \hline \end{array}$$

3. 8 – 8 = ______

4. 9 + ☐ = 8 + 8

5. Color the ovals.

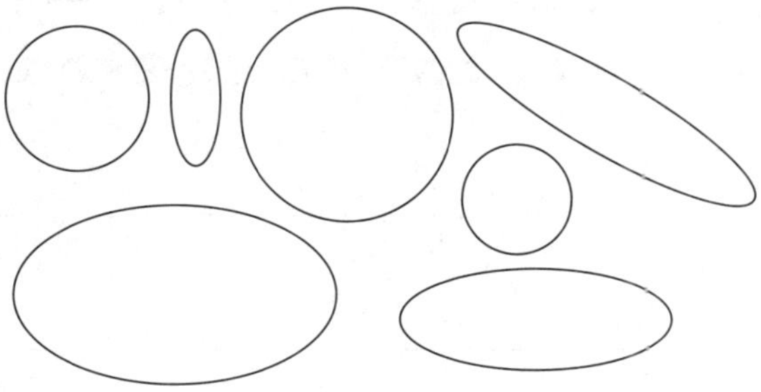

6. True or false?
You can hug another person in less than 1 minute.

____

7.

Pets

	Hamster	Dog	Fish	Cat
Mary	X		X	X
Julia	X	X		X
Evan	X	X		X

Who is the only person who owns a fish?

____

8. Brady gets 25¢ each day in allowance. How much money does he get each week?

____

SCORE

1. ☺ 😐
2. ☺ 😐
3. ☺ 😐
4. ☺ 😐
5. ☺ 😐
6. ☺ 😐
7. ☺ 😐
8. ☺ 😐

____ / 8 Total

DAY
50

NAME: ______________________________

DIRECTIONS Solve each problem.

SCORE

1.

2.

3.

4.

5.

6.

7.

8.

___ / 8

Total

1. Circle about how many pencils are in your desk.

5 50

2. 6 + 0 = ______

3. 9 less than 16 is

____________________.

4. Michael runs 3 miles every day. How many miles does he run in 5 days?

____

1 Day	2 Days	3 Days	4 Days	5 Days
3	6	9	12	

5. Color the correct cross-section.

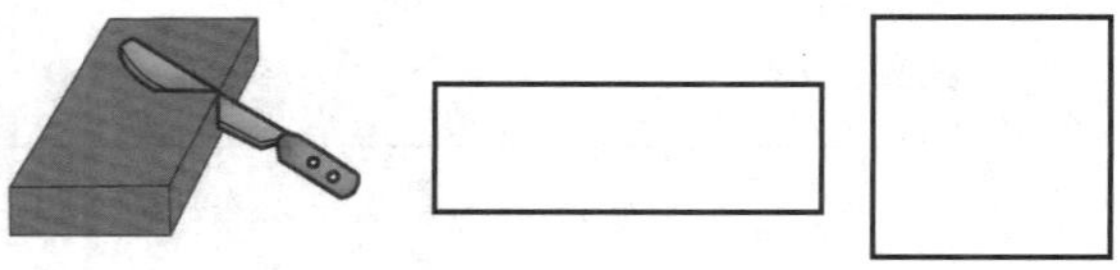

6. Circle the heavier object.

7.

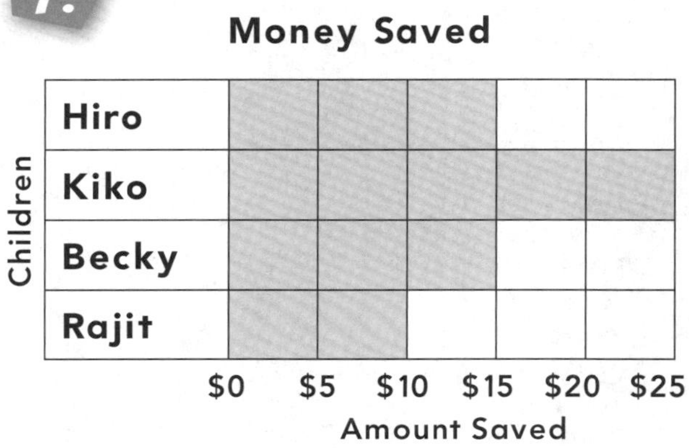

How much did Rajit save?

____________________.

8. Name three solids that can be stacked.

____

____

____

NAME: ______________________

DIRECTIONS Solve each problem.

1. Write the numeral.

____

2. 9 more than 4 is

______________________.

3.

$$\begin{array}{r} 13 \\ -\ \ 8 \\ \hline \end{array}$$

4. Write the missing number.

68		72	74	76

5. Name the solid.

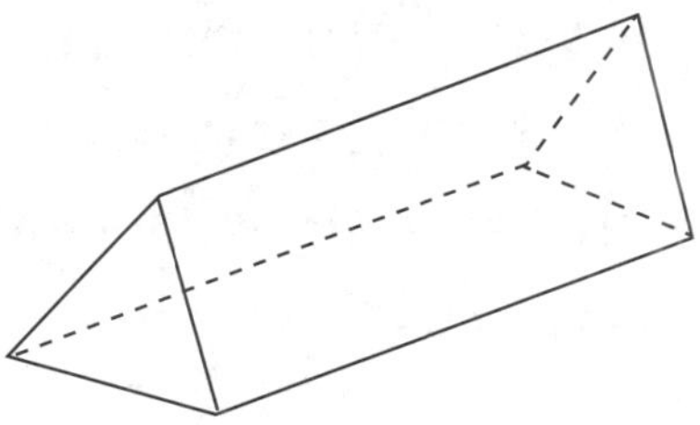

____

6. How many days are in March?

____

7. Teeth Lost

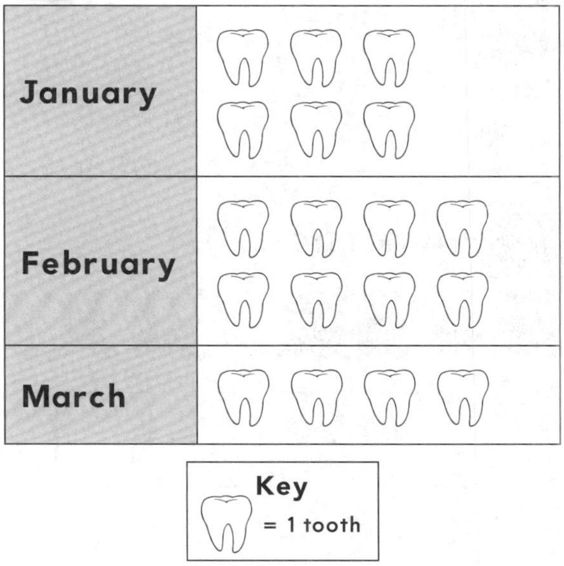

In which month were the fewest teeth lost?

____

8. You can watch TV for $1\frac{1}{2}$ hours. How many of your favorite 30-minute shows can you watch?

____

SCORE

1. ☺ 😐
2. ☺ 😐
3. ☺ 😐
4. ☺ 😐
5. ☺ 😐
6. ☺ 😐
7. ☺ 😐
8. ☺ 😐

___ / 8 Total

NAME: ____________________

DIRECTIONS Solve each problem.

SCORE

1. ☺ 😐
2. ☺ 😐
3. ☺ 😐
4. ☺ 😐
5. ☺ 😐
6. ☺ 😐
7. ☺ 😐
8. ☺ 😐

___ / 8 Total

1. What is the place value of 9 in 93?

____

2. 4 + 3 = ______

3. Subtract.

☐ – ☐ = ☐

4. 6 ☐ 5 = 1

5. Name the shape.

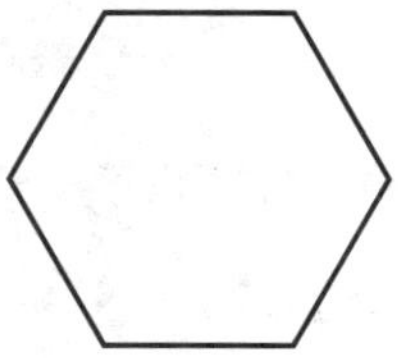

____

6. Circle the longer fish.

7.

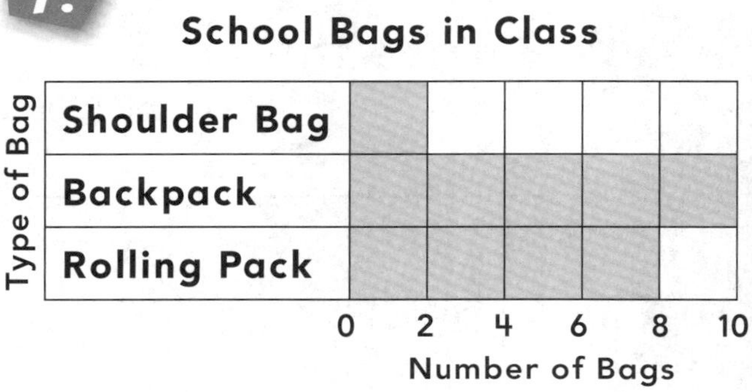

How many kids have backpacks?

____

8. Your mom bakes 2 pans of brownies. Each pan has 10 brownies. You and your friends eat 8 of the brownies. How many brownies are left?

____

NAME: ____________________

DIRECTIONS Solve each problem.

1. Name the shaded fraction.

____

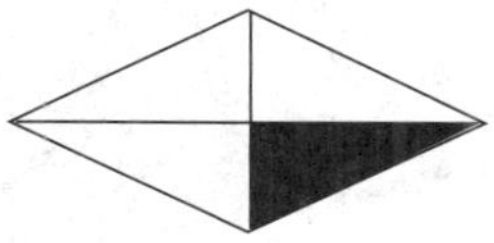

2.

$$\begin{array}{r} 6 \\ +\ 5 \\ \hline \end{array}$$

3. What is 5 less than 12?

____

4. 8 – ☐ = 6 – 4

5. True or false? A cross-section is where two lines come together.

____

6. Write the length.

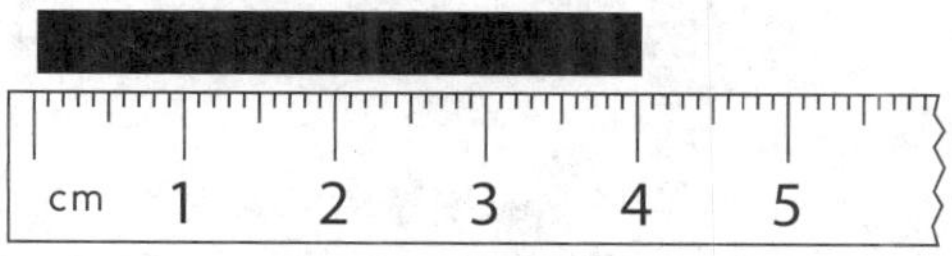

_____ centimeters

7.

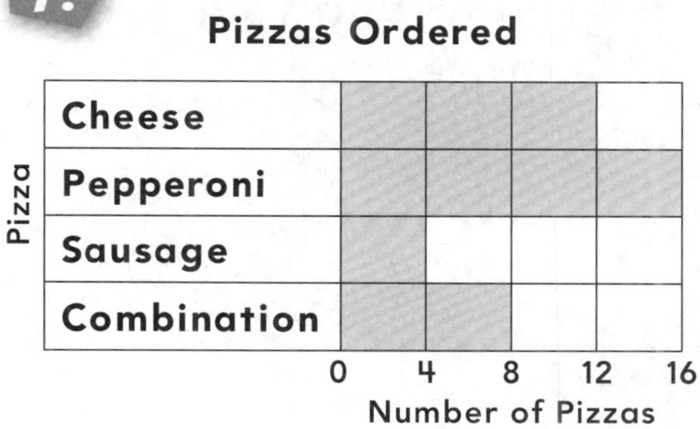

Which type of pizza was ordered least often?

____

8. Maria has 7 markers. She buys a new box that has 8 markers in it. How many markers does she have now?

____

SCORE

1. ☺ ☹
2. ☺ ☹
3. ☺ ☹
4. ☺ ☹
5. ☺ ☹
6. ☺ ☹
7. ☺ ☹
8. ☺ ☹

____ / 8 Total

DAY
54

NAME: ____________________

DIRECTIONS Solve each problem.

SCORE

1. ☺ ☹
2. ☺ ☹
3. ☺ ☹
4. ☺ ☹
5. ☺ ☹
6. ☺ ☹
7. ☺ ☹
8. ☺ ☹

____ / 8
Total

1. Is this a fair share?
Circle: yes no

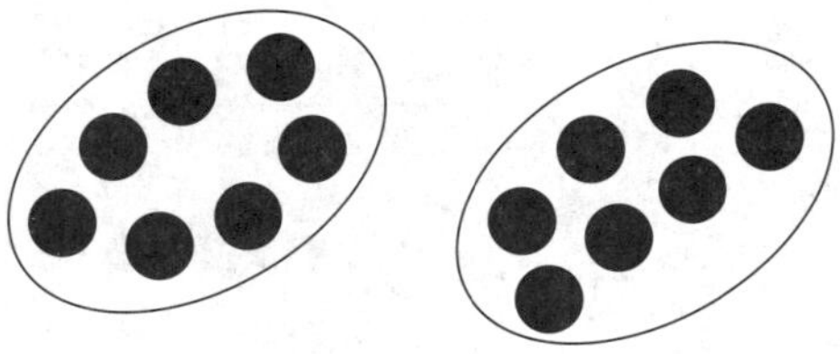

2. Nine and four more is

____________________.

3.

$$\begin{array}{r} 15 \\ -\ \ 8 \\ \hline \end{array}$$

4. 4 + 6 = ☐ + 0

5. Circle the doghouse that has the most dogs.

6. Color the coin with the larger area.

7.

Library Books Checked Out

	Week 1	Week 2	Week 3
Jody	4	5	5
Emily	4	4	4
Brenda	5	7	6
Alison	6	3	6

How many library books did Emily check out the second week?

____

8. Write a subtraction number sentence using the numbers 6, 7, and 13.

____

NAME: ______________________

DIRECTIONS Solve each problem.

1. Write the number that comes right before 62.

____

2. 8 + 10 = ______

3. What is the difference between 11 and 9?

____

4. Continue the pattern.

______ ______

5. Circle the cone.

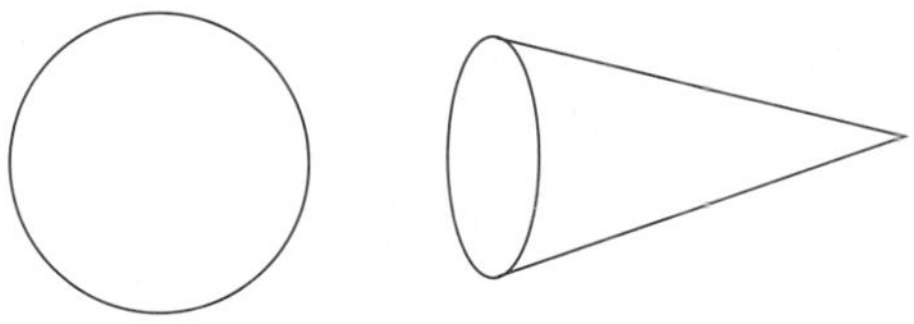

6. Write the time.

______ o'clock

7. Record the data. Write each animal name in the chart.

	Farm Animal	Zoo Animal
Tyrone		
Emile		
Peter		

- Peter likes tigers and cows.
- Tyrone likes goats and zebras.
- Emile likes lions and sheep.

8. A movie begins at 3:30 P.M. and ends at 6:00 P.M. How long was the movie?

____

SCORE

1. ☺ 😐
2. ☺ 😐
3. ☺ 😐
4. ☺ 😐
5. ☺ 😐
6. ☺ 😐
7. ☺ 😐
8. ☺ 😐

____ / 8
Total

NAME: ____________________

DIRECTIONS Solve each problem.

SCORE

1. ☺ 😐
2. ☺ 😐
3. ☺ 😐
4. ☺ 😐
5. ☺ 😐
6. ☺ 😐
7. ☺ 😐
8. ☺ 😐

____ / 8
Total

1. Write the numeral.

5	Tens	8	Ones

____

2.

$$\begin{array}{r} 9 \\ +\ 2 \\ \hline \end{array}$$

3. Subtract.

☐ – ☐ = ☐

4. ☐ + 9 = 15

5. Is this a polygon?

Circle: yes no

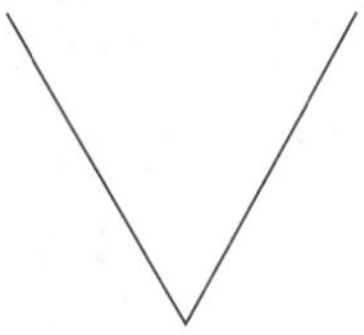

6. Write the month that comes after November.

____

7. Ages

Matthew	
Breanna	
Imogen	
Rory	

 Key = 1 year

Who is the oldest?

____

8. I am 3 less than 21. What number am I?

____

NAME: ____________________

DIRECTIONS Solve each problem.

1. Use >, <, or =.

89 ◯ 89

2. 5 + 5 = ______

3.
$$\begin{array}{r} 20 \\ -\ 10 \\ \hline \end{array}$$

4. 7 − ☐ = 0

5. Color the shape with 3 sides.

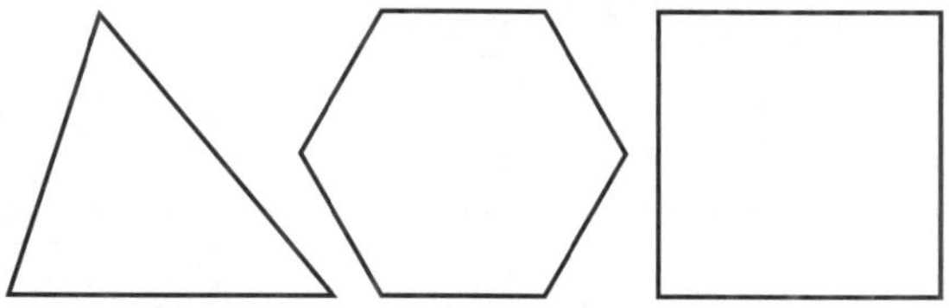

6. What is the volume?

______ cubes

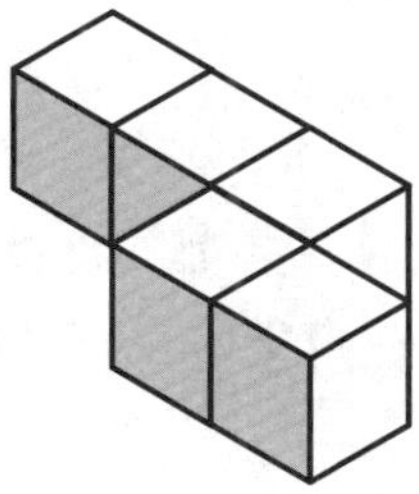

7.

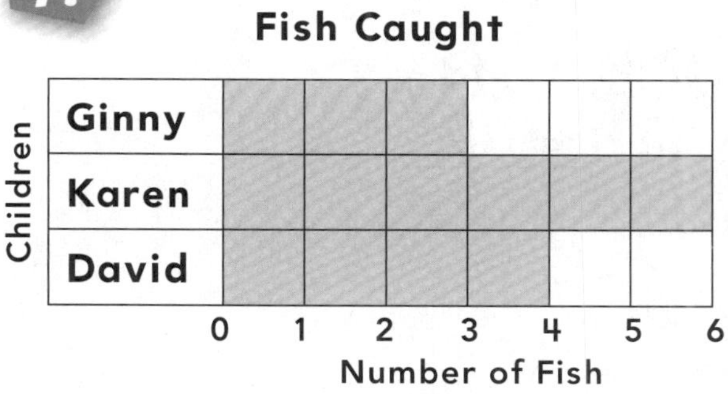

Who caught three fish?

____

8. Yulia brushes her teeth twice a day. How many times does she brush her teeth in 5 days?

____

SCORE

1. ☺ 😐

2. ☺ 😐

3. ☺ 😐

4. ☺ 😐

5. ☺ 😐

6. ☺ 😐

7. ☺ 😐

8. ☺ 😐

____ / 8
Total

DAY
58

NAME: ______________________________

DIRECTIONS Solve each problem.

SCORE

1. ☺ 😐
2. ☺ 😐
3. ☺ 😐
4. ☺ 😐
5. ☺ 😐
6. ☺ 😐
7. ☺ 😐
8. ☺ 😐

____ / 8
Total

1. Color $\frac{1}{2}$.

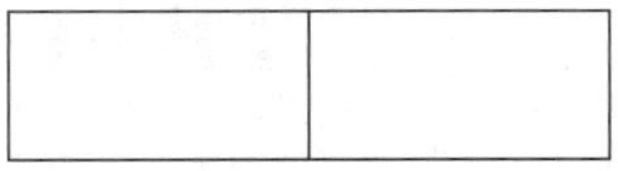

2. What is 8 more than 0?

____

3.

$$\begin{array}{r} 18 \\ -\ \ 7 \\ \hline \end{array}$$

4. 6 – 3 = ☐ – 2

5. Can the object stack?

Circle: yes no

6. Circle the object that would be taller than 1 meter.

7. **Toy Train Sales Last Week**

Mon.	
Tues.	
Wed.	
Thurs.	
Fri.	
Sat.	
Sun.	

Key
 = 1 train

On which day were the fewest trains sold?

____

8. What is the smallest 2-digit number you can make with the numbers 5, 3, and 6?

____

DAY 59

NAME: ______________________________

DIRECTIONS Solve each problem.

1. Write the numeral for four hundred fifty-two.

____

2. 7 + 3 = ______

3. 16 – 8 = ______

4. 7 + 4 = 8 + ☐

5. Draw the top view of the solid.

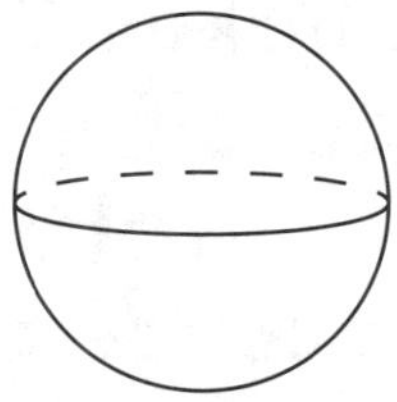

6. Circle the object with more mass.

7. Count the tally marks.

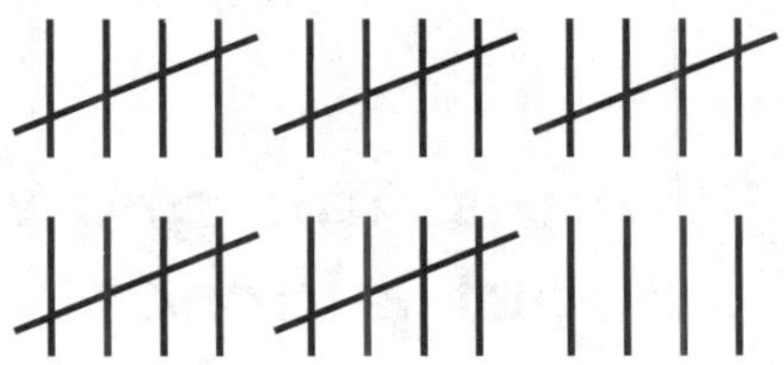

____

8. What is the smallest 3-digit number you can make with the numbers 9, 3, and 6?

____

SCORE

1. ☺ 😐
2. ☺ 😐
3. ☺ 😐
4. ☺ 😐
5. ☺ 😐
6. ☺ 😐
7. ☺ 😐
8. ☺ 😐

____ / 8

Total

DAY 60

NAME: ______________________________

DIRECTIONS Solve each problem.

SCORE

1. ☺ 😐
2. ☺ 😐
3. ☺ 😐
4. ☺ 😐
5. ☺ 😐
6. ☺ 😐
7. ☺ 😐
8. ☺ 😐

____ /8 Total

1. Circle about how many cups of water you drink each day.

5 50

2. $0 + 6 =$ ______

3.

$$\begin{array}{r} 13 \\ -\ \ 6 \\ \hline \end{array}$$

4. Tina's hair grows about 2 inches every month. About how many inches will her hair grow in 3 months?

____

1 Month	2 Months	3 Months
2		

5. Circle the prism.

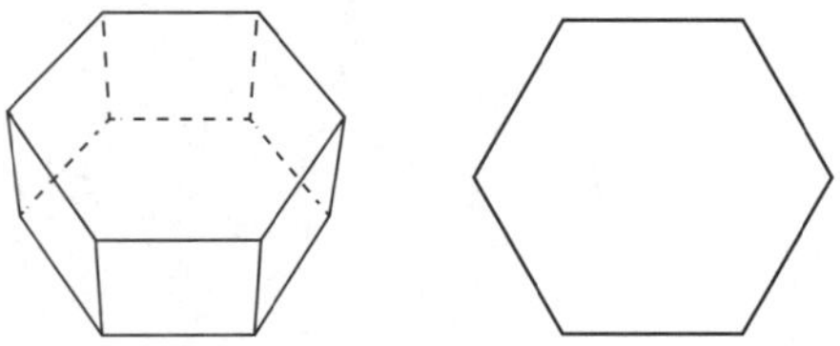

6. Circle the lighter object.

7.

Favorite Pets

Which type of pet is the least favorite?

____

8. Mom bakes 23 cupcakes for a party. At the party, 16 cupcakes are eaten. How many are not eaten?

____

DAY
61

NAME: ____________________

DIRECTIONS Solve each problem.

1. Write the numeral.

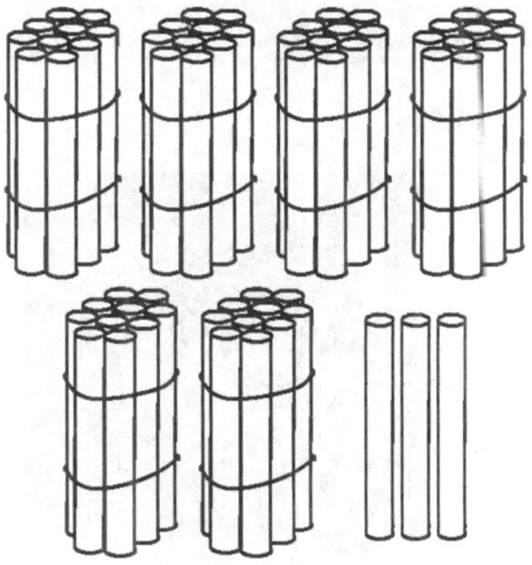

____

2.

$$\begin{array}{r} 4 \\ +\ 0 \\ \hline \end{array}$$

3. 15 – 5 = ______

4. Write the missing number.

30	40		60	70

5. Color one face on the solid.

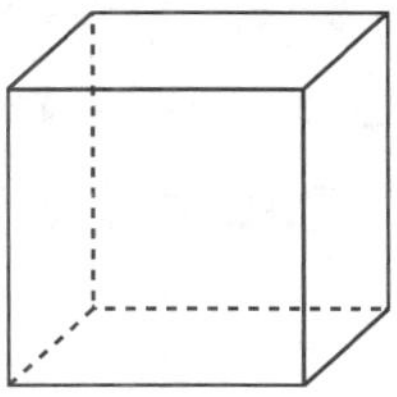

6. Write the time.

______ : ______

7. Car Colors

Red	𝍸 𝍸 |||
Blue	𝍸 𝍸 𝍸 𝍸 |
Yellow	𝍸 ||||
Green	𝍸 𝍸 𝍸 ||

How many cars are red?

____

8. Tina wants to buy a doll that costs $13.00. She gets $2.00 every week in her allowance. How many weeks will she have to save her allowance so she can buy the doll?

____

SCORE

1. ☺ 😐
2. ☺ 😐
3. ☺ 😐
4. ☺ 😐
5. ☺ 😐
6. ☺ 😐
7. ☺ 😐
8. ☺ 😐

____ / 8 Total

DAY
62

NAME: ____________________

DIRECTIONS Solve each problem.

SCORE

1. ☺ 😐
2. ☺ 😐
3. ☺ 😐
4. ☺ 😐
5. ☺ 😐
6. ☺ 😐
7. ☺ 😐
8. ☺ 😐

____ / 8
Total

1. Circle the larger number.

72 70

2. 8 + 8 = ______

3. 11 – 3 = ______

4. 7 – ☐ = 2

5. Circle the hexagon.

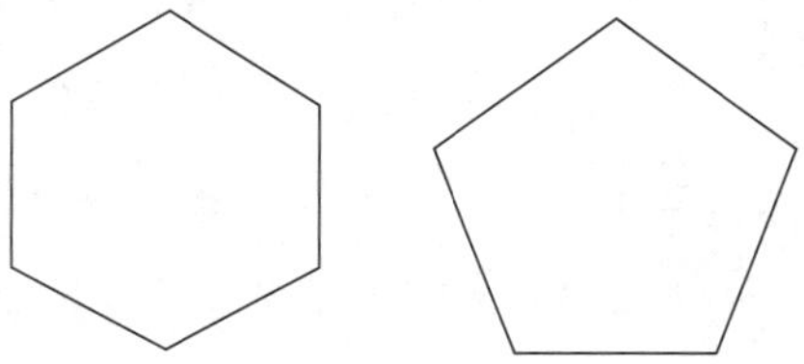

6. Circle how long it takes to sleep at night.

more than 1 hour

less than 1 hour

7. Sports Played

	Soccer	Swimming	Baseball
Mark	X		X
Tracy		X	
Mike		X	X

Which sport do both Mike and Tracy play?

____

8. Write the number that is 2 more tens and 6 more ones than the number 27.

____

DAY 63

NAME: ______________________________

DIRECTIONS Solve each problem.

1. Name the shaded fraction.

____

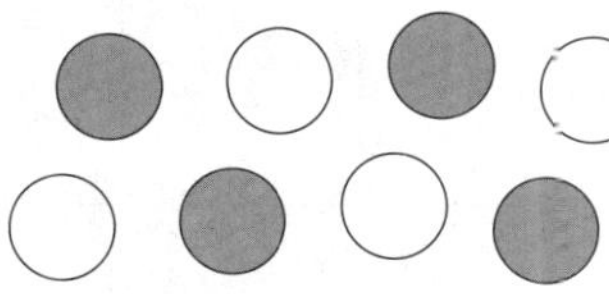

2.

$$\begin{array}{r} 6 \\ +\ 3 \\ \hline \end{array}$$

3. 19 – 7 = ______

4. 4 – 2 = 10 – ☐

5. Circle the polygon.

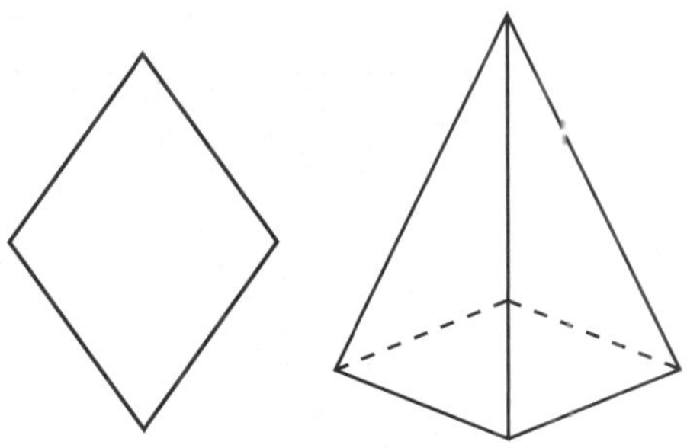

6. Write the length.

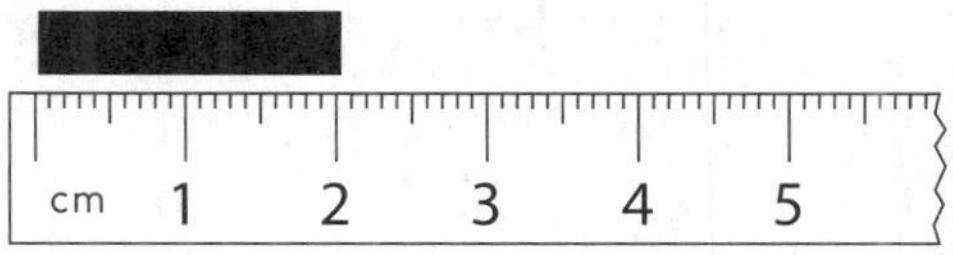

______ centimeters

7. Flower Shop Orders

Rose	16
Daisy	23
Tulip	15
Iris	25

If 7 more roses were added to the order, how many roses should be ordered?

____

8. Michael eats 3 apple slices every day. How many apple slices will he eat in 5 days?

____

SCORE

1. ☺ 😐
2. ☺ 😐
3. ☺ 😐
4. ☺ 😐
5. ☺ 😐
6. ☺ 😐
7. ☺ 😐
8. ☺ 😐

____ / 8 Total

DAY 64

NAME: ______________________

DIRECTIONS Solve each problem.

SCORE

1. ☺ 😐
2. ☺ 😐
3. ☺ 😐
4. ☺ 😐
5. ☺ 😐
6. ☺ 😐
7. ☺ 😐
8. ☺ 😐

____ / 8
Total

1. Is this a fair share?
Circle: yes no

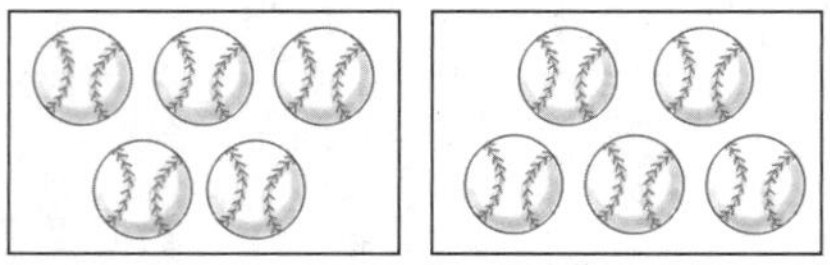

2. 4 + 7 = ______

3. What is the difference between 17 and 6?

____

4. ☐ + 3 = 7 + 5

5. Draw a line of symmetry.

6. Record the area.

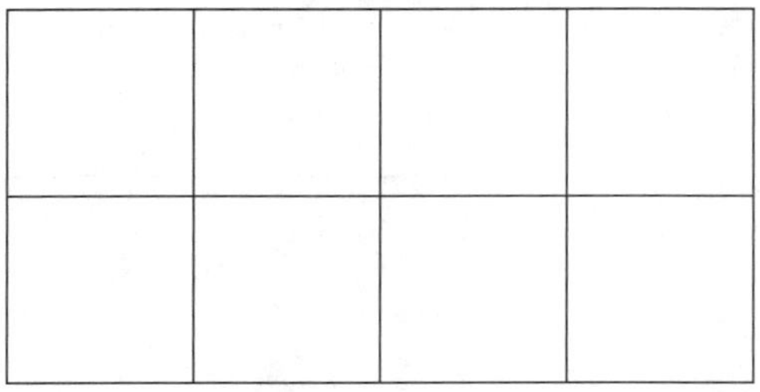

area = ____ squares

7. Make 7 tally marks.

8. Name three solids that can roll.

____

____

____

NAME: ______________________________

DIRECTIONS Solve each problem.

1. Write the number that comes right before 37.

____

2.

$$\begin{array}{r} 9 \\ +\ 1 \\ \hline \end{array}$$

3. 14 – 8 = ______

4. Continue the pattern.

A B C A B ____

5. Color one face of the solid.

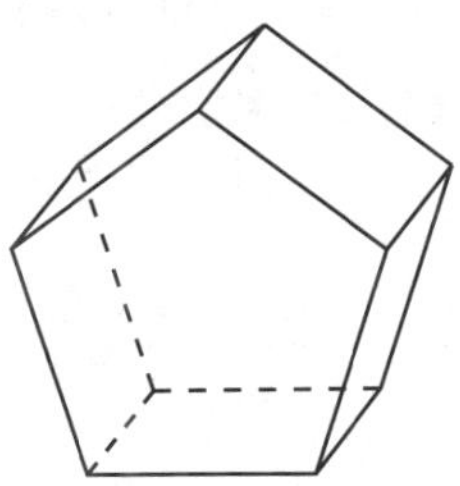

6. Show 1 o'clock.

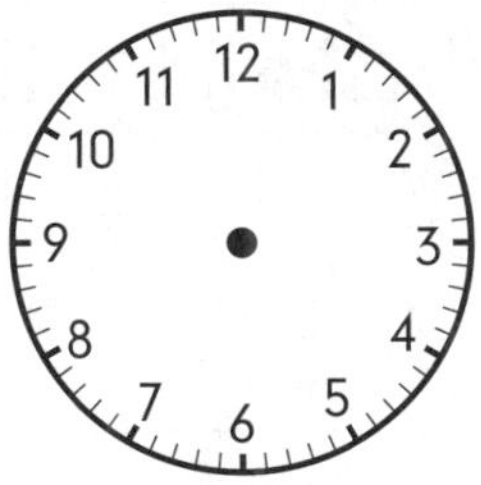

7.

Favorite Activity

Movies	𝍸𝍸𝍷𝍷𝍷
Restaurant	𝍸𝍷𝍷𝍷𝍷
Park	𝍸𝍸𝍷𝍷
Stay Home	𝍸𝍷𝍷𝍷

How many more people like going to the movies than staying home?

____

8. Jack has 15 quarters, 3 dimes, and 7 pennies. If he gets 6 more dimes, how many dimes will he have?

____

SCORE

1. ☺ 😐
2. ☺ 😐
3. ☺ 😐
4. ☺ 😐
5. ☺ 😐
6. ☺ 😐
7. ☺ 😐
8. ☺ 😐

____ / 8 Total

DAY 66

NAME: ______________________

DIRECTIONS Solve each problem.

SCORE

1. ☺ 😐
2. ☺ 😐
3. ☺ 😐
4. ☺ 😐
5. ☺ 😐
6. ☺ 😐
7. ☺ 😐
8. ☺ 😐

___ / 8

Total

1. Write the numeral.

9	Tens	2	Ones

____

2. What is the sum of nine and three?

____

3.

$$\begin{array}{r} 15 \\ -\ \ 9 \\ \hline \end{array}$$

4. $\square - 9 = 9$

5. How many vertices?

______ vertices

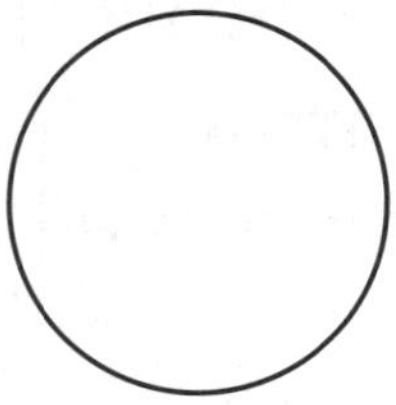

6. Write the day of the week that comes after Monday.

____

7.

How many miles did Cheryl run?

____

8. Which solid has 6 square faces?

____

NAME: ____________________

DIRECTIONS Solve each problem.

1. Order the numbers from largest to smallest.

86 17 49 22

____, ____, ____, ____

2. 8 + 5 = ______

3. 12 − 7 = ______

4. 8 ☐ 4 = 4

5. Color the shape with 4 sides.

6. What is the volume?

____________ cubes

7. Pets

	Hamster	Dog	Fish	Cat
Mary	X		X	X
Julia	X	X		X
Evan	X	X		X

Which animal does Julia not have?

____

8. Allison signed up for a karate class that meets every day for 1 month in March. How many days is the class?

____

SCORE

1. ☺ 😐
2. ☺ 😐
3. ☺ 😐
4. ☺ 😐
5. ☺ 😐
6. ☺ 😐
7. ☺ 😐
8. ☺ 😐

____ / 8 Total

DAY 68

NAME: ____________________

DIRECTIONS Solve each problem.

SCORE

1. ☺ 😐
2. ☺ 😐
3. ☺ 😐
4. ☺ 😐
5. ☺ 😐
6. ☺ 😐
7. ☺ 😐
8. ☺ 😐

____ / 8 Total

1. Color $\frac{1}{2}$.

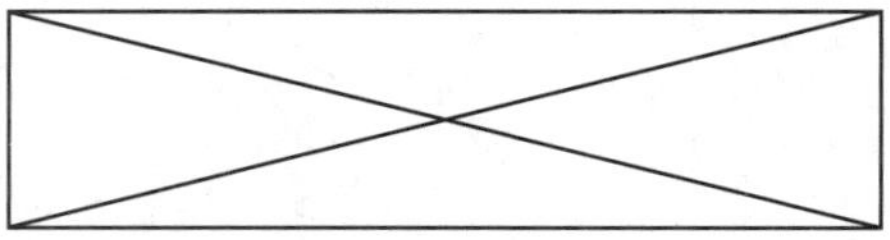

2.

$$\begin{array}{r} 7 \\ +\ 0 \\ \hline \end{array}$$

3. 11 – 5 = ______

4. ☐ – 4 = 7 – 2

5. Circle the object that can roll.

6. Circle the object that is shorter than 1 meter.

7.

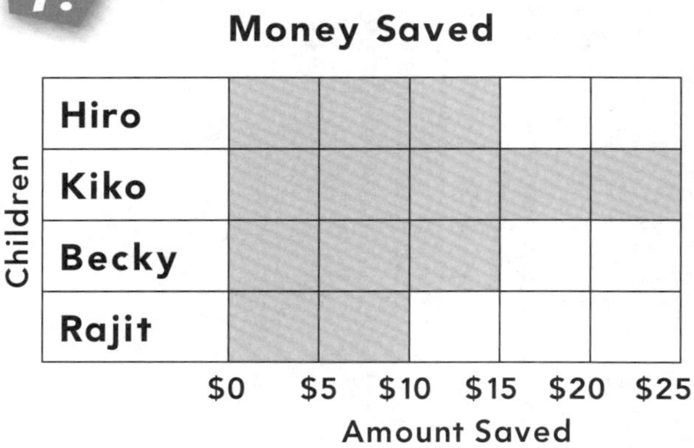

Who saved the least?

____

8. Michael has 16 fish in his tank. He buys 12 more. Michael's friend gives him two more fish. Now how many fish does Michael have?

____

NAME: ____________________

DIRECTIONS Solve each problem.

1. Write the number word for 71.

____

2. 7 + 6 = ______

3. 20 minus 4 is ______.

4. 5 + ☐ = 7 + 6

5. Draw the front view of the solid.

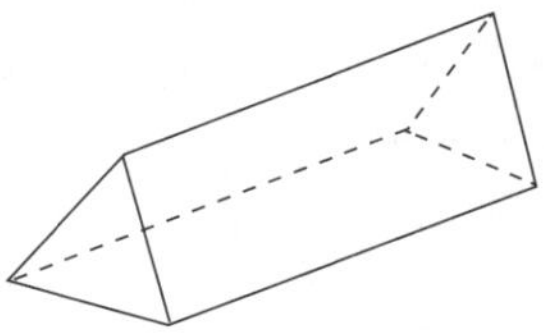

6. Draw the time on the clock.

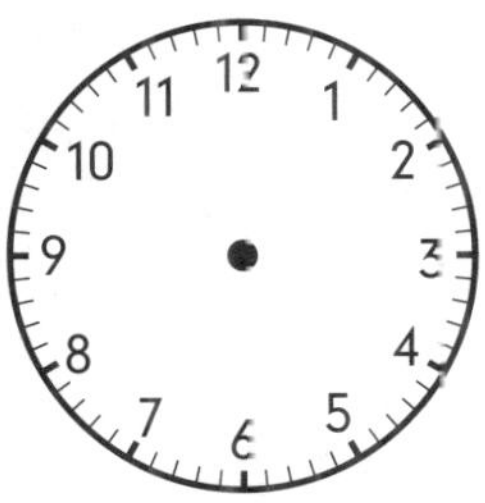

7. Teeth Lost

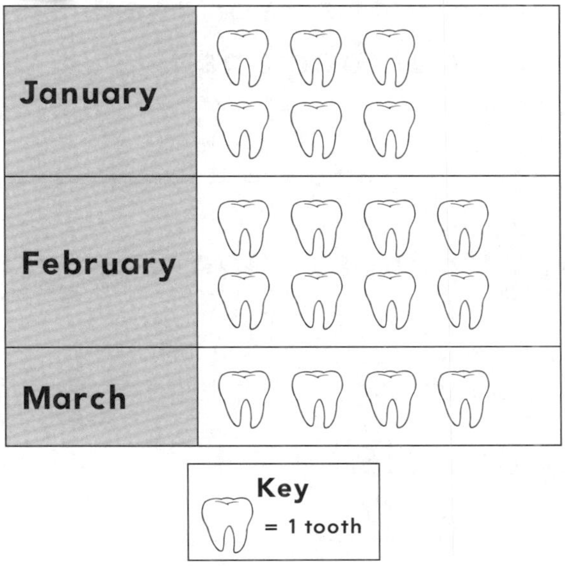

How many teeth were lost in February?

____

8. Michelle bought 9 peaches. Her family ate 5 of them. How many peaches are left?

____

SCORE

1. ☺ 😐
2. ☺ 😐
3. ☺ 😐
4. ☺ 😐
5. ☺ 😐
6. ☺ 😐
7. ☺ 😐
8. ☺ 😐

___ / 8 Total

DAY
70

NAME: ______________________________

DIRECTIONS Solve each problem.

SCORE

1. ☺ 😐
2. ☺ 😐
3. ☺ 😐
4. ☺ 😐
5. ☺ 😐
6. ☺ 😐
7. ☺ 😐
8. ☺ 😐

____ / 8
Total

1. Write the ordinal number for the number one.

____

2. 8 more than 9 is

______________________.

3.

$$\begin{array}{r} 16 \\ -\ \ 7 \\ \hline \end{array}$$

4. Count by twos and color each number counted.

1	2	3	4	5	6	7	8	9	10
11	12	13	14	15	16	17	18	19	20
21	22	23	24	25	26	27	28	29	30
31	32	33	34	35	36	37	38	39	40
41	42	43	44	45	46	47	48	49	50

5. Color the rhombus.

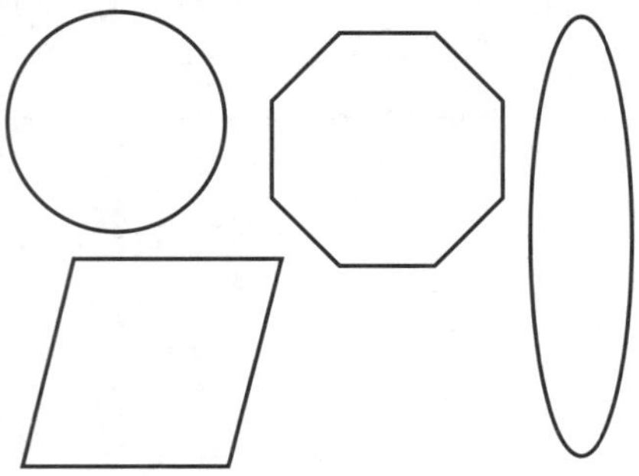

6. Circle the heavier object.

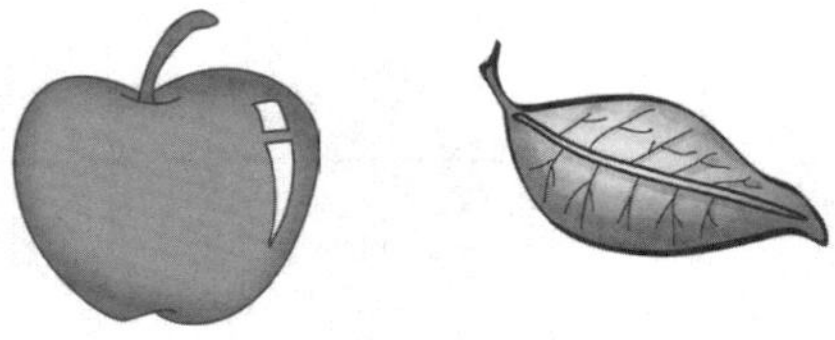

7.

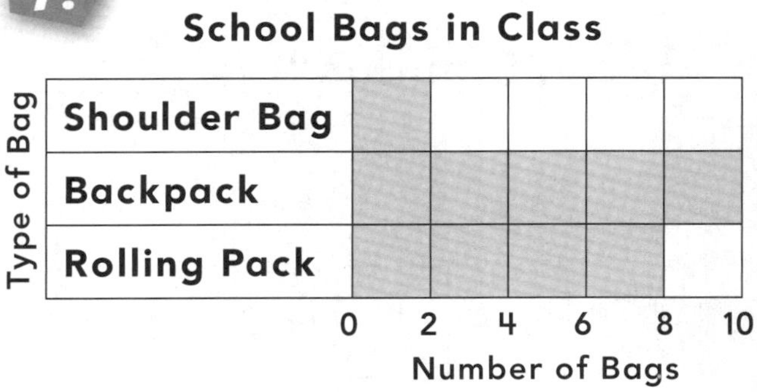

Which kind of school bag did most kids have?

____

8. Double 32, then add 14 more. What is the number?

____

NAME: ______________________

DIRECTIONS Solve each problem.

1. Write the numeral.

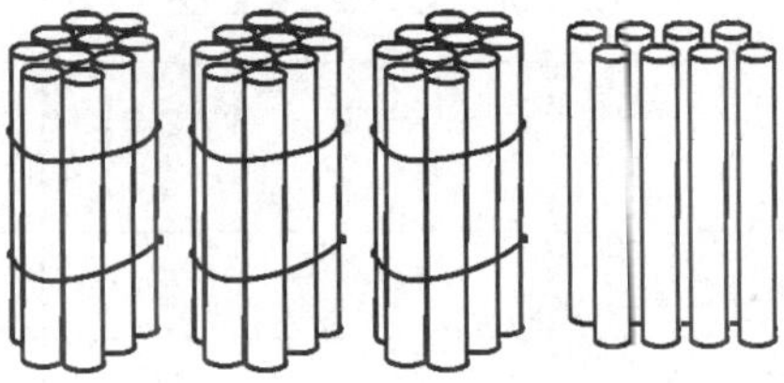

____

2. 9 + 5 = ______

3. What is 9 less than 18?

____

4. Write the missing number.

11	13	15	17	

5. Circle the object that looks like the solid.

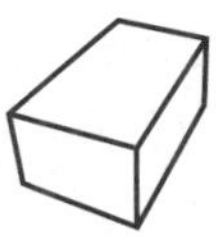

6. Tracy takes a nap from 2:30 P.M. until 3:30 P.M. How long is the nap?

____

7.

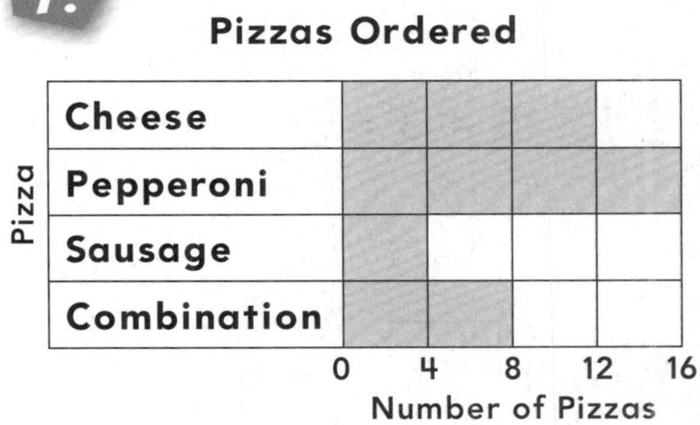

How many sausage pizzas were ordered?

____

8. Write the related subtraction problem.

43 + 56 = 99

____

SCORE

1.
2.
3.
4.
5.
6.
7.
8.

____ / 8 Total

DAY 72

NAME: ____________________

DIRECTIONS Solve each problem.

SCORE

1. ☺ 😐
2. ☺ 😐
3. ☺ 😐
4. ☺ 😐
5. ☺ 😐
6. ☺ 😐
7. ☺ 😐
8. ☺ 😐

____ / 8 Total

1. What is the place value of 7 in 71?

____

2.

$$\begin{array}{r} 4 \\ +\ 10 \\ \hline \end{array}$$

3. 15 – 3 = ______

4. 4 ☐ 0 = 4

5. Name the shape.

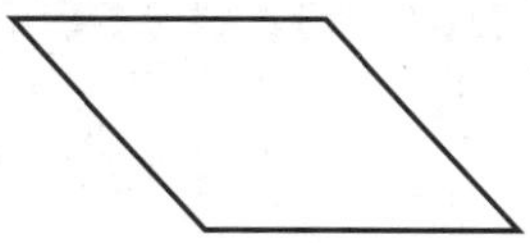

____

6. Circle the longer stick.

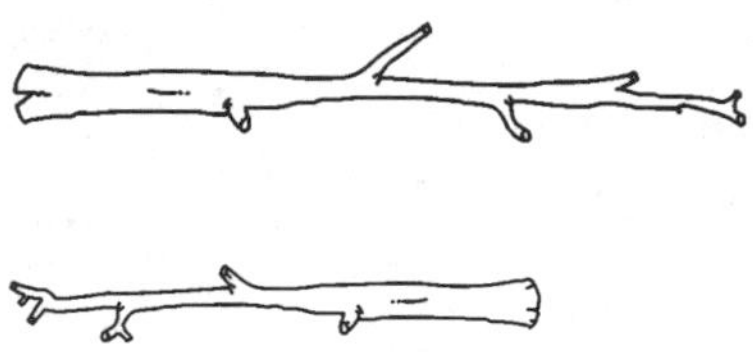

7. Library Books Checked Out

	Week 1	Week 2	Week 3
Jody	4	5	5
Emily	4	4	4
Brenda	5	7	6
Alison	6	3	6

Who checked out the most library books during the second week?

____

8. It is April 16th, and Marco is already planning for his birthday that is exactly three months away. What date is Marco's birthday?

____

DAY
73

NAME: ______________________________

DIRECTIONS Solve each problem.

1. Name the shaded fraction.

____

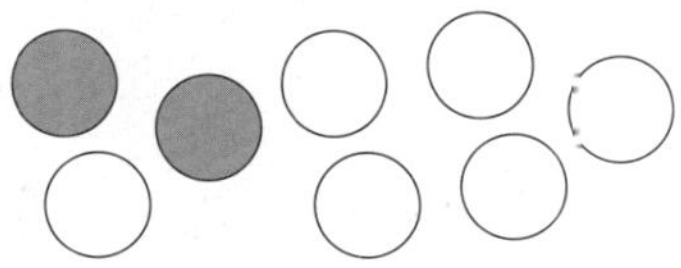

2. 5 + 6 = ______

3.

$$\begin{array}{r} 11 \\ -\ \ 6 \\ \hline \end{array}$$

4. 7 – ☐ = 9 – 7

5. True or false? Some shapes have more than one line of symmetry.

____

6. Write the length.

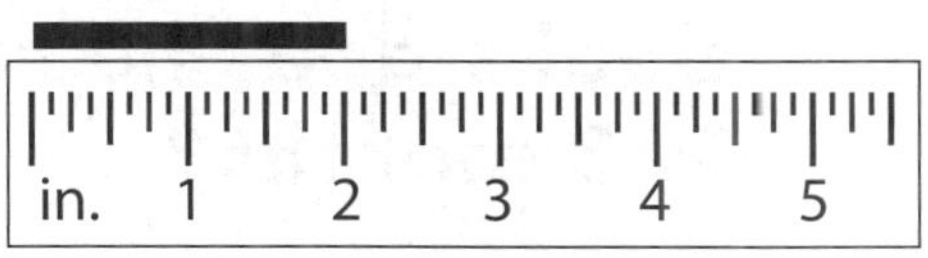

________ inches

7. Record the data in the chart. Use numbers.

- Marshall has fifty-eight trading cards.
- Amar has seventy-nine trading cards.
- Mitch has fifty-two trading cards.
- Esteban has thirty-one trading cards.
- Jose has forty-six trading cards.

Trading Cards

Marshall	
Jose	
Mitch	
Esteban	
Amar	

8. I am 10 less than 34. What number am I?

____

SCORE

1. ☺ 😐
2. ☺ 😐
3. ☺ 😐
4. ☺ 😐
5. ☺ 😐
6. ☺ 😐
7. ☺ 😐
8. ☺ 😐

____ / 8
Total

DAY
74

NAME: ______________________________

DIRECTIONS Solve each problem.

SCORE

1.
2.
3.
4.
5.
6.
7.
8.

____ / 8
Total

1. Is this a fair share?
Circle: yes no

2.
$$\begin{array}{r} 5 \\ +\ 4 \\ \hline \end{array}$$

3. Subtract 7 from 13 to find the difference.

____

4. 9 + 6 = ☐ + 7

5. Draw all lines of symmetry.

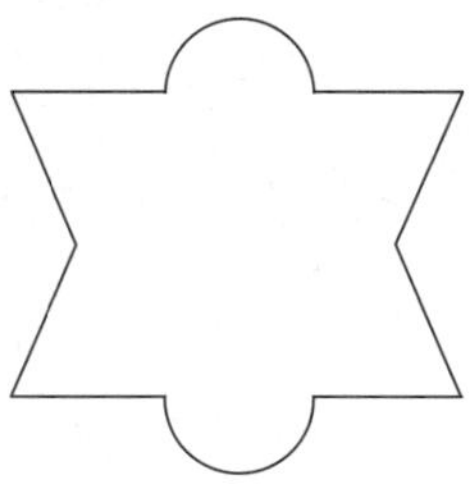

6. Record the area.

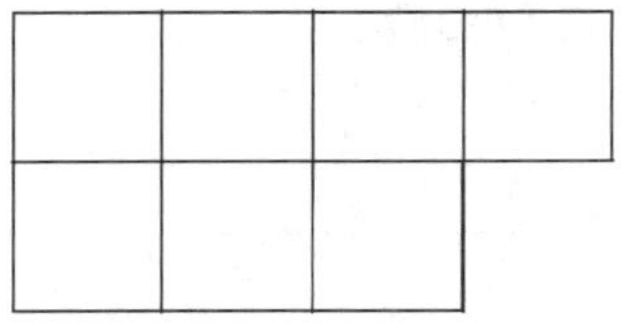

area = ____ squares

7.

Ages

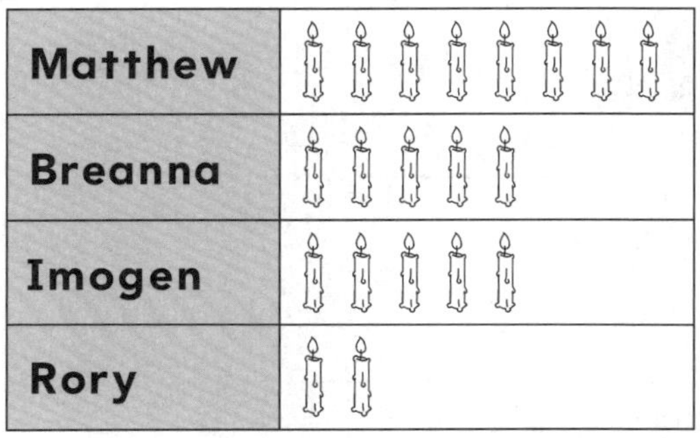

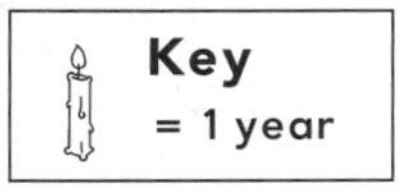

How old is Rory?

____

8. Mark reads 5 chapter books every month. How many books does he read in 3 months?

____

DAY 75

NAME: ____________________

DIRECTIONS Solve each problem.

1. Write the number that comes before 78.

____

2. 4 + 1 = ______

3. 19 – 9 = ______

4. Continue the pattern.

1, 2, 3, 4, 1, ______, ______

5. True or false?

You can see all sides of a cube at the same time.

____

6. Write the time.

______ o'clock

7.

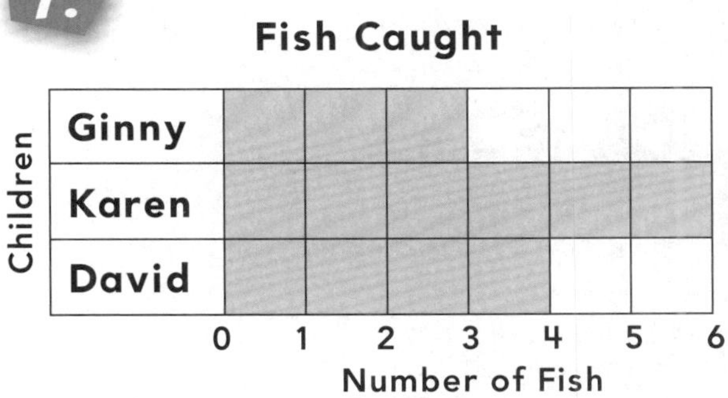

Who caught the fewest fish?

____

8. Circle the container that holds the most water.

swimming pool

bucket

bathtub

SCORE

1. ☺ 😐

2. ☺ 😐

3. ☺ 😐

4. ☺ 😐

5. ☺ 😐

6. ☺ 😐

7. ☺ 😐

8. ☺ 😐

____ / 8

Total

DAY 76

NAME: ____________________

DIRECTIONS Solve each problem.

SCORE

1. ☺ 😐
2. ☺ 😐
3. ☺ 😐
4. ☺ 😐
5. ☺ 😐
6. ☺ 😐
7. ☺ 😐
8. ☺ 😐

____ / 8 Total

1. Write the numeral.

2	Hundreds	3	Tens	5	Ones

____

2.

$$\begin{array}{r} 9 \\ +\ 9 \\ \hline \end{array}$$

3. 17 – 8 = ______

4. 6 + ☐ = 13

5. How many vertices?

______ vertices

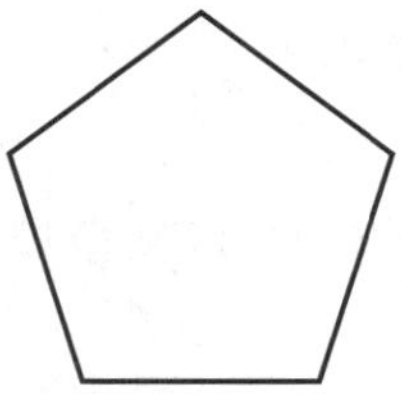

6. Write the month that comes after March.

____

7. Toy Train Sales Last Week

Mon.	
Tues.	
Wed.	
Thurs.	
Fri.	
Sat.	
Sun.	

Key
 = 1 train

How many trains were sold on the weekdays?

____

8. A group of cats has 16 legs. How many cats are there?

____

NAME: ______________________

DIRECTIONS Solve each problem.

SCORE

1. Use >, <, or =.

56 ◯ 65

2. 6 + 7 = ______

3. 14 – 6 = ______

4. ☐ – 8 = 1

5. How many sides does the shape have?

__________ sides

6. What is the volume?

______ cubes

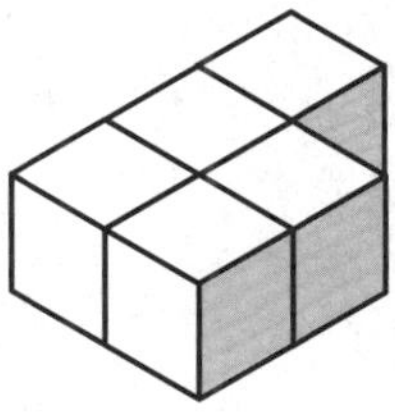

7. How many tally marks?

____

8. Write the number sentence:

Forty-eight minus thirty-two equals sixteen.

____

1. ☺ 😐
2. ☺ 😐
3. ☺ 😐
4. ☺ 😐
5. ☺ 😐
6. ☺ 😐
7. ☺ 😐
8. ☺ 😐

____ / 8

Total

NAME: ____________________

DIRECTIONS Solve each problem.

SCORE

1. ☺ ☹
2. ☺ ☹
3. ☺ ☹
4. ☺ ☹
5. ☺ ☹
6. ☺ ☹
7. ☺ ☹
8. ☺ ☹

____ / 8 Total

1. Color $\frac{1}{2}$.

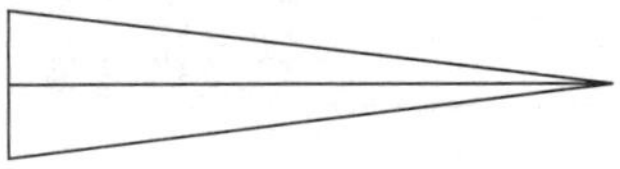

2.

$$\begin{array}{r} 8 \\ +\ 4 \\ \hline \end{array}$$

3. 15 – 7 = ______

4. 5 – 5 = ☐ – 8

5. Circle the object that can stack.

6. Is a ladder less than 1 meter, about 1 meter, or more than 1 meter?

____

7.

Favorite Pets

How many more votes for fish are there than mice?

____

8. What is the largest 3-digit number you can make with the numbers 4, 9, and 0?

____

NAME: ______________________

DIRECTIONS Solve each problem.

1. Write the numeral for six hundred forty-three.

____

2. Complete.

Double 2 = ______

3. What is 9 less than 12?

____

4. 4 + 7 = 11 + ☐

5. Color the correct cross-section.

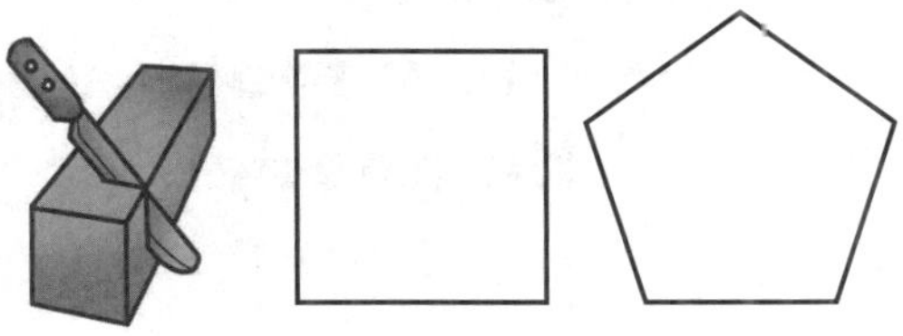

6. Is a cat longer or shorter than a yard?

____

7. Car Colors

Red	卌 卌 |||
Blue	卌 卌 卌 卌 |
Yellow	卌 ||||
Green	卌 卌 卌 ||

How many cars are green?

____

8. There are 9 mommy ducks. There are 43 ducklings. How many more ducklings are there than mommy ducks?

____

SCORE

1. ☺ 😐
2. ☺ 😐
3. ☺ 😐
4. ☺ 😐
5. ☺ 😐
6. ☺ 😐
7. ☺ 😐
8. ☺ 😐

____ / 8
Total

DAY 80

NAME: ____________________

DIRECTIONS Solve each problem.

SCORE

1. ☺ 😐
2. ☺ 😐
3. ☺ 😐
4. ☺ 😐
5. ☺ 😐
6. ☺ 😐
7. ☺ 😐
8. ☺ 😐

____ / 8 Total

1. Circle about how many children can fit on a school bus.

60 300

2. 7 + 2 = ______

3. 11 – 7 = ______

4. Haroo can read 3 chapter books in a month. How many books will he read in 3 months?

____

1 Month	2 Months	3 Months
3		

5. Circle the rectangular prism.

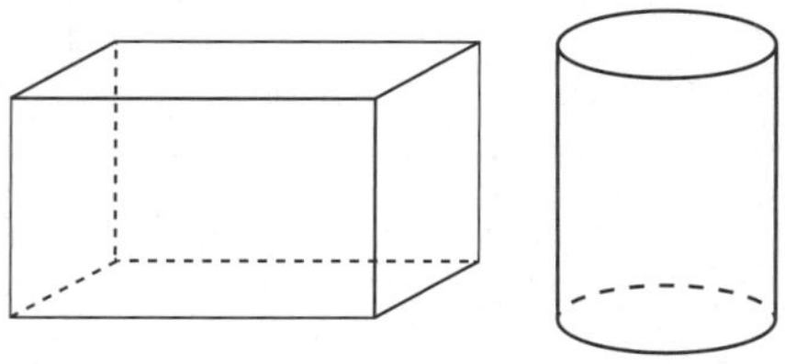

6. Order from the least volume to the greatest volume.

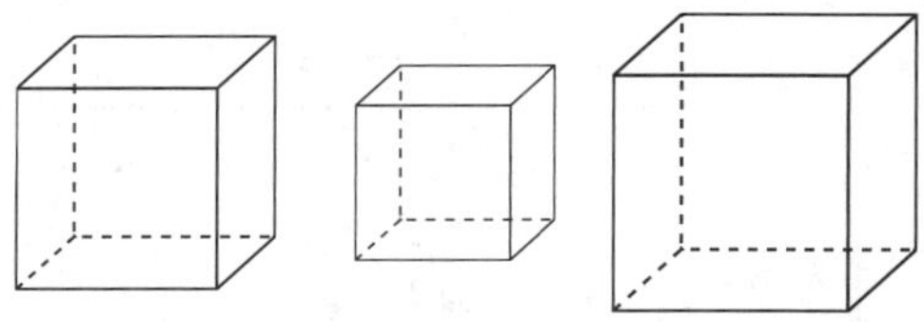

______ ______ ______

7. Sports Played

	Soccer	Swimming	Baseball
Mark	X		X
Tracy		X	
Mike		X	X

Which children do not play soccer?

____

8. A van will hold 9 people. If a class of 23 students is going on a field trip, how many vans will be needed?

____

NAME: ______________________________

DIRECTIONS Solve each problem.

1. Write the numeral.

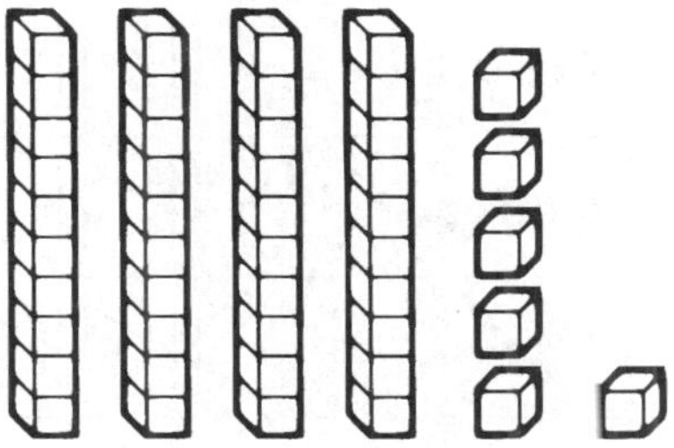

____

2.

$$\begin{array}{r} 4 \\ +\ 9 \\ \hline \end{array}$$

3. 20 – 8 = ______

4. Write the missing number.

34		38	40	42

5. Color one face on the solid.

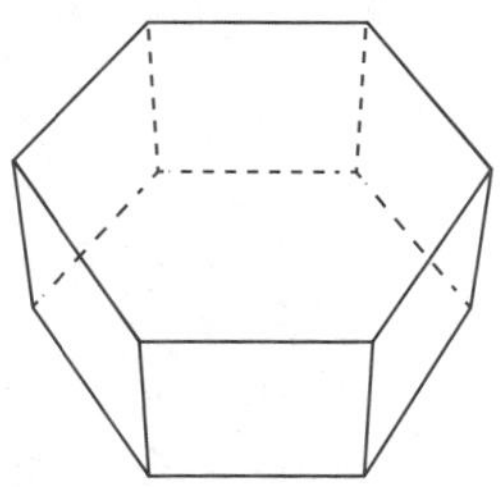

6. How many days are in May?

____

7. Flower Shop Orders

Rose	16
Daisy	23
Tulip	15
Iris	25

Which type of flower had the smallest order?

____

8.

Circle the number sentence that matches the picture.

4 + 4 + 4 = 12

3 + 4 = 7

3 x 3 = 9

SCORE

1.

2.

3.

4.

5.

6.

7.

8.

___ / 8
Total

DAY 82

NAME: ____________________

DIRECTIONS Solve each problem.

SCORE

1. 🙂 😐
2. 🙂 😐
3. 🙂 😐
4. 🙂 😐
5. 🙂 😐
6. 🙂 😐
7. 🙂 😐
8. 🙂 😐

____ /8 Total

1. Circle the smaller number.

148 184

2. 6 + 0 = ______

3. Subtract 8 from 18 to find the difference.

____

4. 6 – ☐ = 5

5. True or false?

A triangle has four vertices.

____

6. What tool would you use to measure weight? Circle one.

ruler scale clock

7. Favorite Activity

Movies	卌 卌 |||
Restaurant	卌 ||||
Park	卌 卌 ||
Stay Home	卌 |||

If 3 more people report that they like to go to the movies, what will the new total be?

____

8. Kelly counts the cars that drive by her house. She counts 16 red cars, 13 blue cars, and 9 green cars. How many more red cars did Kelly see than green cars?

____

DAY 83

NAME: ____________________

DIRECTIONS Solve each problem.

1. Name the shaded fraction.

____

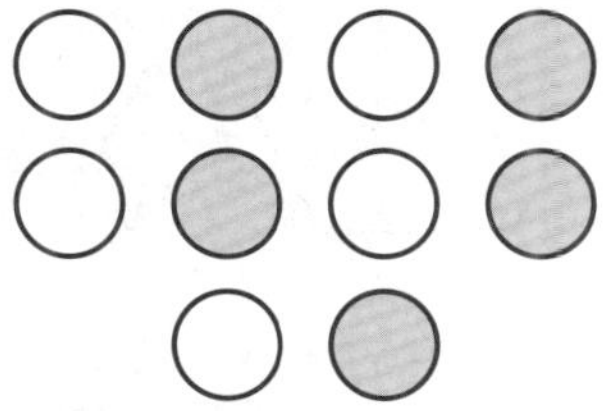

2. 9 more than 8 is

____________________.

3.

$$\begin{array}{r} 16 \\ -\ \ 5 \\ \hline \end{array}$$

4. 3 – 1 = 7 – ☐

5. Complete the chart.

Shape	Number of Sides	Number of Angles

6. Write the length.

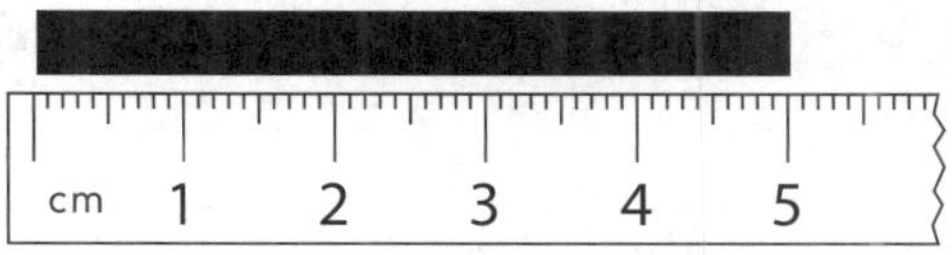

______ centimeters

7. Make 18 tally marks.

8. Jovani has 2 quarters and 2 dimes. How much money does he have?

____

SCORE

1. ☺ 😐
2. ☺ 😐
3. ☺ 😐
4. ☺ 😐
5. ☺ 😐
6. ☺ 😐
7. ☺ 😐
8. ☺ 😐

____ / 8 Total

DAY 84

NAME: ____________________

DIRECTIONS Solve each problem.

SCORE

1. ☺ ☹
2. ☺ ☹
3. ☺ ☹
4. ☺ ☹
5. ☺ ☹
6. ☺ ☹
7. ☺ ☹
8. ☺ ☹

____ / 8
Total

1. Is this a fair share?
Circle: yes no

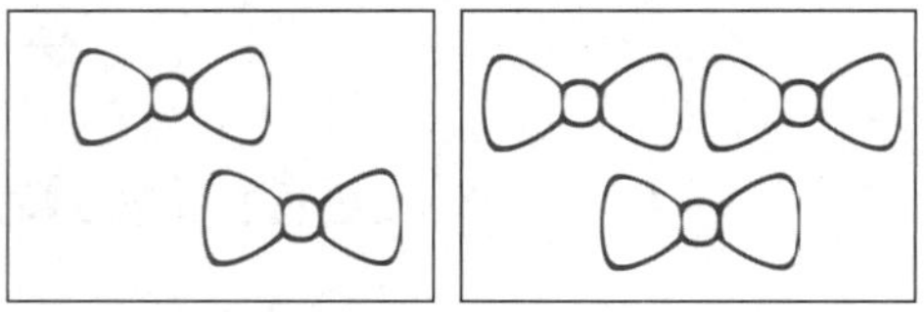

2. 7 + 7 = ______

3.

$$\begin{array}{r} 15 \\ -\ \ 6 \\ \hline \end{array}$$

4. ☐ + 5 = 10 + 3

5. Circle the fan in the middle.

6. Color the hexagon with the larger area.

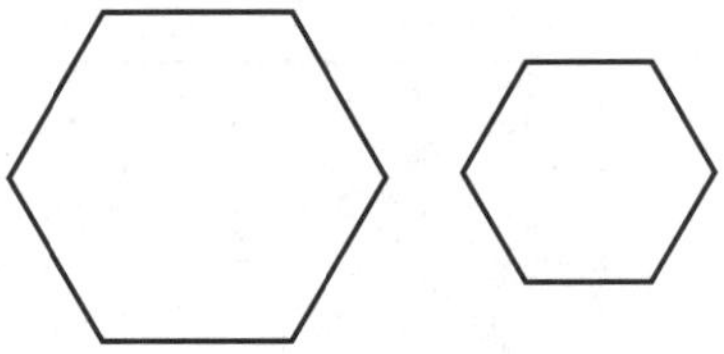

7.

How many miles did Brandon run?

____

8. You pay for a pack of gum that costs 55¢ with 3 quarters. How much change will you get back?

____

NAME: ______________________

DIRECTIONS Solve each problem.

1. Write the number that comes before 91.

____

2. 5 plus 3 equals

______________________.

3. 13 minus 4 equals

______________________.

4. Continue the pattern.

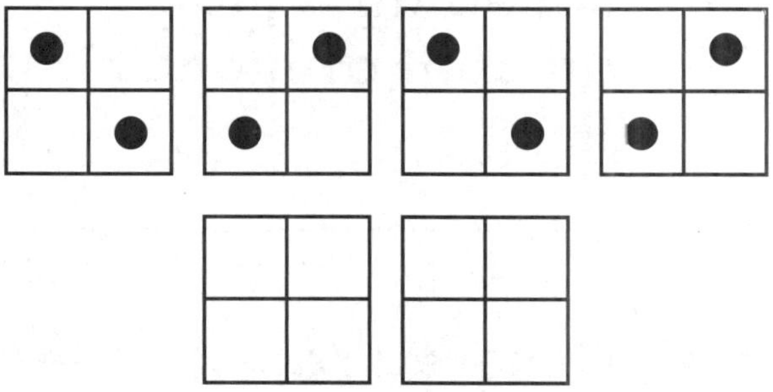

5. Circle the cylinder.

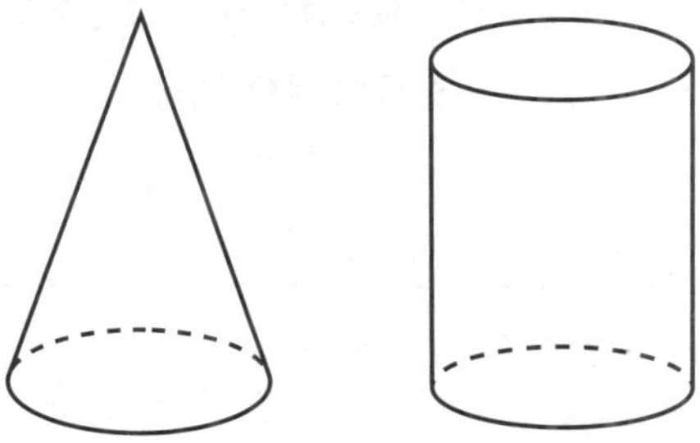

6. Show half past 2:00.

7. Pets

	Hamster	Dog	Fish	Cat
Mary	X		X	X
Julia	X	X		X
Evan	X	X		X

How many pets does Evan have?

____

8. You have 34 trading cards. You win 15 more in a game. Then you lose 12. How many trading cards do you have now?

____

SCORE

1.
2.
3.
4.
5.
6.
7.
8.

____ / 8
Total

DAY 86

NAME: ____________________

DIRECTIONS Solve each problem.

SCORE

1. ☺ 😐
2. ☺ 😐
3. ☺ 😐
4. ☺ 😐
5. ☺ 😐
6. ☺ 😐
7. ☺ 😐
8. ☺ 😐

____ / 8 Total

1. Write the numeral.

4	Hundreds	1	Tens	7	Ones

____

2.

$$\begin{array}{r} 5 \\ +\ 9 \\ \hline \end{array}$$

3. 12 – 3 = ______

4. 15 – ☐ = 10

5. Does a rhombus have 4 vertices?

Circle: yes no

6. Write the day of the week that comes after Wednesday.

____

7.

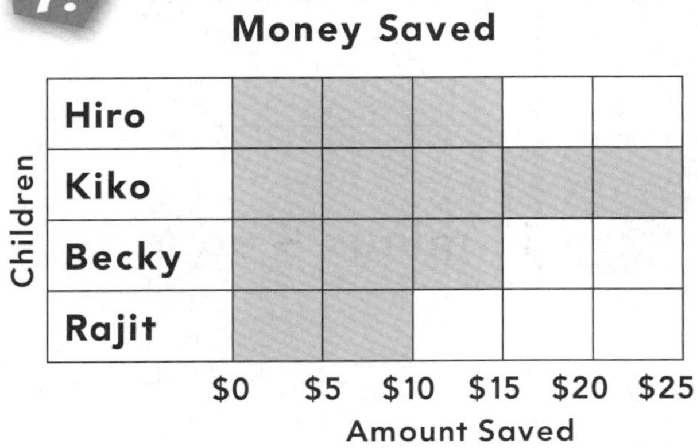

Which 2 children saved an equal amount of money?

____

8. Deserea ran 15 miles last week. She ran 6 miles this week. How many miles did she run in all?

____

NAME: ______________________

DIRECTIONS Solve each problem.

1. Order the numbers from smallest to largest.

43 82 39 99

____

2. 6 + 1 = ______

3.
$$\begin{array}{r} 20 \\ -\ \ 6 \\ \hline \end{array}$$

4. 6 − ☐ = 2

5. Color the shape with 3 sides.

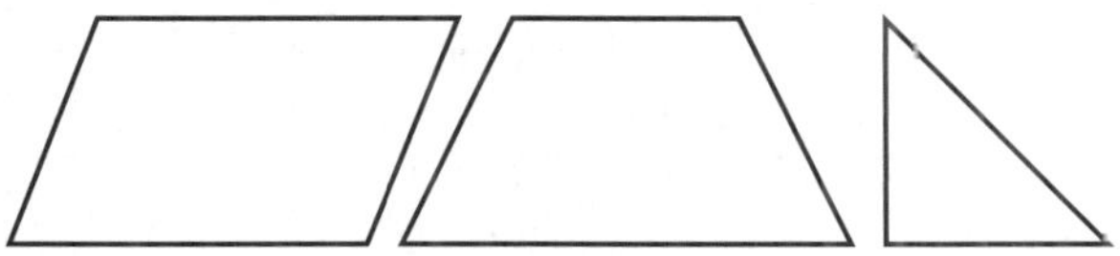

6. What is the volume?

______ cubes

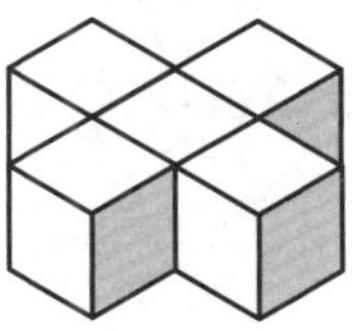

7. Teeth Lost

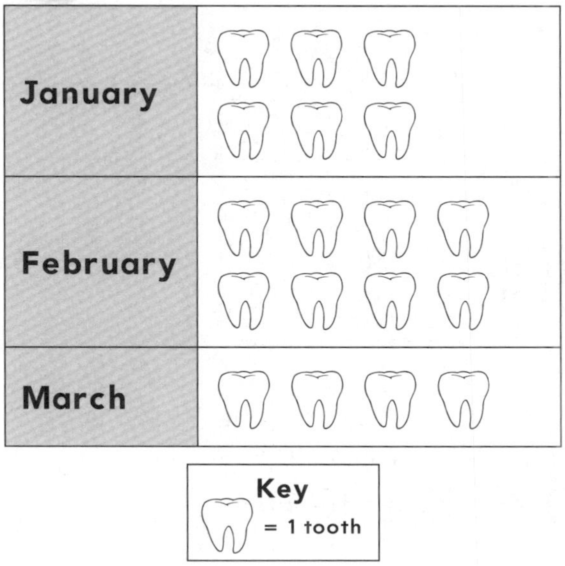

How many more teeth were lost in February than in January?

____

8. Write an addition number sentence using the numbers 15, 23, and 38.

____

SCORE

1. ☺ 😐
2. ☺ 😐
3. ☺ 😐
4. ☺ 😐
5. ☺ 😐
6. ☺ 😐
7. ☺ 😐
8. ☺ 😐

____ / 8 Total

DAY 88

NAME: ______________________

DIRECTIONS Solve each problem.

SCORE

1. ☺ 😐
2. ☺ 😐
3. ☺ 😐
4. ☺ 😐
5. ☺ 😐
6. ☺ 😐
7. ☺ 😐
8. ☺ 😐

____ / 8 Total

1. Color $\frac{1}{2}$.

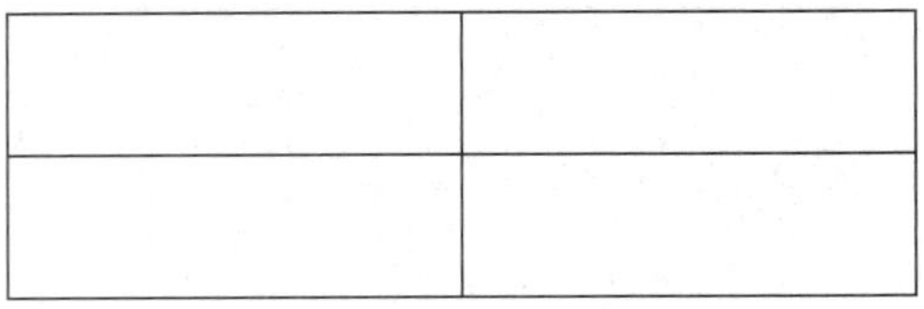

2.

$$\begin{array}{r} 8 \\ +\ 7 \\ \hline \end{array}$$

3. 18 − 10 = ______

4. 8 − 3 = ☐ − 5

5. Can the object stack?

Circle: yes no

6. Circle the better estimate for the width.

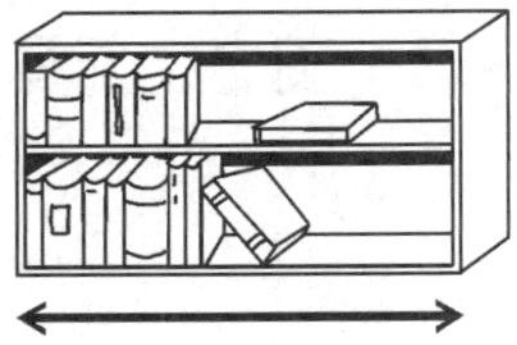

2 m 10 m

7.

School Bags in Class

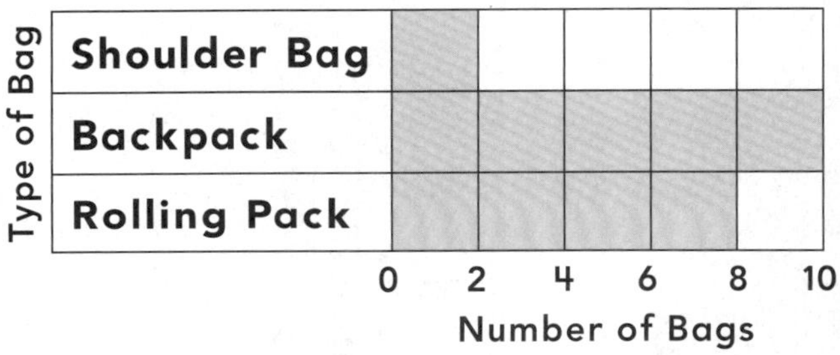

Which kind of school bag do the fewest kids have?

____

8. Today is Thursday. Sam has a baseball game in 6 days. On what day is Sam's baseball game?

____

NAME: ______________________________

DIRECTIONS Solve each problem.

1. Write the number word for the number 47.

____

2. Complete.

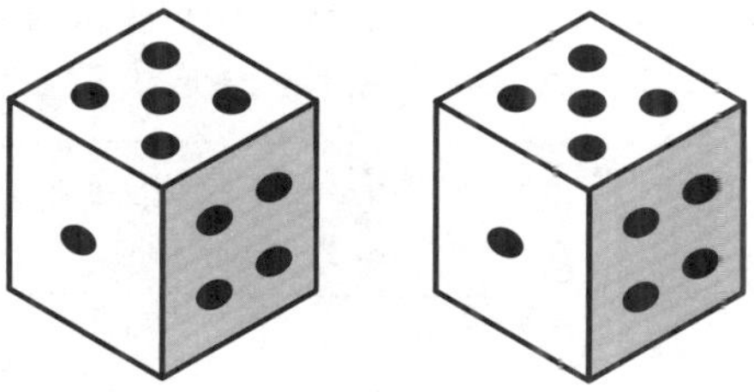

Double 5 = ______

3. 16 – 6 = ______

4. 25 + 30 = 30 + ☐

5. Draw the top view of the solid.

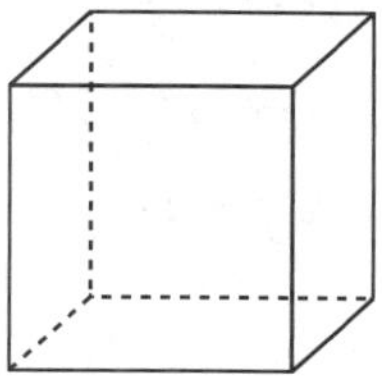

6. Show 10:30.

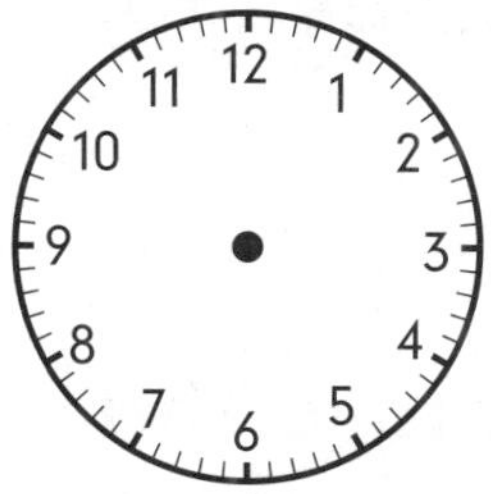

7.

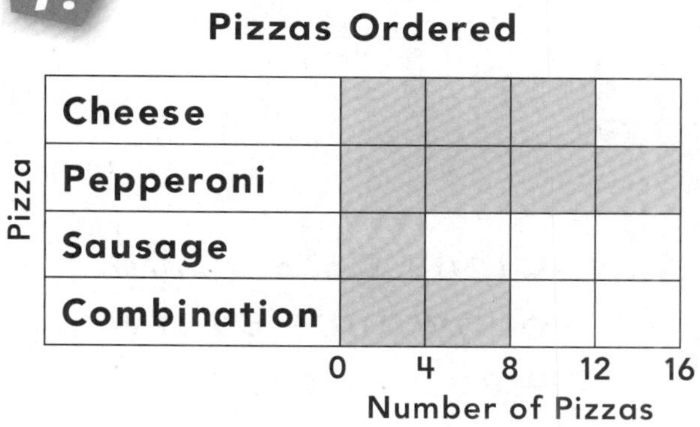

How many cheese and pepperoni pizzas were ordered?

____

8. I am 16 more than 23. What number am I?

____

SCORE

1. ☺ ☹
2. ☺ ☹
3. ☺ ☹
4. ☺ ☹
5. ☺ ☹
6. ☺ ☹
7. ☺ ☹
8. ☺ ☹

____ / 8 Total

NAME: ____________________

DIRECTIONS Solve each problem.

SCORE

1. ☺ 😐
2. ☺ 😐
3. ☺ 😐
4. ☺ 😐
5. ☺ 😐
6. ☺ 😐
7. ☺ 😐
8. ☺ 😐

____ / 8

Total

1. Write the ordinal number for six.

____

2. 9 more than 10 is

____________________.

3. 13 – 9 = ______

4. Ginny gets $2.00 allowance every week. How much allowance does she get in 4 weeks?

____

1 Week	2 Weeks	3 Weeks	4 Weeks
$2.00			

5. Color the circles.

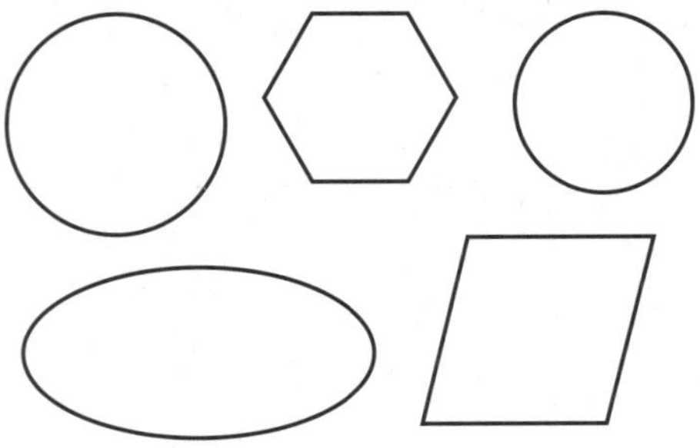

6. Circle the lightest animal in the group.

7. Library Books Checked Out

	Week 1	Week 2	Week 3
Jody	4	5	5
Emily	4	4	4
Brenda	5	7	6
Alison	6	3	6

How many library books did Brenda check out during the third week?

____

8. Peter drinks 4 cups of water every day. How many cups of water will he drink in 2 days?

____

NAME: ____________________

DIRECTIONS Solve each problem.

1. Write the numeral.

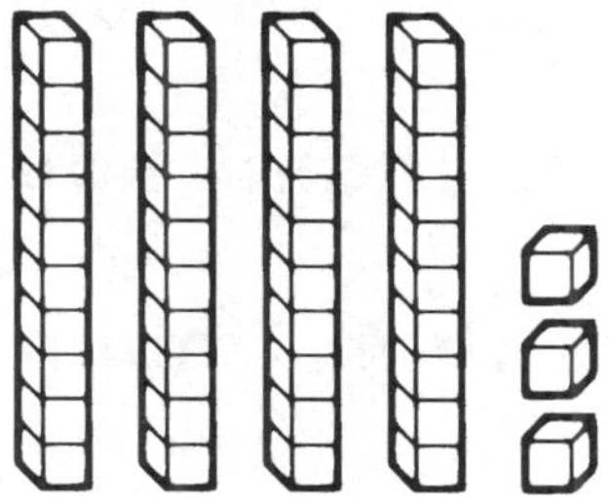

____

2. Add.

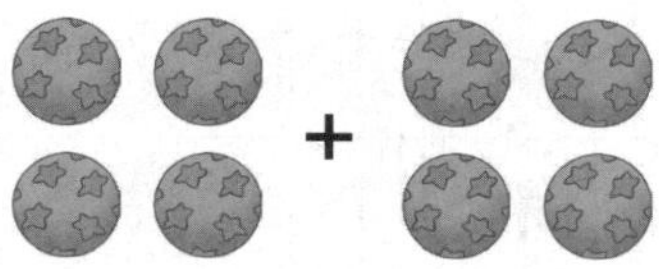

☐ + ☐ = ☐

3. 15 minus 10 equals

____________________.

4. Write the missing number.

65	70	75		85

5. Circle the object that looks like the solid.

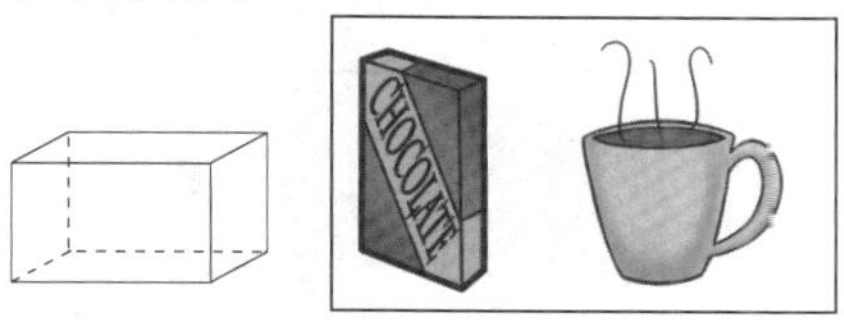

6. Write the time.

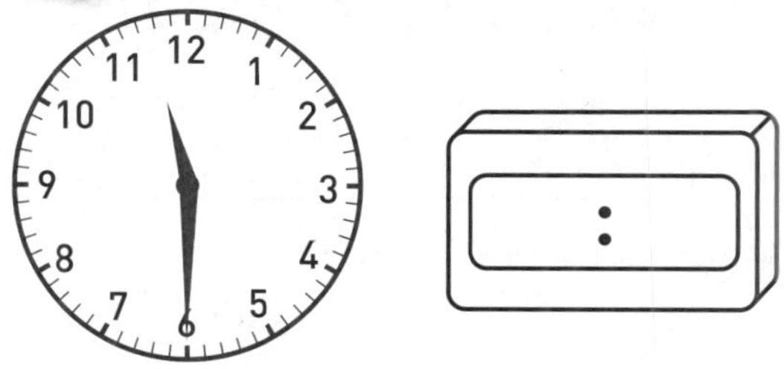

7. Record the data in the bar graph.

Pairs of Shoes

Children								
Tanya								
Daniel								
Lauren								
	0 1	2	3	4	5	6	7	8

Number of Pairs

- Lauren has 7 pairs of shoes.
- Daniel has 4 pairs of shoes.
- Tanya has 5 pairs of shoes.

8. Is a house about 15 feet or 15 inches tall?

____

SCORE

1. ☺ ☹
2. ☺ ☹
3. ☺ ☹
4. ☺ ☹
5. ☺ ☹
6. ☺ ☹
7. ☺ ☹
8. ☺ ☹

____ / 8
Total

DAY 92

NAME: ____________________

DIRECTIONS Solve each problem.

SCORE

1.
2.
3.
4.
5.
6.
7.
8.

___ / 8 Total

1. What is the place value of 2 in 29?

____

2. 12 + 5 = ______

3.

$$\begin{array}{r} 11 \\ -\ \ 4 \\ \hline \end{array}$$

4. 9 ☐ 7 = 16

5. Circle the triangles.

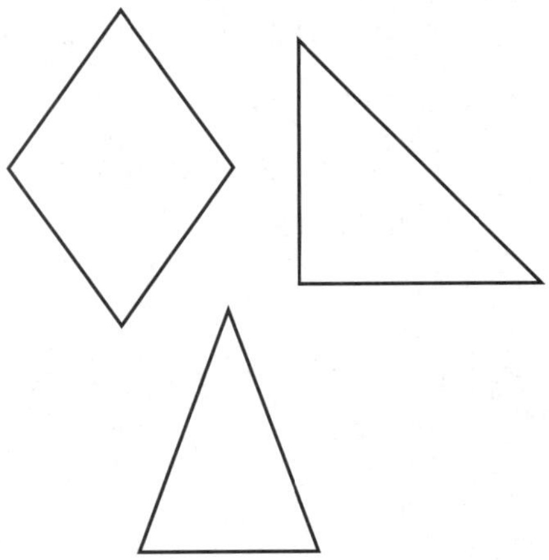

6. Circle how long it takes to eat lunch.

more than 1 hour

less than 1 hour

7.

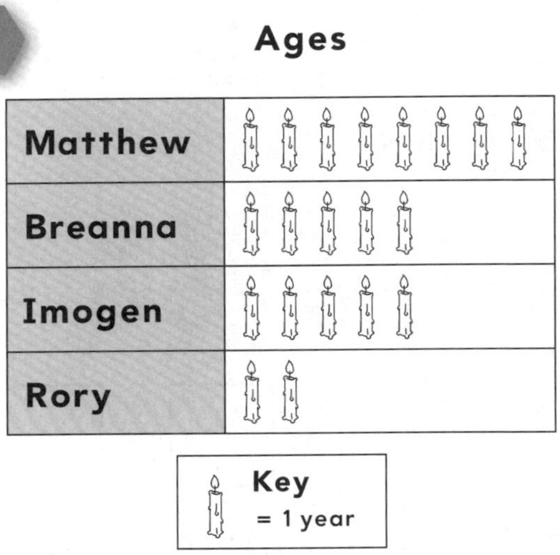

How much older is Imogen than Rory?

____

8. Write the number that has 6 in the tens place and 1 in the ones place.

____

NAME: ______________________

DIRECTIONS Solve each problem.

1. Name the shaded fraction.

____

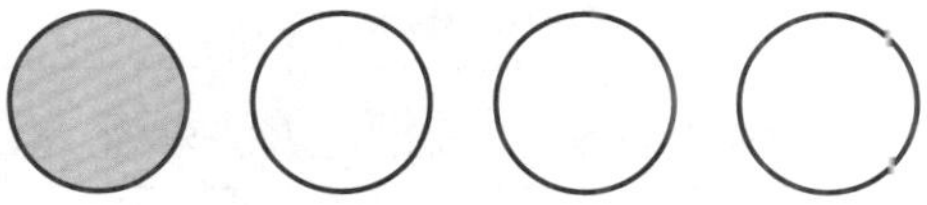

2.

$$\begin{array}{r} 15 \\ +\ \ 7 \\ \hline \end{array}$$

3. What is 8 less than 19?

____

4. 8 + 2 = 10 – ☐

5. True or false? A prism can have a square or a triangle as a base.

____

6. Write the length.

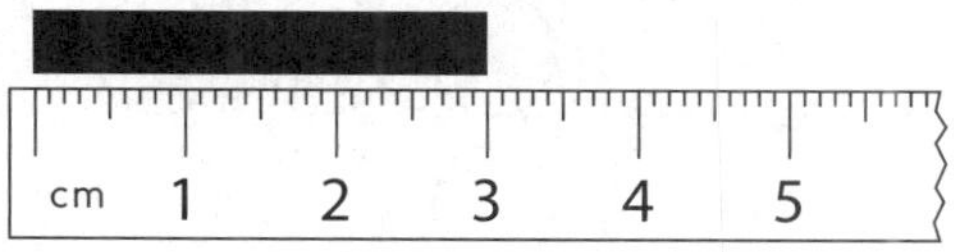

______ centimeters

7.

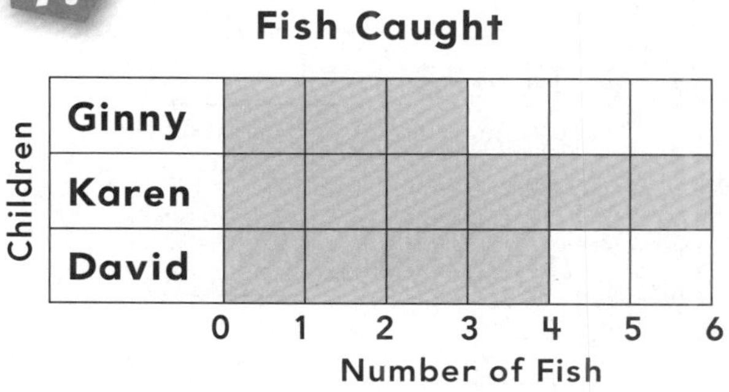

How many more fish did David catch than Ginny?

____

8. List all the 1-digit and 2-digit numbers you make with the digits 4, 3, and 6.

____

____

____

SCORE

1. ☺ ☹
2. ☺ ☹
3. ☺ ☹
4. ☺ ☹
5. ☺ ☹
6. ☺ ☹
7. ☺ ☹
8. ☺ ☹

____ / 8 Total

DAY 94

NAME: ____________________

DIRECTIONS Solve each problem.

1. Circle groups of 2.

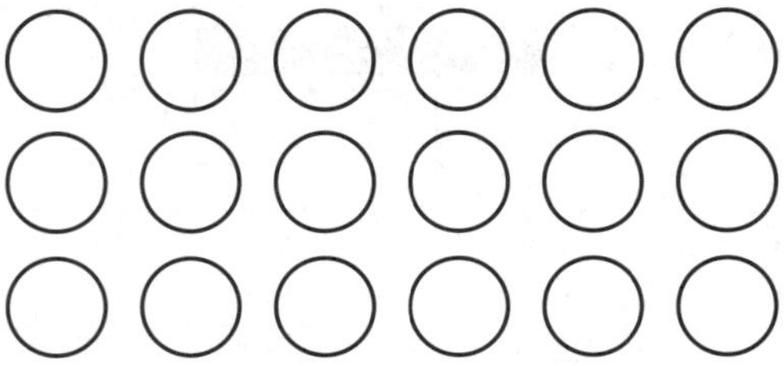

_______ groups

2. 14 + 3 = ______

3. 45 – 32 = ______

4. ☐ + 72 = 72 + 25

5. Draw a line of symmetry.

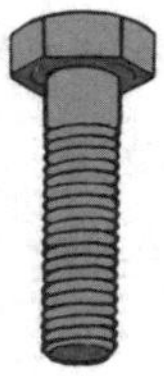

6. Record the area.

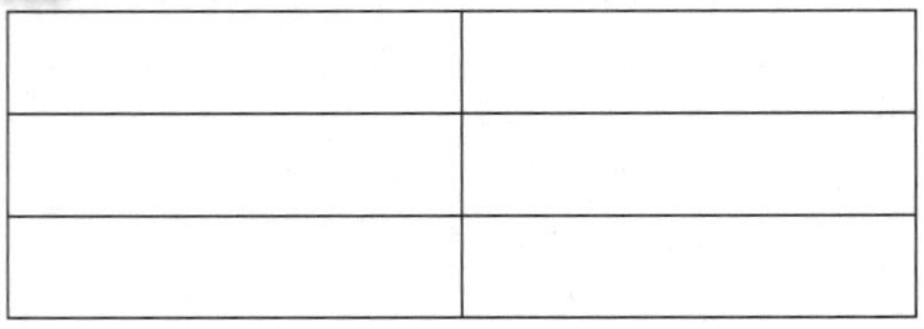

area = _____ rectangles

7. Toy Train Sales Last Week

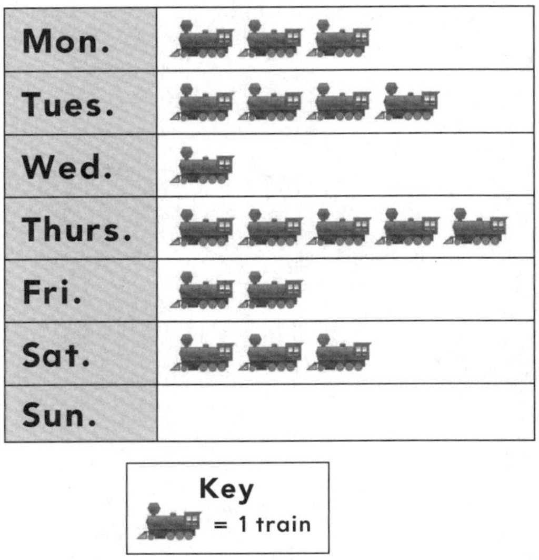

How many more trains were sold on Thursday than on Friday?

____

8. In one month, Hillary read 46 books. Her goal was to read 30 books. How many more books did she read than her goal?

____

SCORE

1. ☺ 😐
2. ☺ 😐
3. ☺ 😐
4. ☺ 😐
5. ☺ 😐
6. ☺ 😐
7. ☺ 😐
8. ☺ 😐

____ / 8 Total

NAME: ______________________________

DIRECTIONS Solve each problem.

1. Write the number that comes before 46.

____

2.

$$\begin{array}{r} 18 \\ +\ \ 2 \\ \hline \end{array}$$

3. 11 minus 10 equals

______________________.

4. Continue the pattern.

girl, boy, girl, boy, girl,

_______, _______

5. Circle the cone.

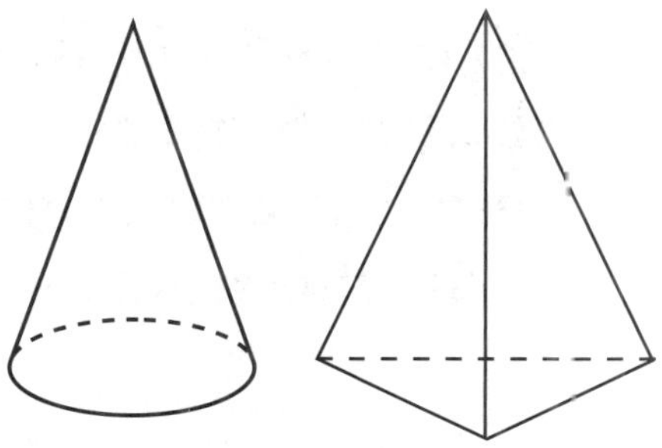

6. Write the time shown.

half past _______

7. Count the tally marks.

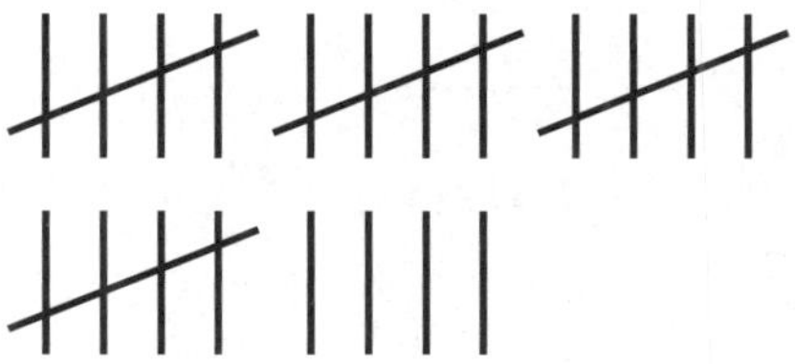

____

8. Erasers come in packs of 10. Mrs. Cane has 37 students in her class. She wants to give each student an eraser. How many packs of erasers should she buy?

____

SCORE

1. ☺ 😐

2. ☺ 😐

3. ☺ 😐

4. ☺ 😐

5. ☺ 😐

6. ☺ 😐

7. ☺ 😐

8. ☺ 😐

___ / 8
Total

DAY 96

NAME: ______________________________

DIRECTIONS Solve each problem.

SCORE

1. ☺ 😐
2. ☺ 😐
3. ☺ 😐
4. ☺ 😐
5. ☺ 😐
6. ☺ 😐
7. ☺ 😐
8. ☺ 😐

____ / 8
Total

1. Write the numeral.

3	Hundreds	5	Tens	6	Ones

____

2. Add.

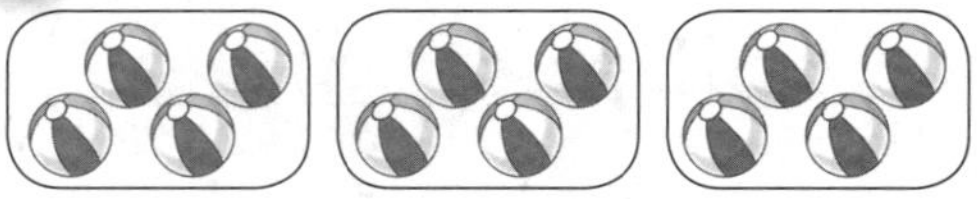

☐ + ☐ + ☐ = ☐

3. 14 minus 7 equals

______________________.

4. ☐ + 5 = 11

5. How many angles does a square have?

____

6. Write the month that comes after July.

____

7.

Favorite Pets

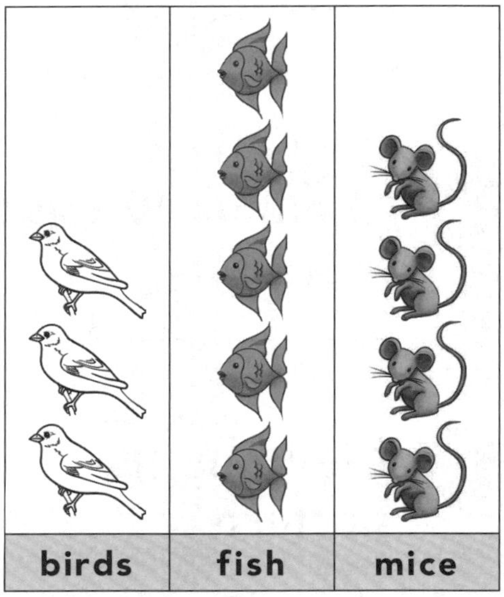

How many votes for mice are there?

____

8. Write the number that is 6 more tens and 8 more ones than the number 30.

____

NAME: ______________________

DIRECTIONS Solve each problem.

1. Use >, <, or =.

120 ◯ 24

2. 19 + 5 = ______

3.

$$\begin{array}{r} 89 \\ -\ 30 \\ \hline \end{array}$$

4. □ + 10 = 15

5. Color the shape with 4 sides.

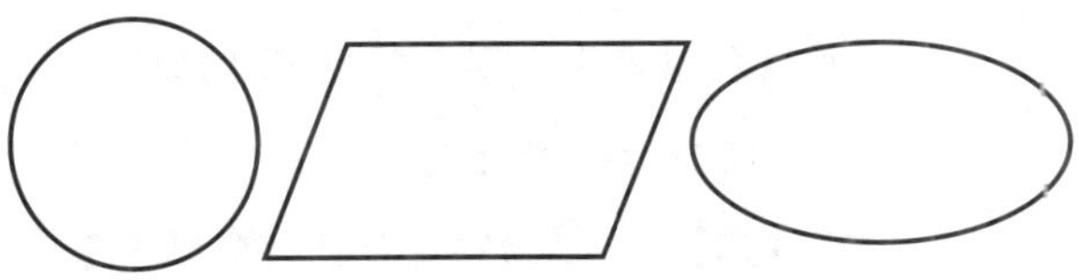

6. Circle the solid that takes up the most space.

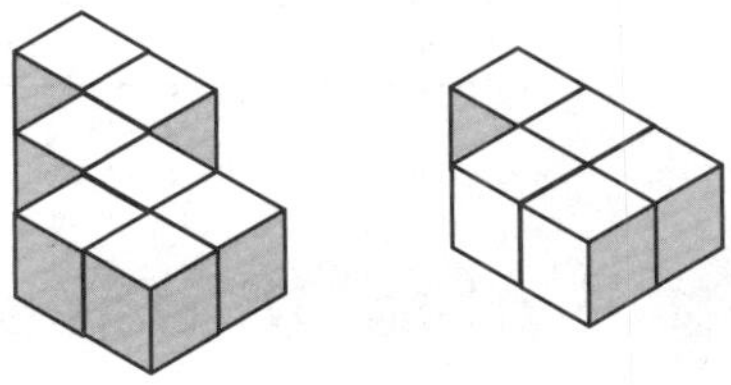

7. Car Colors

Red	卌 卌 |||
Blue	卌 卌 卌 卌 |
Yellow	卌 ||||
Green	卌 卌 卌 ||

How many cars are blue?

____

8. Tim's dad is 74 inches tall. Tim is 56 inches tall. How much does Tim need to grow to be as tall as his dad?

____

SCORE

1. ☺ 😐
2. ☺ 😐
3. ☺ 😐
4. ☺ 😐
5. ☺ 😐
6. ☺ 😐
7. ☺ 😐
8. ☺ 😐

____ / 8 Total

DAY 98

NAME: ____________________

DIRECTIONS Solve each problem.

SCORE

1. ☺😐
2. ☺😐
3. ☺😐
4. ☺😐
5. ☺😐
6. ☺😐
7. ☺😐
8. ☺😐

____ / 8 Total

1. Color $\frac{1}{2}$.

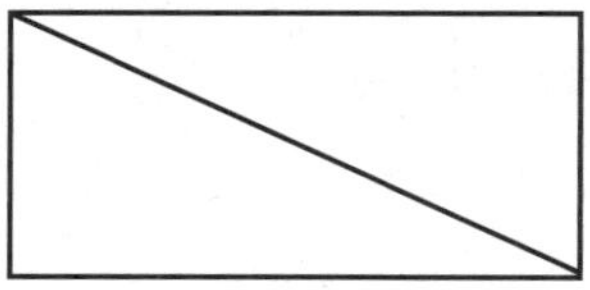

2. 4 plus 18 equals

____________________.

3.

$$\begin{array}{r} 15 \\ -\ \ 4 \\ \hline \end{array}$$

4. $\square - 8 = 3 + 3$

5. Circle the object that can roll.

6. Circle the object that would be taller than 1 meter.

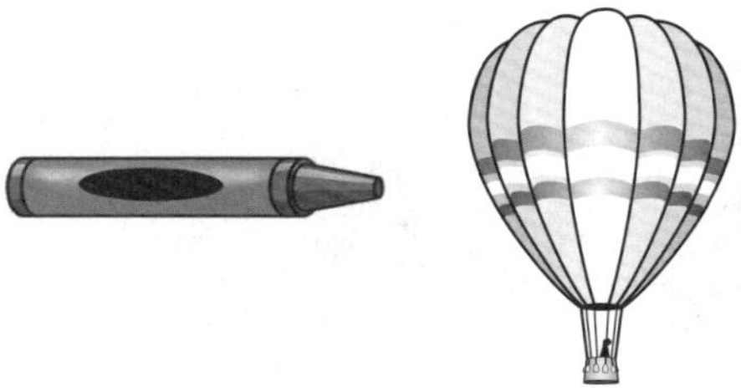

7. Sports Played

	Soccer	Swimming	Baseball
Mark	X		X
Tracy		X	
Mike		X	X

Which sport do both of the boys play?

____

8. Juan rides his bike 5 miles, walks 2 miles, and roller skates 4 miles. If he walks 3 more miles, how many miles will he have walked in all?

____

NAME: ______________________

DIRECTIONS Solve each problem.

1. Write the numeral for two hundred seventy-two.

____

2. Complete.

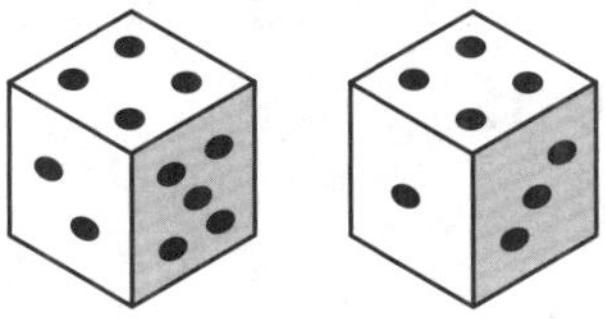

Double 4 = ______

3. 16 – 10 = ______

4. 52 + 28 = ☐ + 52

5. Draw the front view of the solid.

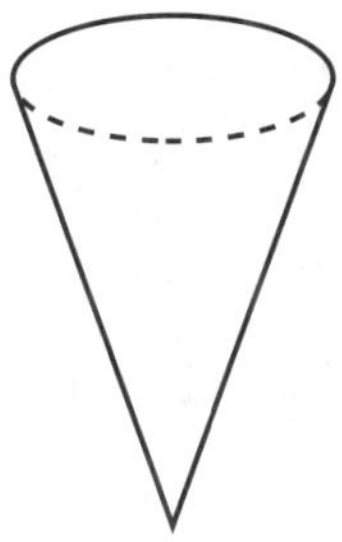

6. Is a car longer or shorter than a yard?

____

7. Flower Shop Orders

Rose	16
Daisy	23
Tulip	15
Iris	25

What was the total number of flowers ordered?

____

8. Which two plane shapes have only curved lines?

____

____

SCORE

1. ☺ 😐
2. ☺ 😐
3. ☺ 😐
4. ☺ 😐
5. ☺ 😐
6. ☺ 😐
7. ☺ 😐
8. ☺ 😐

____ / 8 Total

NAME: ____________________

DIRECTIONS Solve each problem.

SCORE

1. ☺ ☹
2. ☺ ☹
3. ☺ ☹
4. ☺ ☹
5. ☺ ☹
6. ☺ ☹
7. ☺ ☹
8. ☺ ☹

___ / 8 Total

1. Circle about how many phones are in your house.

3   50

2. 17 + 5 = ______

3.

$$\begin{array}{r} 12 \\ -\ \ 6 \\ \hline \end{array}$$

4. Kyle mows 4 lawns every week for extra money. He charges $2.00 to mow a lawn. How much money does he make after 4 weeks?

____

5. Circle the plane figure.

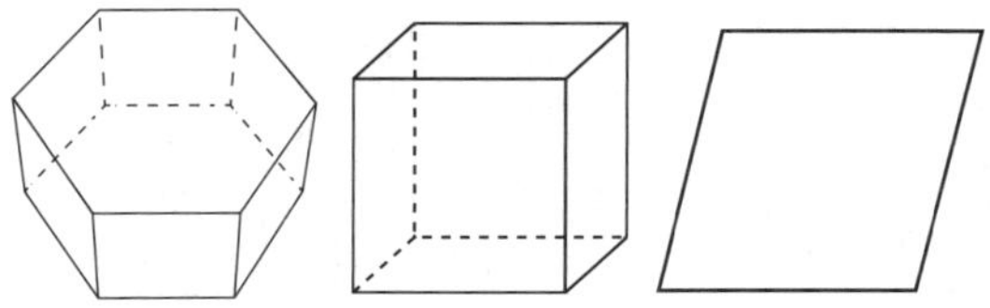

6. Circle the heaviest item.

7. Make 30 tally marks.

8. Marcus wakes up at 7:00 A.M. He is awake for 13 hours and then he goes to bed. What is Marcus' bedtime?

____

NAME: ______________________

DIRECTIONS Solve each problem.

1. Write the numeral.

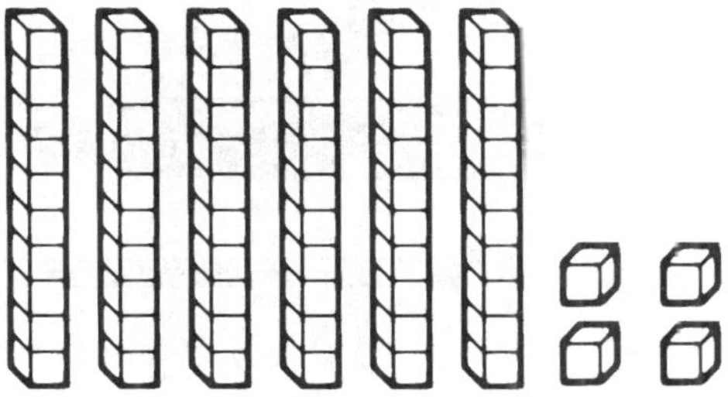

____

2. Add.

☐ + ☐ + ☐ = ☐

3. 17 – 10 = ______

4. Write the missing number.

58	60		64	66

5. Name the solid.

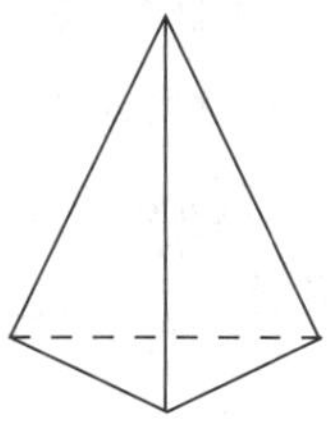

____

6. A family goes out to dinner at 6:00 P.M. and arrives home at 7:00 P.M. How long were they gone?

____

7. Favorite Activity

Movies	𝍸 𝍸 |||
Restaurant	𝍸 ||||
Park	𝍸 𝍸 ||
Stay Home	𝍸 |||

Which activity did the fewest people like?

____

8. Mitch scored 35 points in a game. Steve scored 23 points. Alba scored 20 points. How many points did they score in all?

____

SCORE

1. ☺ 😐
2. ☺ 😐
3. ☺ 😐
4. ☺ 😐
5. ☺ 😐
6. ☺ 😐
7. ☺ 😐
8. ☺ 😐

____ / 8 Total

DAY
102

NAME: ______________________________

DIRECTIONS Solve each problem.

SCORE

1. ☺ 😐
2. ☺ 😐
3. ☺ 😐
4. ☺ 😐
5. ☺ 😐
6. ☺ 😐
7. ☺ 😐
8. ☺ 😐

____ / 8

Total

1. Circle the larger number.

92   29

2. 7 plus 16 equals

______________________.

3.

$$\begin{array}{r} 34 \\ -\ 20 \\ \hline \end{array}$$

4. 4 + ☐ = 11

5. Name the shape.

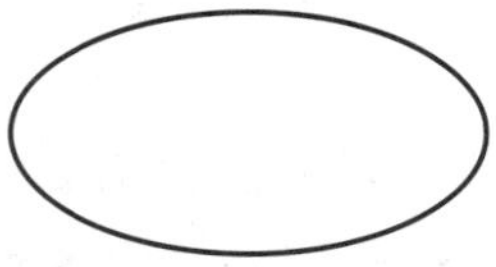

____

6. Circle the longer object.

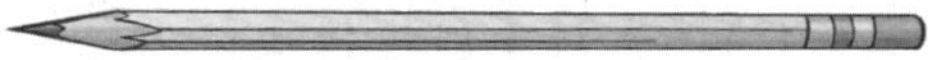

7.

Miles Run

Max	
Cheryl	
Brandon	

Key  = 10 miles

How many more miles did Max run than Cheryl?

____

8. Kazim has 14 toy cars. He gives 6 to his brother. How many toy cars does he still have?

____

NAME: ______________________________

DIRECTIONS Solve each problem.

1. Name the shaded fraction.

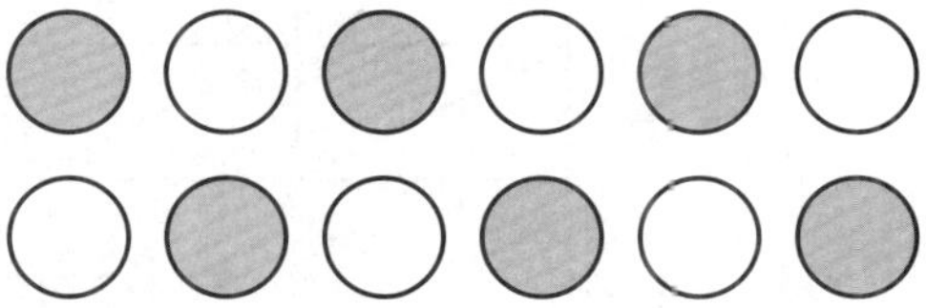

______________________.

2. 18 + 6 = ______

3. 18 minus 6 equals

______________________.

4. 19 – 9 = ☐ + 3

5. True or false? Shapes can only have one line of symmetry.

____

6. Circle the season that matches the months in the box below.

winter spring

summer fall

June
July
August

7.

Pets

	Hamster	Dog	Fish	Cat
Mary	X		X	X
Julia	X	X		X
Evan	X	X		X

Which animals were owned by all three kids?

____

8. Write a related addition problem.

82 – 24 = 58

____

SCORE

1. ☺ 😐

2. ☺ 😐

3. ☺ 😐

4. ☺ 😐

5. ☺ 😐

6. ☺ 😐

7. ☺ 😐

8. ☺ 😐

____ / 8 Total

DAY
104

NAME: ____________________

DIRECTIONS Solve each problem.

SCORE

1. ☺ ☹
2. ☺ ☹
3. ☺ ☹
4. ☺ ☹
5. ☺ ☹
6. ☺ ☹
7. ☺ ☹
8. ☺ ☹

____ / 8 Total

1. Circle groups of 3.

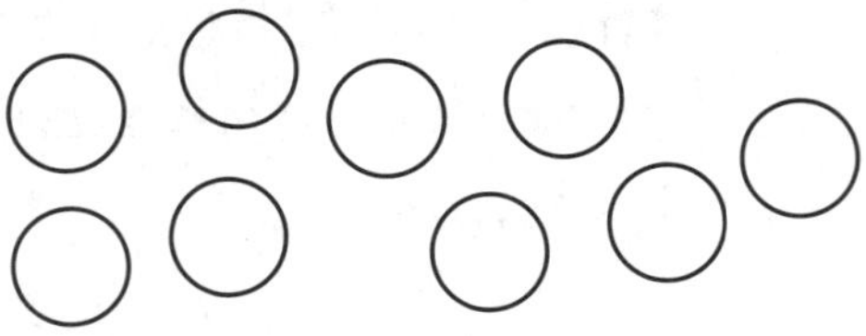

________ groups

2.

$$\begin{array}{r} 15 \\ +\ \ 8 \\ \hline \end{array}$$

3. 61 – 40 = ______

4. 56 + ☐ = 73 + 56

5. Draw all lines of symmetry.

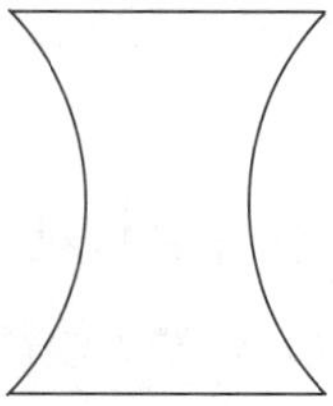

6. Write the area.

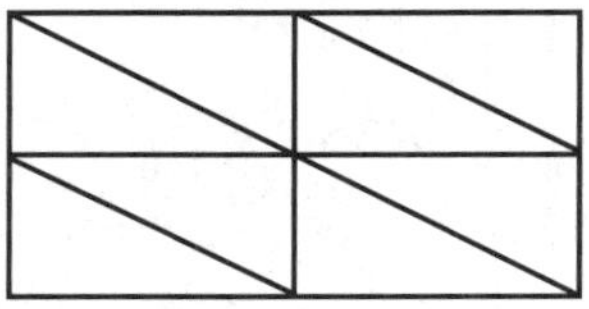

area = ______ triangles

7.

Money Saved

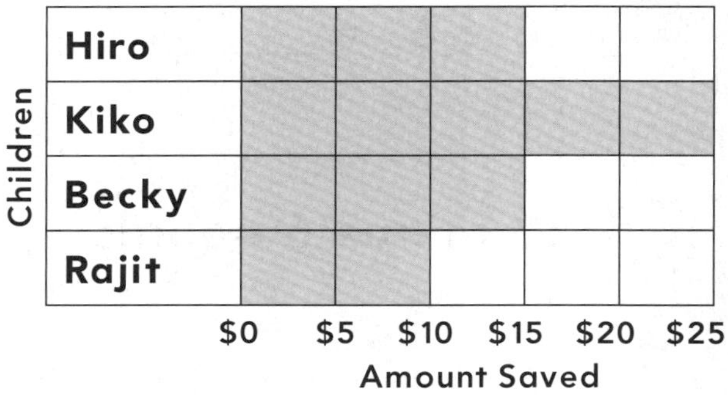

How much more money did Kiko save than Becky?

____

8. Jayden goes for a walk that takes $\frac{1}{2}$ hour. How many minutes did he walk?

____

NAME: ______________________________

DIRECTIONS Solve each problem.

1. Write the number that comes before 85.

____

2.

$$\begin{array}{r} 4 \\ 1 \\ +\ 2 \\ \hline \end{array}$$

3. 19 – 6 = ______

4. Continue the pattern.

A, A, B, B, A, A,

______, ______

5. Color the base of the solid.

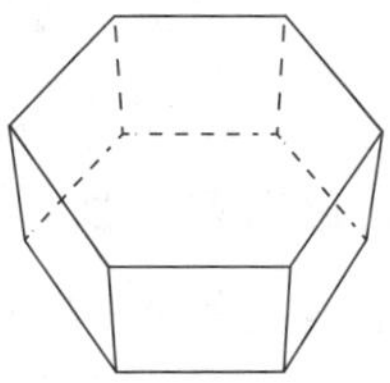

6. Show half past 8:00.

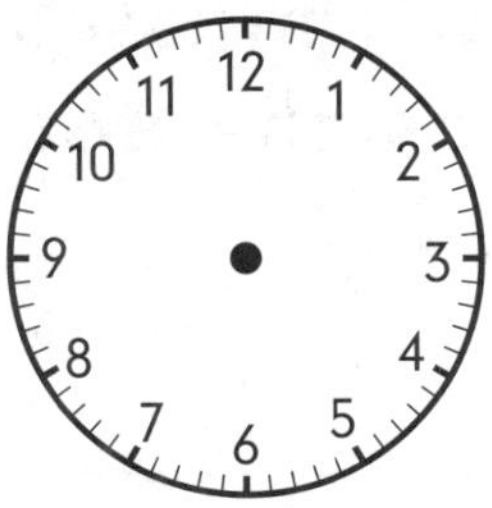

7. Teeth Lost

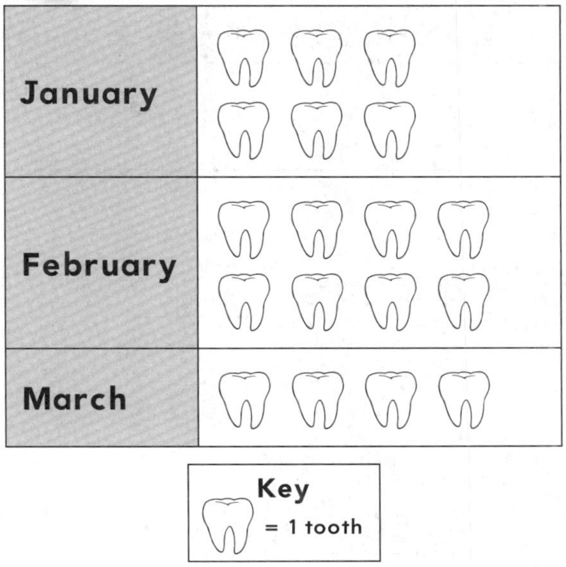

In which month were twice as many teeth lost than in March?

____

8. I am 13 less than 46. What number am I?

____

SCORE

1. ☺ 😐
2. ☺ 😐
3. ☺ 😐
4. ☺ 😐
5. ☺ 😐
6. ☺ 😐
7. ☺ 😐
8. ☺ 😐

___ / 8 Total

DAY 106

NAME: ____________________

DIRECTIONS Solve each problem.

SCORE

1. ☺☹
2. ☺☹
3. ☺☹
4. ☺☹
5. ☺☹
6. ☺☹
7. ☺☹
8. ☺☹

____ / 8

Total

1. Write the numeral.

5	Hundreds	8	Tens	2	Ones

____

2. 4 + 19 = ______

3.

$$\begin{array}{r} 73 \\ -\ 50 \\ \hline \end{array}$$

4. 11 – ☐ = 2

5. Count the angles.

____

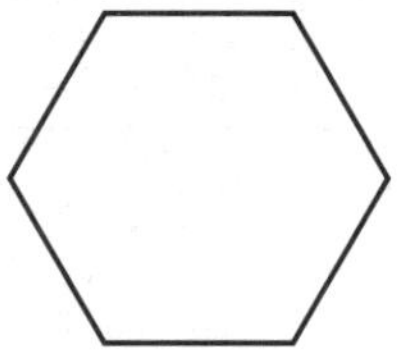

6. Write the day of the week that comes after Saturday.

____

7.

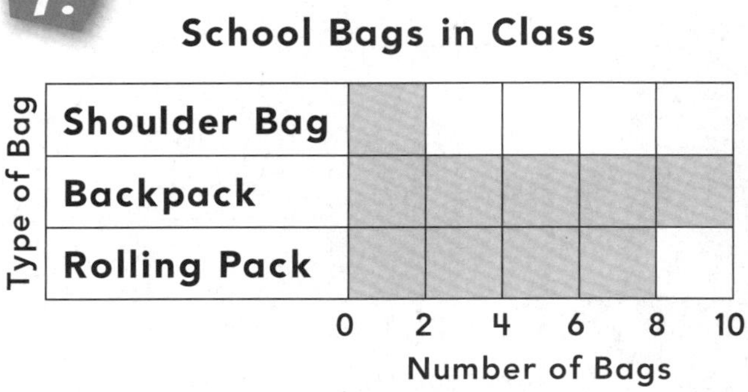

How many more backpacks are there than rolling packs?

____

8. Lilo eats 5 strawberries every day for breakfast. How many strawberries does she eat in one week?

____

NAME: ____________________

DIRECTIONS Solve each problem.

1. Order the numbers from largest to smallest.

176 43 149 73

____, ____, ____, ____

2. What is the sum of 25 and 6?

____

3. 14 – 5 = ______

4. 7 ☐ 3 = 10

5. How many sides does the shape have?

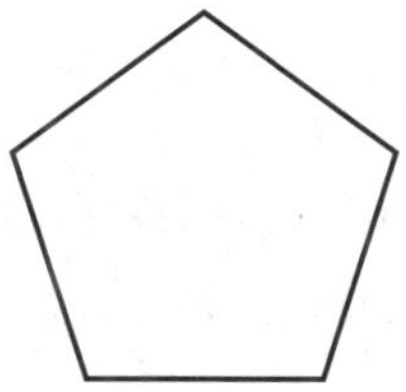

__________ sides

6. What is the volume?

______ cubes

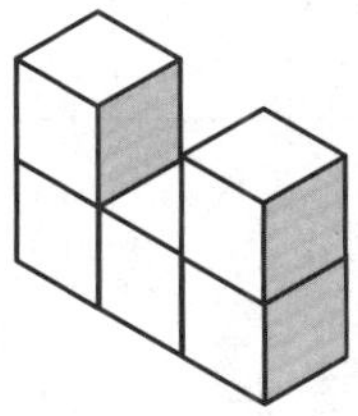

7.

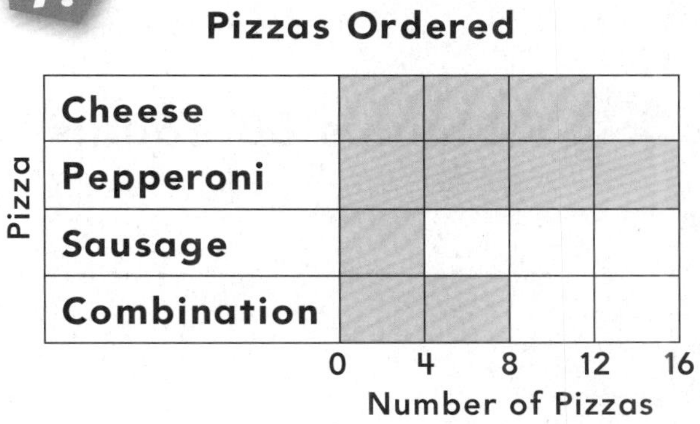

What was the total number of pizzas ordered?

____

8. Would a cold day be about 19°F, 49°F, or 89°F?

____

SCORE

1. ☺ 😐

2. ☺ 😐

3. ☺ 😐

4. ☺ 😐

5. ☺ 😐

6. ☺ 😐

7. ☺ 😐

8. ☺ 😐

____ / 8

Total

DAY

108

NAME: ____________________

DIRECTIONS Solve each problem.

SCORE

1. 🙂 😐
2. 🙂 😐
3. 🙂 😐
4. 🙂 😐
5. 🙂 😐
6. 🙂 😐
7. 🙂 😐
8. 🙂 😐

___ / 8
Total

1. Color $\frac{1}{2}$.

2. 26 + 7 = ______

3. 82 minus 80 equals

______________________.

4. 4 + ☐ = 12 – 5

5. Circle the object that can stack.

6. Circle the object that is shorter than 1 meter.

7. Library Books Checked Out

	Week 1	Week 2	Week 3
Jody	4	5	5
Emily	4	4	4
Brenda	5	7	6
Alison	6	3	6

Who checked out the most library books during the first week?

____

8. How many eyes are there on 18 dogs?

____

NAME: ______________________________

DIRECTIONS Solve each problem.

1. Write the number word for the number 96.

____

2. Double 9 = ______

3.

$$\begin{array}{r} 13 \\ -\ 5 \\ \hline \end{array}$$

4. 82 + 12 = 12 + ☐

5. Color one face of the prism.

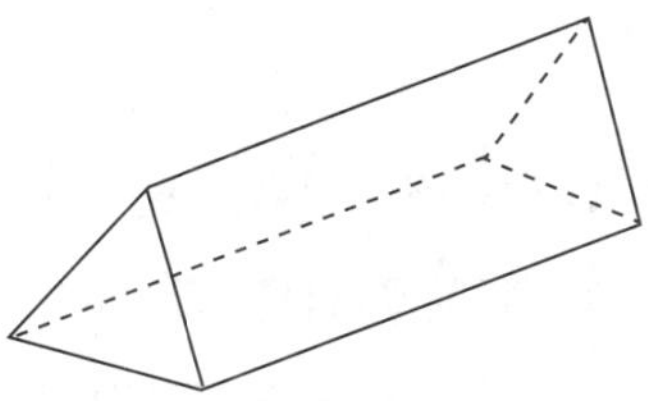

6. True or false? You can walk a mile in less than 1 minute.

____

7. Record the data in the pictograph.

Number of Points Scored

The Tigers	
The Jets	
The Troopers	

Key ☺ = 10 Points

- The Jets scored 60 points.
- The Tigers scored 70 points.
- The Troopers scored 50 points.

8. Write the number that has 0 in the ones place and 5 in the tens place.

____

SCORE

1. ☺ 😐
2. ☺ 😐
3. ☺ 😐
4. ☺ 😐
5. ☺ 😐
6. ☺ 😐
7. ☺ 😐
8. ☺ 😐

____ / 8 Total

DAY
110

NAME: ____________________

DIRECTIONS Solve each problem.

SCORE

1.
2.
3.
4.
5.
6.
7.
8.

____ / 8
Total

1. Write the ordinal number for two.

____

2.

$$\begin{array}{r} 28 \\ +\ \ 5 \\ \hline \end{array}$$

3. 92 minus 40 equals ____________________.

4. Count by threes and color each number counted.

1	2	3	4	5	6	7	8	9	10
11	12	13	14	15	16	17	18	19	20
21	22	23	24	25	26	27	28	29	30
31	32	33	34	35	36	37	38	39	40
41	42	43	44	45	46	47	48	49	50

5. Color the square.

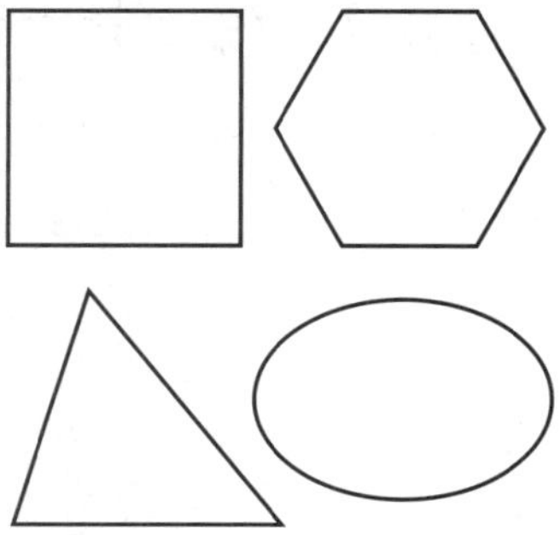

6. Circle the object that weighs the least.

7.

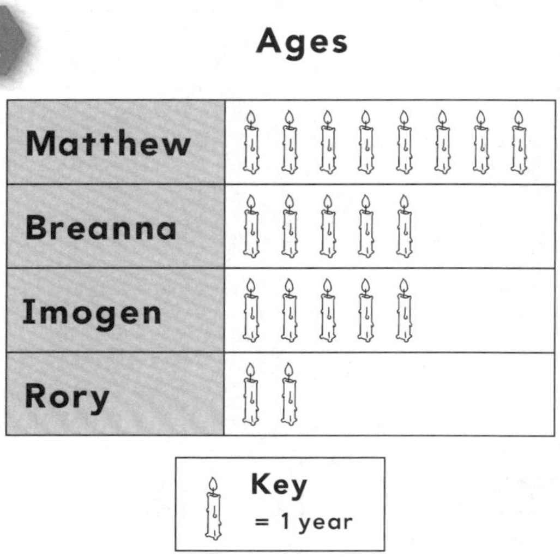

Who is the youngest?

____

8. What is the smallest 3-digit number you can make using each of the digits 4, 7, and 3?

____

NAME: ______________________________

DIRECTIONS Solve each problem.

1. Write the numeral.

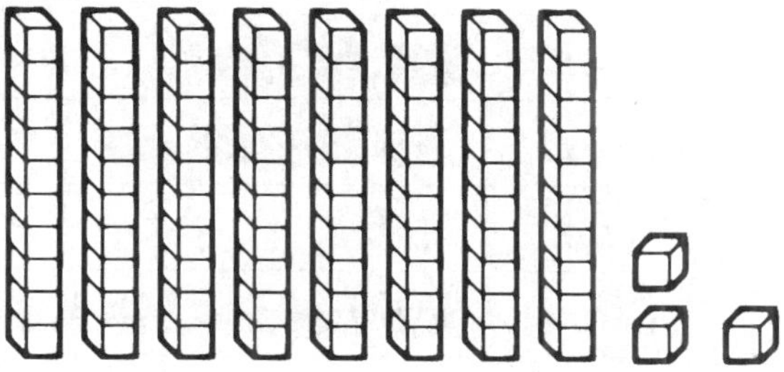

____

2. 1 + 1 + 7 = ______

3. 17 – 9 = ______

4. Write the missing number.

61	71	81		101

5. Is the solid a prism?

Circle: yes no

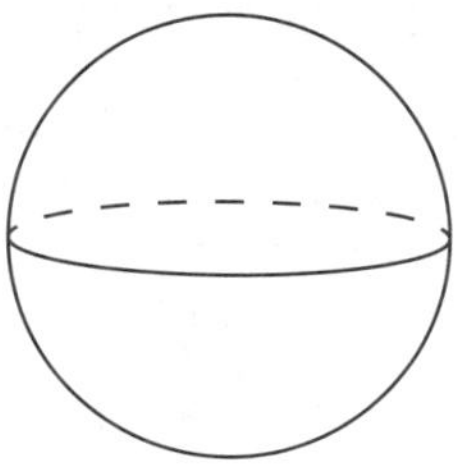

6. School begins at 8:00 A.M. and ends at 2:00 P.M. How long is the school day?

____

7.

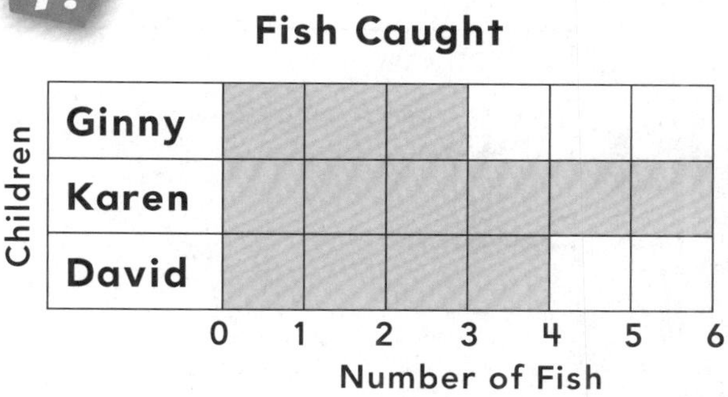

What was the total number of fish caught?

____

8. Roger's goal is to have 75 shells in his collection. He has 32. How many more shells does Roger need to collect?

____

SCORE

1. ☺ 😐

2. ☺ 😐

3. ☺ 😐

4. ☺ 😐

5. ☺ 😐

6. ☺ 😐

7. ☺ 😐

8. ☺ 😐

____ / 8

Total

DAY

112

NAME: ____________________

DIRECTIONS Solve each problem.

SCORE

1. ☺ 😐
2. ☺ 😐
3. ☺ 😐
4. ☺ 😐
5. ☺ 😐
6. ☺ 😐
7. ☺ 😐
8. ☺ 😐

____ / 8

Total

1. Round 64 to the nearest ten.

____

2. What is 3 more than 29?

____

3.

$$\begin{array}{r} 49 \\ -\ 30 \\ \hline \end{array}$$

4. ☐ + 1 = 10

5. Circle the hexagon.

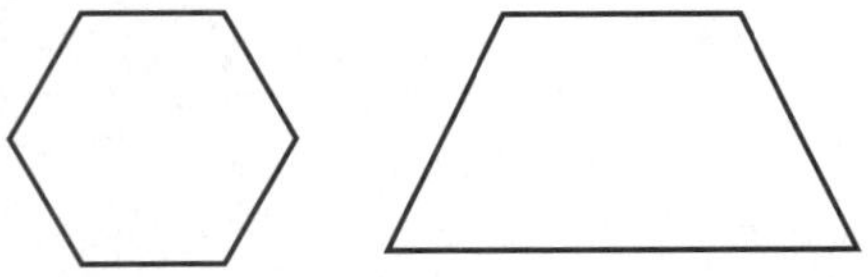

6. Circle how long it takes to get dressed.

more than 1 hour

less than 1 hour

7. Toy Train Sales Last Week

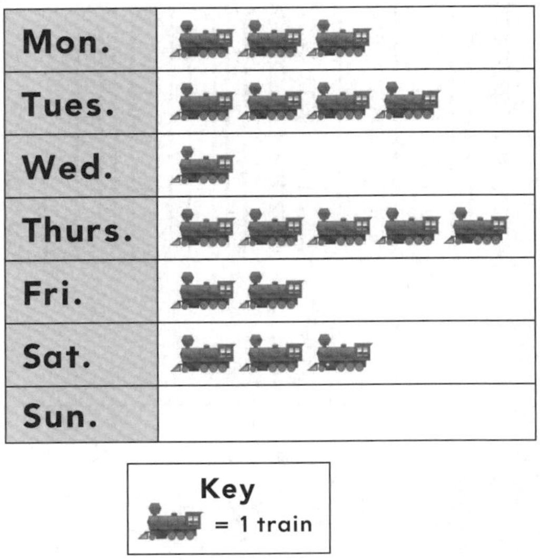

On which day were no trains sold?

____

8. At a pet store, the owner can fit 5 mice in one cage. If the store owner has 17 mice, how many cages will he need?

____

NAME: ____________________

DIRECTIONS Solve each problem.

1. Name the shaded fraction.

____

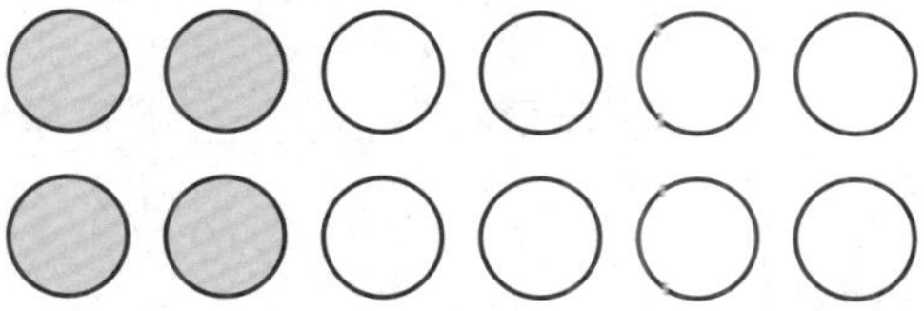

2. 89 + 5 = ______

3.

$$\begin{array}{r} 19 \\ -\ \ 3 \\ \hline \end{array}$$

4. 15 – 6 = 5 + ☐

5. Circle the prism.

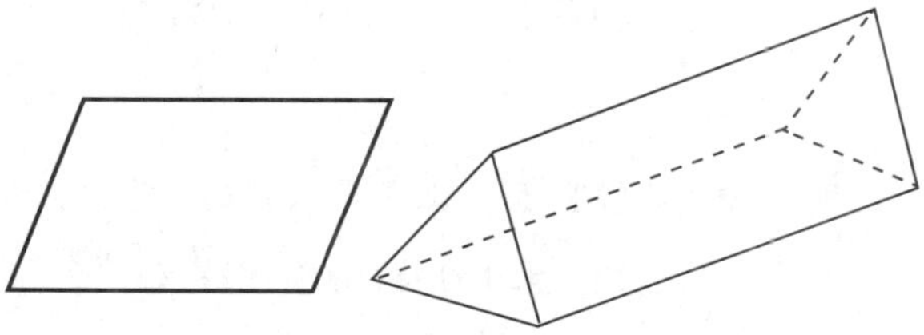

6. Write the length.

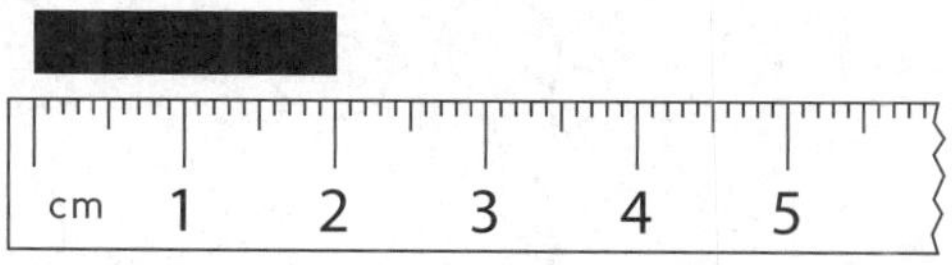

______ centimeters

7. Count the tally marks.

____

8. Write the number that is 4 more ones than the number 43.

____

SCORE

1. ☺ ☹
2. ☺ ☹
3. ☺ ☹
4. ☺ ☹
5. ☺ ☹
6. ☺ ☹
7. ☺ ☹
8. ☺ ☹

____ / 8
Total

DAY
114

NAME: ______________________

DIRECTIONS Solve each problem.

SCORE

1.
2.
3.
4.
5.
6.
7.
8.

____ / 8
Total

1. Circle groups of 4.

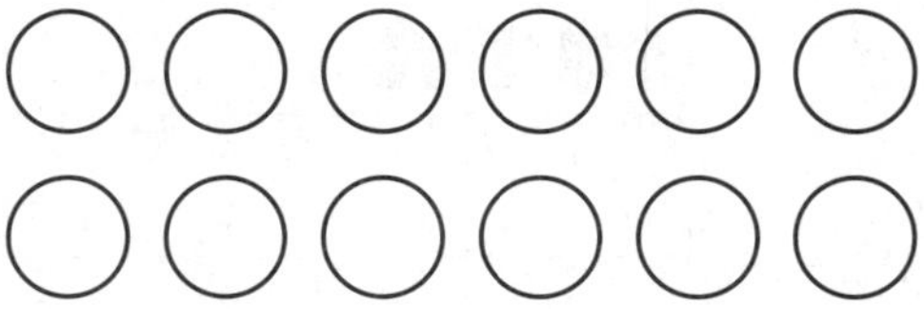

________ groups

2. 6 plus 72 equals

______________________.

3. 12 – 8 = ______

4. 5 + 4 = 7 + ☐

5. What is to the left of the plate?

____

6. Record the area.

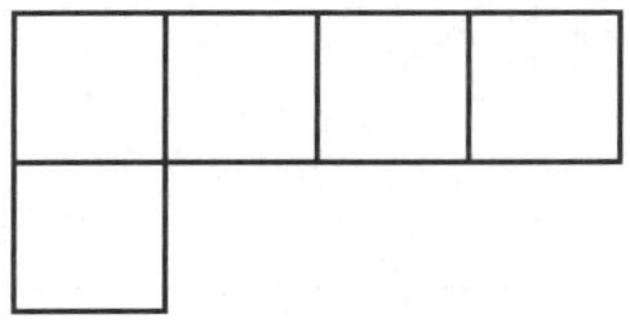

area = ____ squares

7.

Favorite Pets

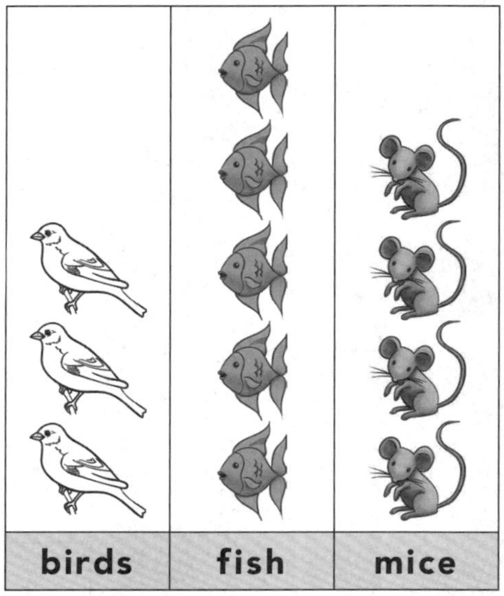

Are there more votes for mice than fish?

Circle: yes no

8. What is 35¢ more than 3 dimes and 2 nickels?

____

NAME: ____________________

DIRECTIONS Solve each problem.

SCORE

1. Write the next even number that follows 12.

____

2.

$$\begin{array}{r} 4 \\ 3 \\ +\ 1 \\ \hline \end{array}$$

3.

$$\begin{array}{r} 66 \\ -\ 50 \\ \hline \end{array}$$

4. Continue the pattern.

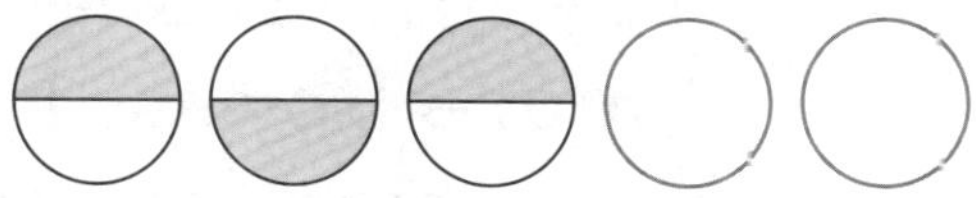

5. Circle the cylinder.

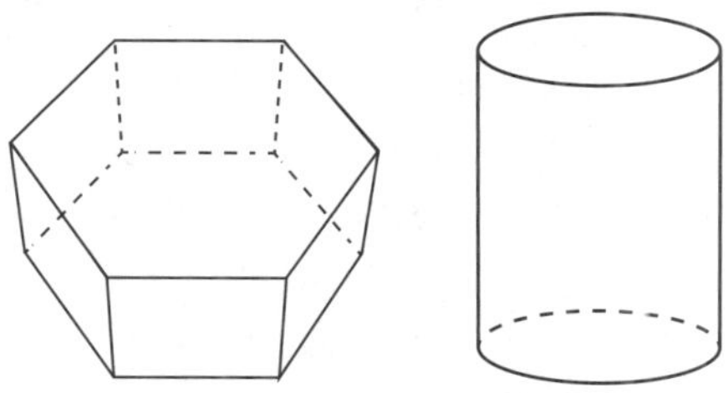

6. Write the time shown.

half past ______

7. Car Colors

Red	卌 卌 |||
Blue	卌 卌 卌 卌 |
Yellow	卌 ||||
Green	卌 卌 卌 ||

Are there more blue cars than green cars?

Circle: yes no

8. Marcia has 2 dogs, 3 cats, and 15 fish. If she buys 4 more fish, how many total fish will she have now?

____

1. ☺ 😐
2. ☺ 😐
3. ☺ 😐
4. ☺ 😐
5. ☺ 😐
6. ☺ 😐
7. ☺ 😐
8. ☺ 😐

___ / 8
Total

DAY 116

NAME: ____________________

DIRECTIONS Solve each problem.

SCORE

1. ☺ ☹
2. ☺ ☹
3. ☺ ☹
4. ☺ ☹
5. ☺ ☹
6. ☺ ☹
7. ☺ ☹
8. ☺ ☹

___ / 8

Total

1. Write the numeral.

1	Hundreds	9	Tens	4	Ones

____

2. 9 + 61 = ______

3.

$$\begin{array}{r} 17 \\ -\ \ 7 \\ \hline \end{array}$$

4. ☐ + 8 = 16

5. Does a hexagon have 5 angles?

Circle: yes no

6. Write the month that comes after October.

____

7. Sports Played

	Soccer	Swimming	Baseball
Mark	X		X
Tracy		X	
Mike		X	X

Which sport does Mark *not* play?

____

8. Joy has a box of 12 crayons. If she buys 2 more boxes, how many total crayons will she have?

____

DAY 117

NAME: ____________________

DIRECTIONS Solve each problem.

1. Use >, <, or =.

279 ◯ 43

2. 49 plus 7 equals

____________________.

3.

$$\begin{array}{r} 56 \\ -\ 40 \\ \hline \end{array}$$

4. 6 + ☐ = 13

5. Color the shape with 3 sides.

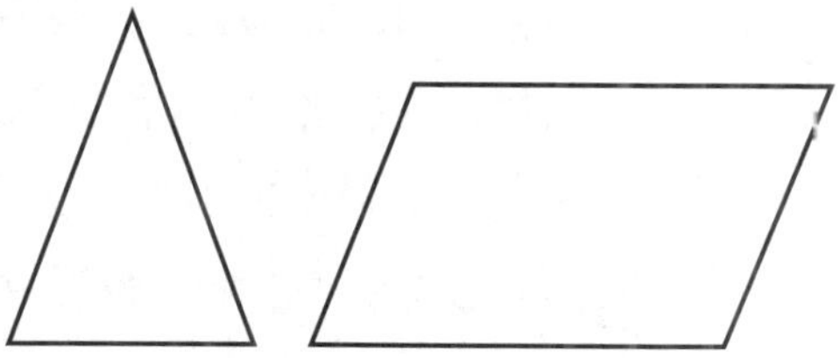

6. What is the volume?

______ cubes

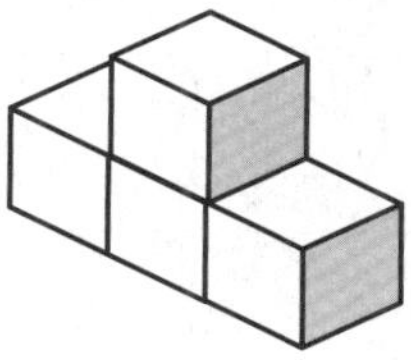

7. **Flower Shop Orders**

Rose	16
Daisy	23
Tulip	15
Iris	25

How many more roses should be ordered to equal the number of irises ordered?

____

8. David can get a lizard when he turns 8. It is his 7th birthday today. In how many months will he get a lizard?

____

SCORE

1.

2.

3.

4.

5.

6.

7.

8.

___ / 8
Total

DAY
118

NAME: ____________________

DIRECTIONS Solve each problem.

SCORE

1. ☺ 😐
2. ☺ 😐
3. ☺ 😐
4. ☺ 😐
5. ☺ 😐
6. ☺ 😐
7. ☺ 😐
8. ☺ 😐

____ / 8
Total

1. Color $\frac{1}{2}$.

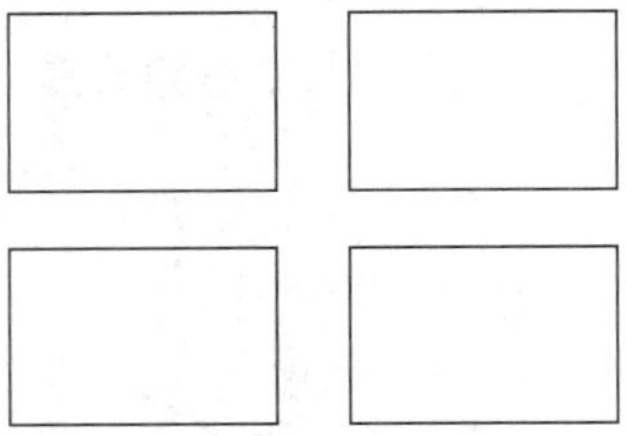

2. 37 + 6 = ______

3. What is 9 less than 14? ______

4. ☐ + 5 = 14 − 1

5. Can the object roll?
Circle: yes no

6. Is the object less than 1 meter, about 1 meter, or more than 1 meter?

____

7. Make 26 tally marks.

8. Dad filled up the gas tank with 24 gallons of gas last week. He used 13 gallons last week. He used 7 gallons of gas this week. How many gallons of gas does he have left?

____

NAME: ______________________________

DIRECTIONS Solve each problem.

1. Write the number word for the number 53.

____

2. Double 6.

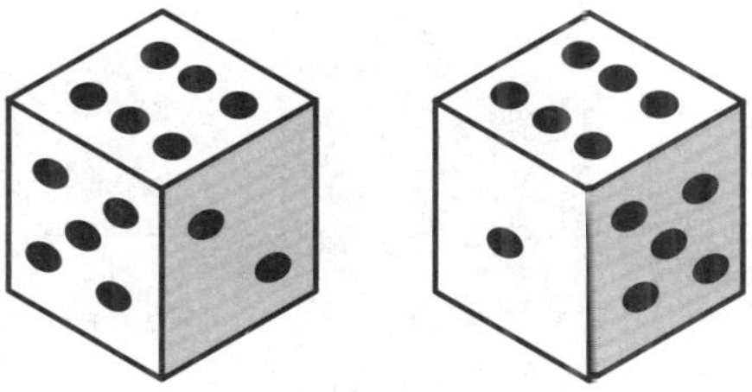

____

3. 74 – 50 = ______

4. ☐ + 46 = 46 + 37

5. Draw the top view of the solid.

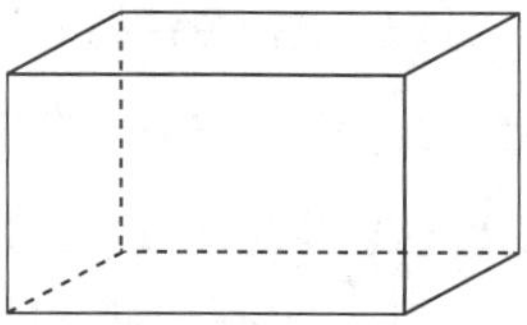

6. Circle the object with less mass.

7. Favorite Activity

Movies	𝍸 𝍸 |||
Restaurant	𝍸 ||||
Park	𝍸 𝍸 ||
Stay Home	𝍸 |||

How many fewer people like going to a restaurant than going to the park?

____

8. Twila has 6 toy ponies, 5 toy puppies, and 7 toy kitties. How many toy animals does she have in all?

____

SCORE

1. ☺ 😐
2. ☺ 😐
3. ☺ 😐
4. ☺ 😐
5. ☺ 😐
6. ☺ 😐
7. ☺ 😐
8. ☺ 😐

___ / 8 Total

DAY
120

NAME: ______________________________

DIRECTIONS Solve each problem.

SCORE

1.

2.

3.

4.

5.

6.

7.

8.

___ / 8

Total

1. Circle about how many pennies would fit in your hand.

20 200

2. 73 + 8 = ______

3.
$$\begin{array}{r} 20 \\ -\ \ 9 \\ \hline \end{array}$$

4. Marcy's sticker book has 10 stickers on each page. There are 6 pages in her book. How many stickers are in her book?

____

Page 1	Page 2	Page 3	Page 4	Page 5	Page 6
10					

5. Circle the pyramid.

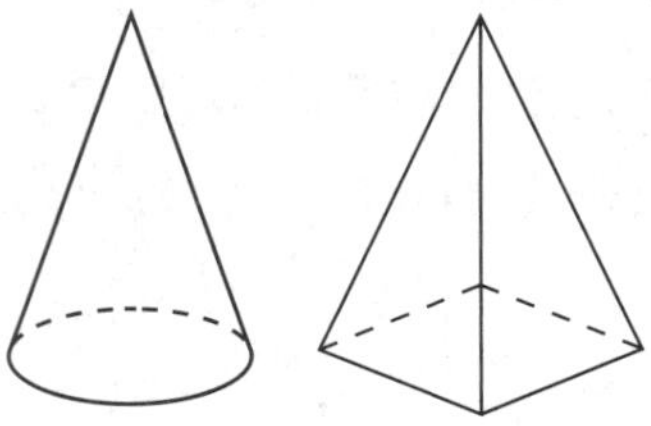

6. Circle the heaviest item.

7.

Max's goal is to run 60 miles during this school year. How many more miles does he have to run?

____

8. Write a subtraction number sentence using the numbers 23, 26, and 49.

____

NAME: ______________________________

DIRECTIONS Solve each problem.

1. Write the numeral.

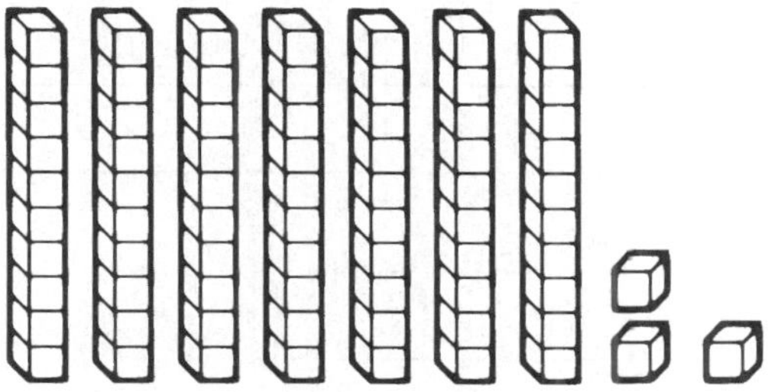

____

2. 2 + 3 + 1 = ______

3. What is the difference between 34 and 10?

____

4. Write the missing number.

55	50		40	35

5. Circle the object that looks like the solid.

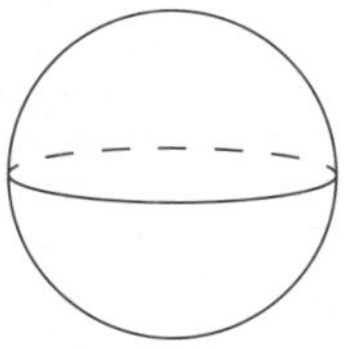

6. How many days are in November?

____

7.

Pets

	Hamster	Dog	Fish	Cat
Mary	X		X	X
Julia	X	X		X
Evan	X	X		X

How many more kids own dogs than fish?

____

8. A baby takes a $2\frac{1}{2}$ hour nap. If the baby went to sleep at 1:00 P.M., what time did she wake up?

____

SCORE

1. ☺ 😐

2. ☺ 😐

3. ☺ 😐

4. ☺ 😐

5. ☺ 😐

6. ☺ 😐

7. ☺ 😐

8. ☺ 😐

____ / 8 Total

DAY
122

NAME: ______________________

DIRECTIONS Solve each problem.

SCORE

1.
2.
3.
4.
5.
6.
7.
8.

____ / 8
Total

1. Circle the smaller number.

190   150

2. 69 + 4 = ______

3. What is 4 less than 14?

____

4. 8 ☐ 0 = 8

5. True or false? Rectangles have four vertices.

____

6. Circle the longer bar.

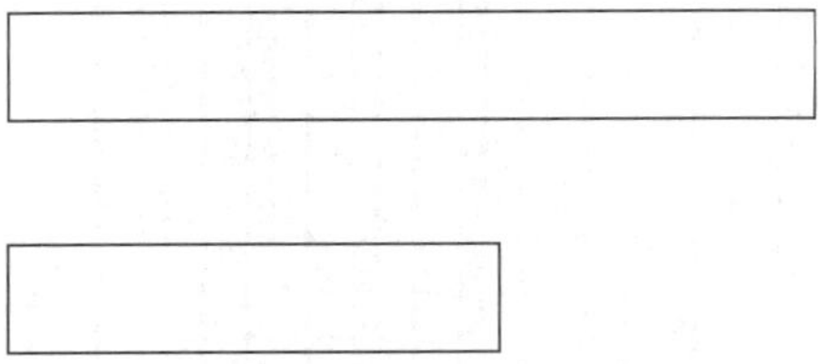

7.

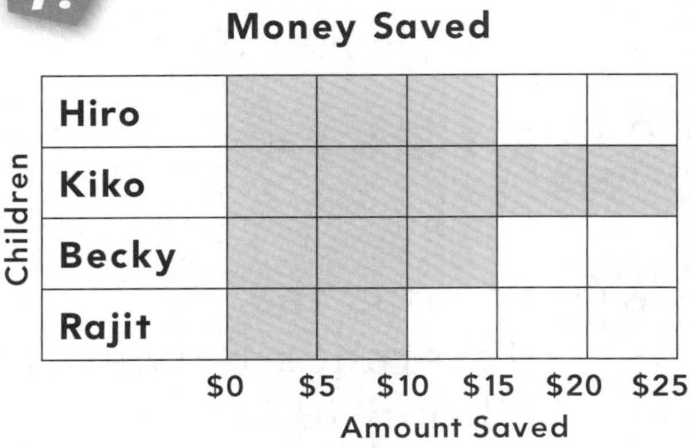

How much less money did Rajit save than Hiro?

____

8. I am 43 more than 32. What number am I?

____

NAME: ______________________

DIRECTIONS Solve each problem.

1. Name the shaded fraction.

____

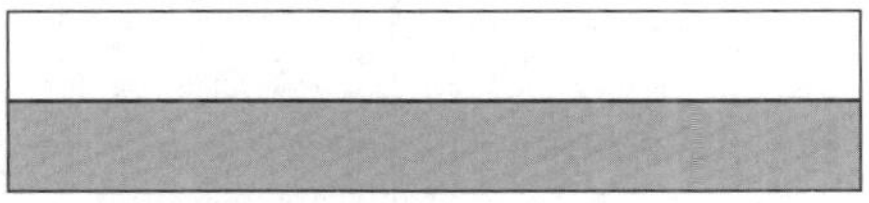

2. What is 5 more than 7?

____

3.

$$\begin{array}{r} 83 \\ -\ 40 \\ \hline \end{array}$$

4. 13 – 8 = ☐ + 0

5. True or false? Every surface is flat.

____

6. Write the length.

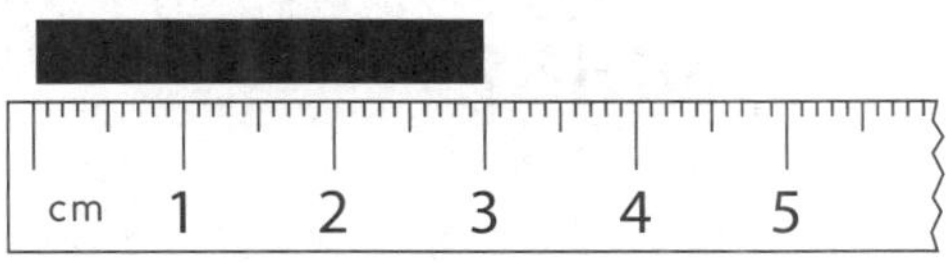

______ centimeters

7.

If children get $2.00 per lost tooth, how much money was given for teeth lost in March?

____

8. Raj can type 42 words per minute on the computer. How many words can Raj type in 2 minutes?

____

SCORE

1. ☺ ☹
2. ☺ ☹
3. ☺ ☹
4. ☺ ☹
5. ☺ ☹
6. ☺ ☹
7. ☺ ☹
8. ☺ ☹

____ / 8 Total

DAY
124

NAME: ______________________

DIRECTIONS Solve each problem.

SCORE

1.
2.
3.
4.
5.
6.
7.
8.

____ / 8
Total

1. Circle groups of 3.

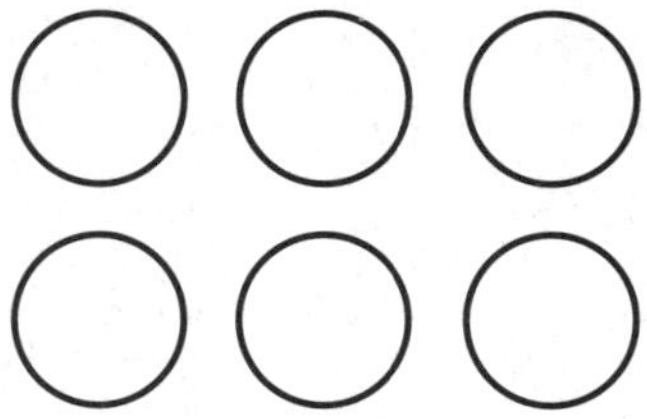

______ groups

2. 75 + 7 = ______

3.

$$\begin{array}{r} 9 \\ -\ 5 \\ \hline \end{array}$$

4. 63 + 28 = ☐ + 63

5. Draw a line of symmetry.

6. Color the polygon with the larger area.

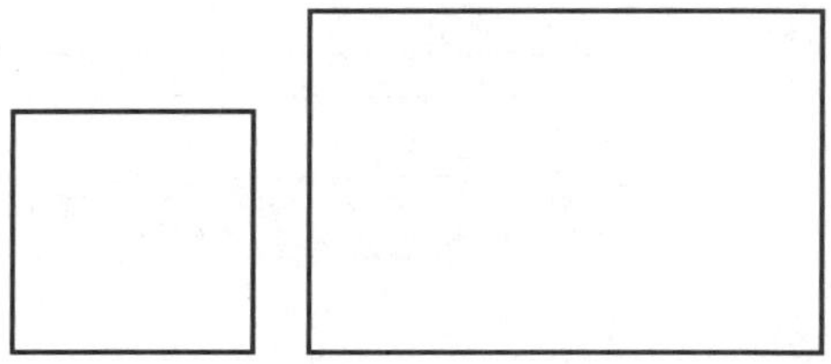

7.

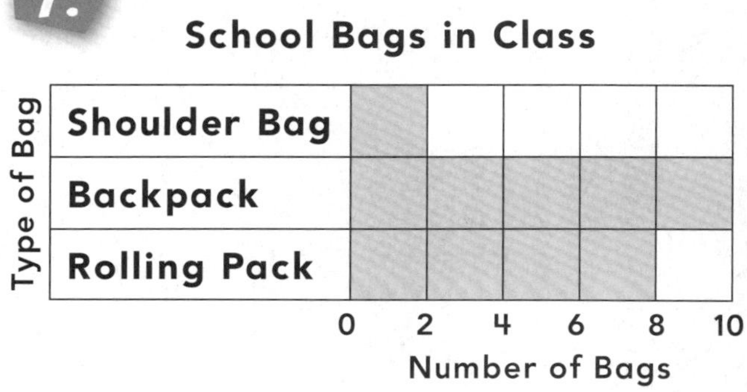

How many kids in the class have school bags?

____

8. Is a classroom about 30 yards, 30 feet, or 30 inches wide?

____

NAME: ______________________

DIRECTIONS Solve each problem.

1. Write the even number that follows 18.

____

2. 3 + 2 + 5 = ______

3. What is the difference between 45 and 20?

____

4. Continue the pattern.

5. Circle the cone.

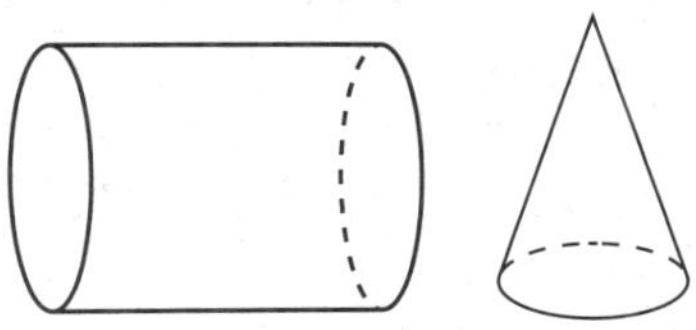

6. Show half past 4:00.

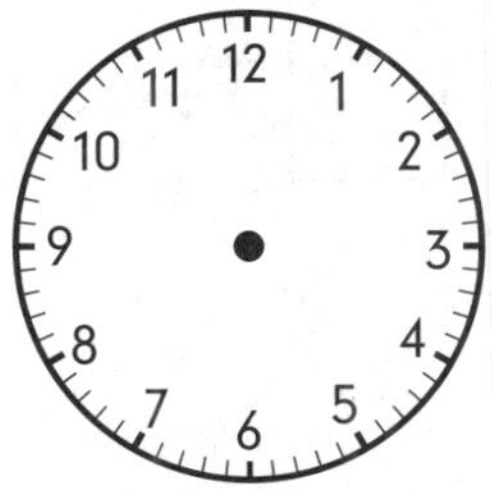

7.

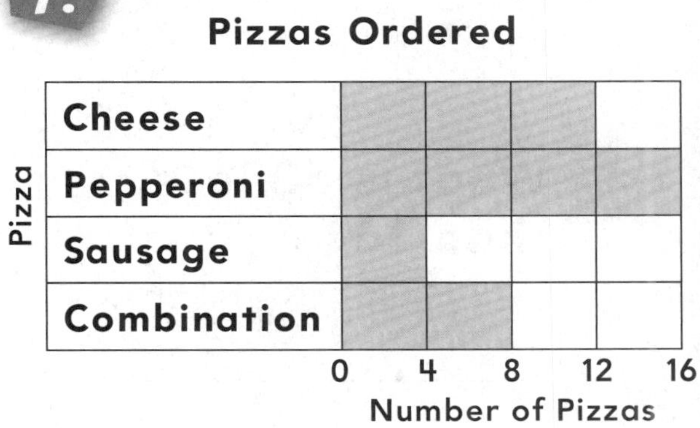

How many more pepperoni pizzas than cheese pizzas were ordered?

____

8. There are 15 wheels on a group of tricycles. How many tricycles are there?

____

SCORE

1. ☺ 😐
2. ☺ 😐
3. ☺ 😐
4. ☺ 😐
5. ☺ 😐
6. ☺ 😐
7. ☺ 😐
8. ☺ 😐

____ / 8
Total

DAY
126

NAME: ____________________

DIRECTIONS Solve each problem.

SCORE

1. ☺ 😐
2. ☺ 😐
3. ☺ 😐
4. ☺ 😐
5. ☺ 😐
6. ☺ 😐
7. ☺ 😐
8. ☺ 😐

___ / 8
Total

1.

66 = ☐ Tens ☐ Ones

2. 3 + 49 = ______

3. What is 50 less than 76?

____

4. 15 – ☐ = 7

5. Count the angles.

____

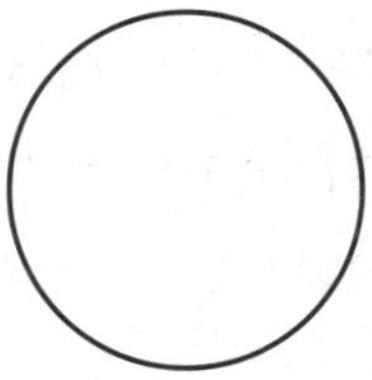

6. Write the month that comes after April.

____

7.

Library Books Checked Out

	Week 1	Week 2	Week 3
Jody	4	5	5
Emily	4	4	4
Brenda	5	7	6
Alison	6	3	6

What was the total number of library books that Jody checked out?

____

8. Write the number sentence.

Seventy-three plus seventeen equals ninety.

____

NAME: ______________________________

DIRECTIONS Solve each problem.

1. Order the numbers from smallest to largest.

473 827 552 791

____

2. 91 + 5 = ______

3.

$$\begin{array}{r} 13 \\ -\ \ 3 \\ \hline \end{array}$$

4. ☐ + 8 = 13

5. Color the shape with 4 sides.

6. What is the volume?

______ cubes

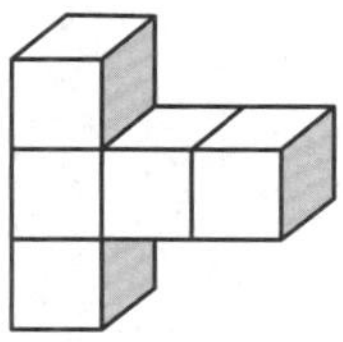

7. Record the data in the graph.

Family Members

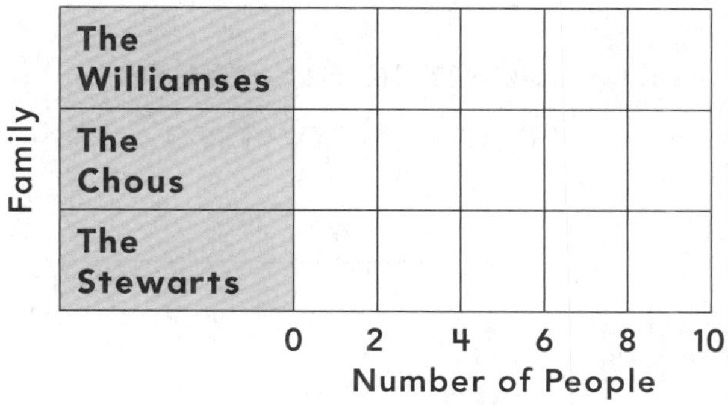

- The Stewarts have 6 people in their family.
- The Williamses have 8 people in their family.
- The Chous have 4 people in their family.

8. What is the largest 3-digit number you can make with the numbers 0, 5, and 7?

____

SCORE

1. ☺ 😐
2. ☺ 😐
3. ☺ 😐
4. ☺ 😐
5. ☺ 😐
6. ☺ 😐
7. ☺ 😐
8. ☺ 😐

____ / 8

Total

DAY
128

NAME: ______________________

DIRECTIONS Solve each problem.

SCORE

1.
2.
3.
4.
5.
6.
7.
8.

____ / 8
Total

1. Circle $\frac{1}{2}$.

2. What is six more than thirty-two?

____

3.

$$\begin{array}{r} 57 \\ -\ 40 \\ \hline \end{array}$$

4. 9 + ☐ = 18 − 8

5. Circle the object that can roll.

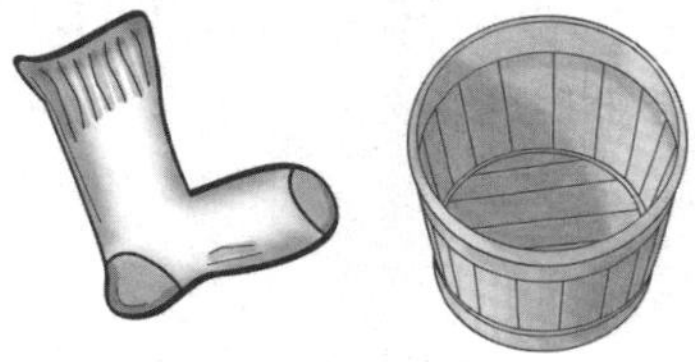

6. Circle the best estimate for the height.

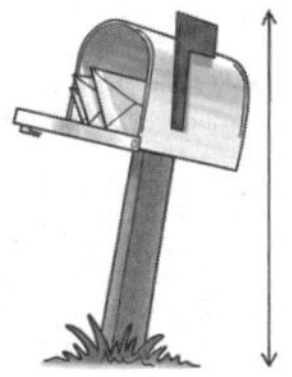

5 m   1 m

7.

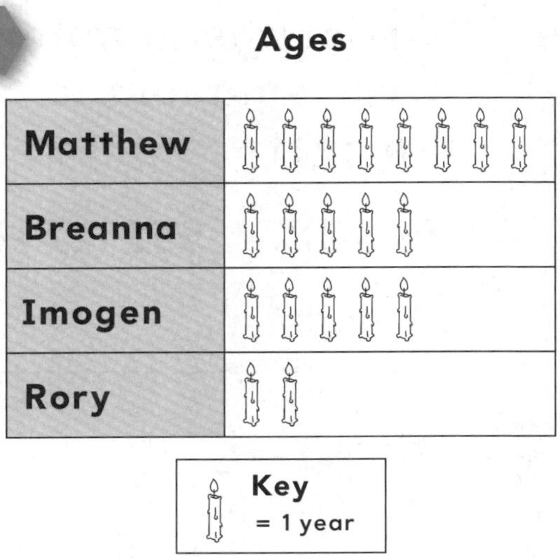

Is Imogen older than Matthew?

Circle: yes   no

8. A survey was taken by the cafeteria.

Eighty-three children like pizza. Fifty-seven like spaghetti. How many more children like pizza than spaghetti?

____

DAY 129

NAME: ______________________________

DIRECTIONS Solve each problem.

1. Write the number word for the number 62.

____

2. 66 + 8 = ______

3. 12 minus 4 equals

______________________.

4. 67 + ☐ = 43 + 67

5. Draw the front view of the solid.

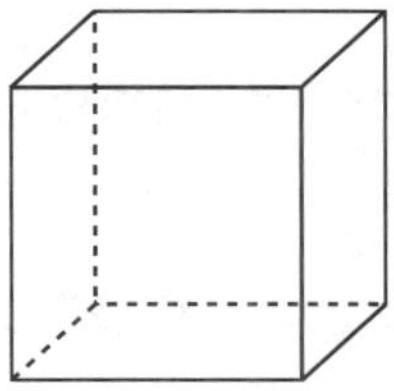

6. Show 2:00.

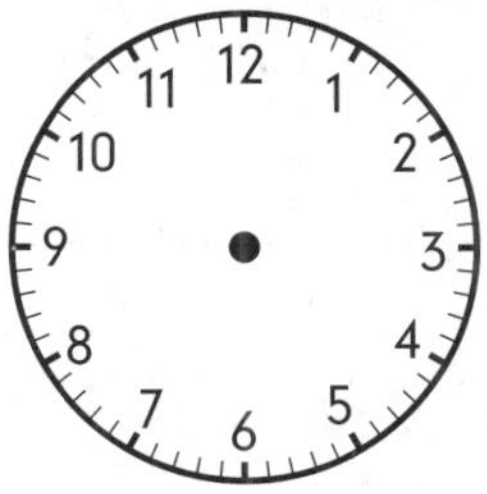

7.

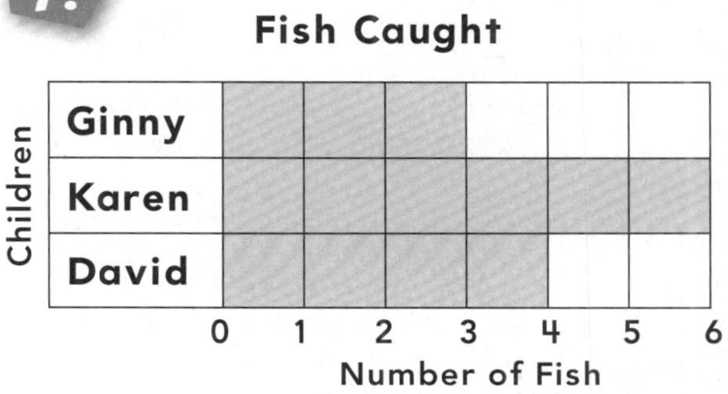

How many fish did Ginny catch?

____

8. A custodian is going to paint a school. He needs 3 cans of paint for each classroom. There are twenty classrooms. How many cans of paint will he need to buy?

____

SCORE

1. ☺ 😐
2. ☺ 😐
3. ☺ 😐
4. ☺ 😐
5. ☺ 😐
6. ☺ 😐
7. ☺ 😐
8. ☺ 😐

____ / 8
Total

NAME: ______________________

DIRECTIONS Solve each problem.

SCORE

1. ☺ ☹
2. ☺ ☹
3. ☺ ☹
4. ☺ ☹
5. ☺ ☹
6. ☺ ☹
7. ☺ ☹
8. ☺ ☹

____ / 8 Total

1. Write the ordinal number for four.

____

2. 29 + 4 = ______

3.

$$\begin{array}{r} 53 \\ -\ 40 \\ \hline \end{array}$$

4. Each page in a poetry book has 4 poems. How many poems are on 5 pages?

____

1 Page	2 Pages	3 Pages	4 Pages	5 Pages
4				

5. Color the triangles.

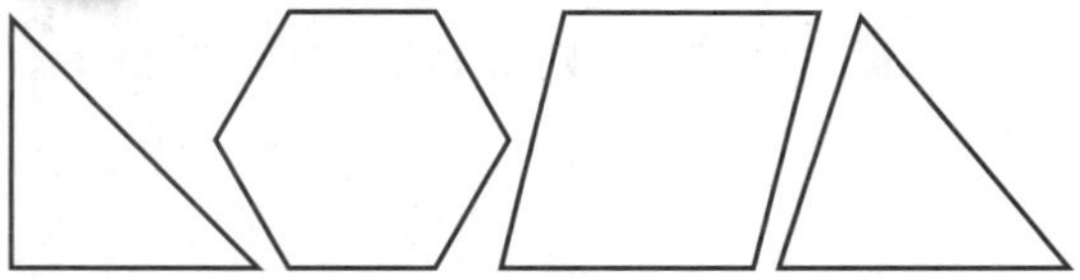

6. Circle the object that holds less.

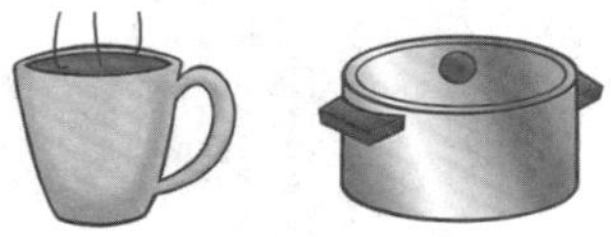

7. Toy Train Sales Last Week

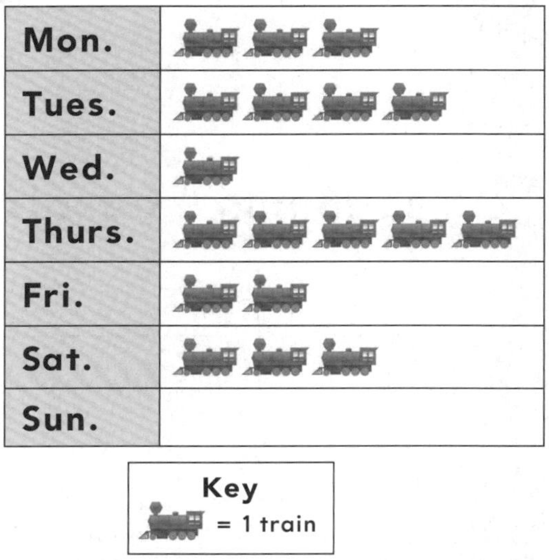

What is the total number of trains that were sold?

____

8. Write the number that is 1 more hundred, 3 more tens, and 5 more ones than the number 123.

____

NAME: ______________________

DIRECTIONS Solve each problem.

1. Write the numeral.

2	Hundreds	1	Tens	7	Ones

____

2. 4 plus 7 plus 1 equals

______________________.

3. 11 – 8 = ______

4. Write the missing number.

45	47		51	53

5. Color one surface on the solid.

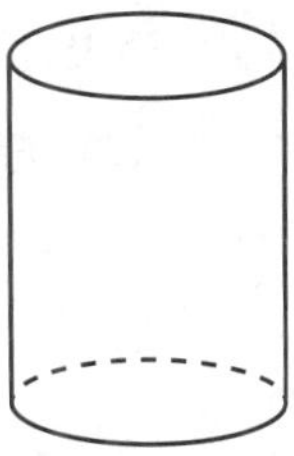

6. Write the time.

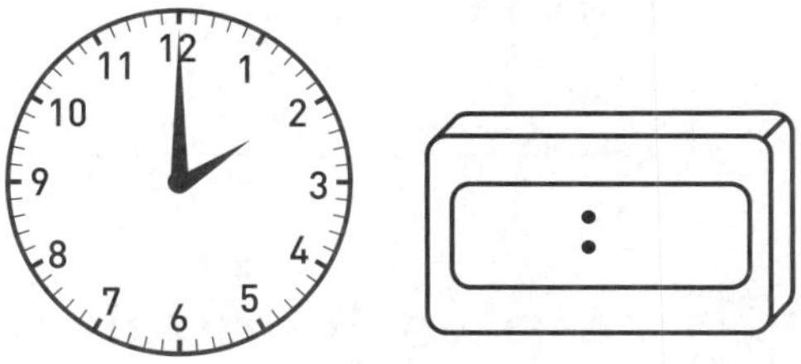

7. Count the tally marks.

____

8. Match the transportation with the boy who uses it. Ralph does not ride the bike. Ian rides the skateboard. Darren does not ride the scooter.

Ralph: ______________

Ian: ______________

Darren: ______________

SCORE

1.
2.
3.
4.
5.
6.
7.
8.

____ / 8

Total

NAME: ______________________________

DIRECTIONS Solve each problem.

SCORE

1. ☺ ☹
2. ☺ ☹
3. ☺ ☹
4. ☺ ☹
5. ☺ ☹
6. ☺ ☹
7. ☺ ☹
8. ☺ ☹

____ / 8
Total

1. Round 78 to the nearest ten.

____

2. 76 plus 9 equals

______________________________.

3. What is 20 less than 25?

____

4. 7 + ☐ = 15

5. Name the shape.

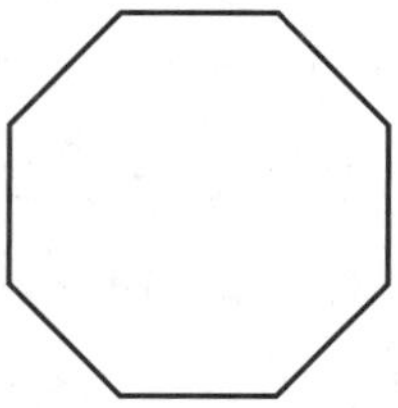

____

6. Circle the larger container.

7.

Favorite Pets

How many votes for birds and mice are there altogether?

____

8. A banana costs 19¢, an apple costs 26¢, and a pear costs 35¢. Rita has 65¢. Can she buy all three pieces of fruit?

____

NAME: ____________________

DIRECTIONS Solve each problem.

1. Name the shaded fraction.

____

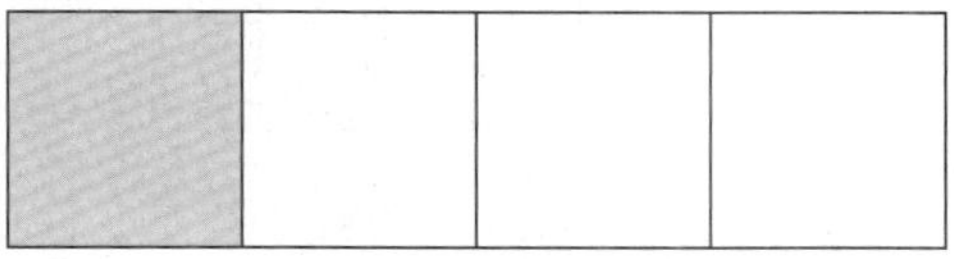

2. 58 + 3 = ______

3.

$$\begin{array}{r} 20 \\ -\ \ 7 \\ \hline \end{array}$$

4. 11 – 8 = ☐ + 1

5. True or false? The side view of a solid is always the same as the top view.

____

6. Write the length.

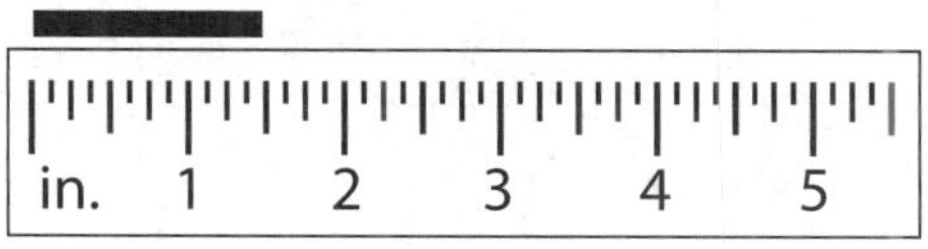

______ inches

7.

Car Colors

Red	𝍸 𝍸 |||
Blue	𝍸 𝍸 𝍸 𝍸	
Yellow	𝍸 ||||
Green	𝍸 𝍸 𝍸 ||

How many cars are green or red?

____

8. List three solids that have a cross-section that is a circle.

____

____

____

SCORE

1. ☺ 😐

2. ☺ 😐

3. ☺ 😐

4. ☺ 😐

5. ☺ 😐

6. ☺ 😐

7. ☺ 😐

8. ☺ 😐

____ / 8

Total

DAY
134

NAME: ______________________________

DIRECTIONS Solve each problem.

SCORE

1. ☺☹
2. ☺☹
3. ☺☹
4. ☺☹
5. ☺☹
6. ☺☹
7. ☺☹
8. ☺☹

____ / 8
Total

1. Circle groups of 5.

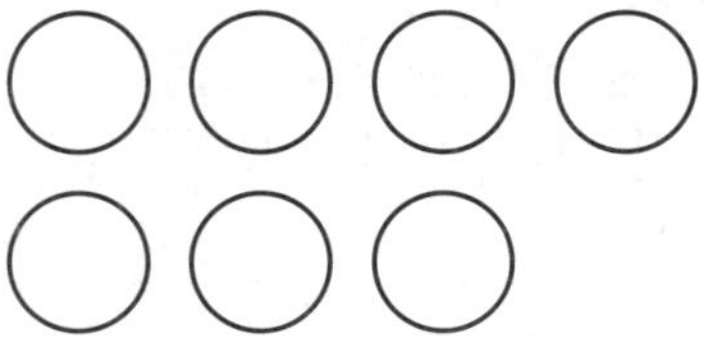

_______ group of 5

_______ left over

2. 7 + 43 = ______

3. 12 minus 10 equals

____________________.

4. 91 + 57 = 57 + ☐

5. Draw all lines of symmetry.

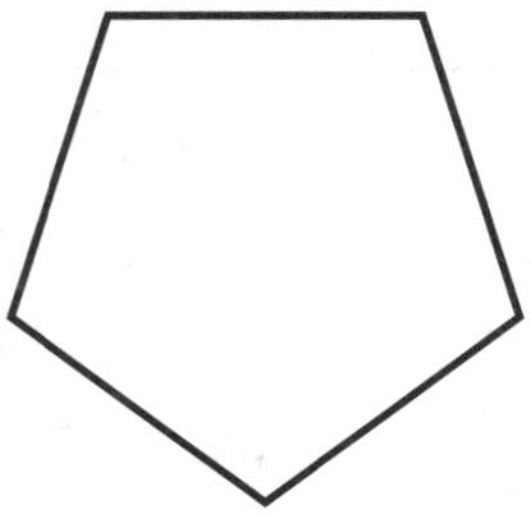

6. Record the area.

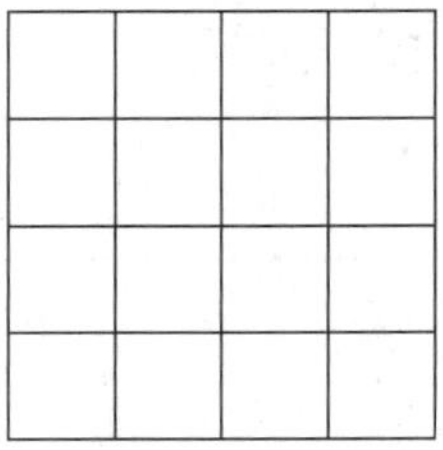

area = ____ squares

7. Sports Played

	Soccer	Swimming	Baseball
Mark	X		X
Tracy		X	
Mike		X	X

If we add Kim to the chart and she plays soccer, how many children play soccer?

____

8. You have 45¢. Your grandma gives you 2 dimes. You spend 15¢. Now how much money do you have?

____

NAME: ______________________________

DIRECTIONS Solve each problem.

1. Write the even number that follows 10.

____

2. 6 + 4 + 3 = ______

3. What is the difference between 99 and 60?

____

4. Continue the pattern.

__________ __________

5. Color a face of the solid.

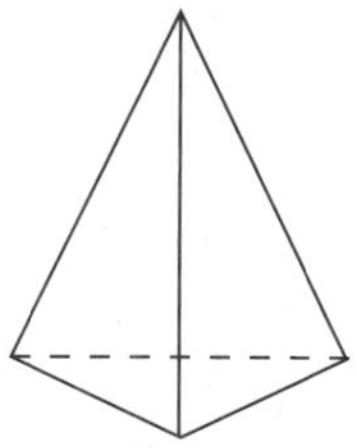

6. Write the time.

half past ______

7. Flower Shop Orders

Rose	16
Daisy	23
Tulip	15
Iris	25

If 7 daisies are sold, how many daisies are left?

____

8. You have 62¢ in your piggy bank. Your mom gives you a quarter and a dime. You spend 35¢. How much money do you have left?

____

SCORE

1. ☺ 😐
2. ☺ 😐
3. ☺ 😐
4. ☺ 😐
5. ☺ 😐
6. ☺ 😐
7. ☺ 😐
8. ☺ 😐

____ / 8
Total

DAY 136

NAME: ______________________________

DIRECTIONS Solve each problem.

SCORE

1. ☺ 😐
2. ☺ 😐
3. ☺ 😐
4. ☺ 😐
5. ☺ 😐
6. ☺ 😐
7. ☺ 😐
8. ☺ 😐

____ / 8
Total

1.

31	=		Tens		Ones

2. 23 + 14 = ______

3.

$$\begin{array}{r} 86 \\ -\ 40 \\ \hline \end{array}$$

4. ☐ + 9 = 14

5. Count the angles.

____

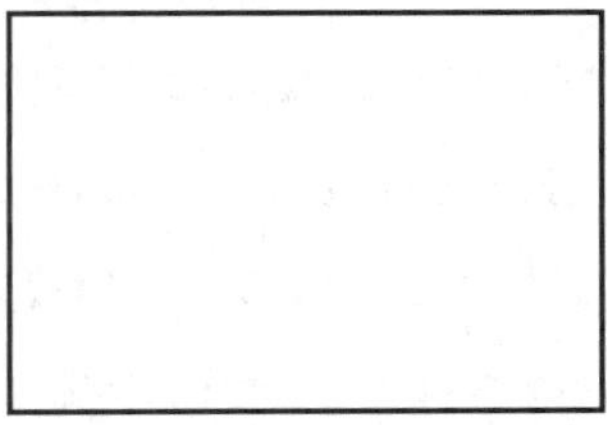

6. Write the day that comes after Thursday.

____

7. Make 15 tally marks.

8. Aneal bought 23 trading cards. He put 15 in a box and he traded the rest. How many cards did Aneal trade?

____

NAME: ______________________________

DIRECTIONS Solve each problem.

1. Round 35 to the nearest ten.

____

2. 78 + 52 = ______

3. 31 minus 20 equals

__________________.

4. 4 ☐ 1 = 5

5. How many sides does the shape have?

____

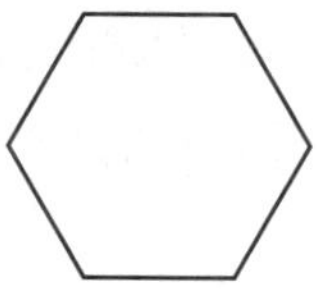

6. What is the volume?

______ cubes

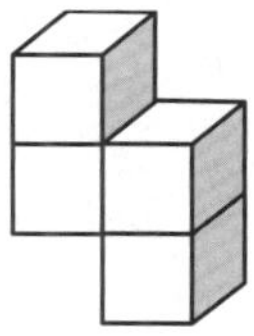

7. Favorite Activity

Movies	卌 卌 |||
Restaurant	卌 ||||
Park	卌 卌 ||
Stay Home	卌 |||

If half of the people who like to stay home change their mind and choose the park, what will the new total be for the park?

____

8. Write a related addition problem.

56 – 21 = 35

____

SCORE

1. ☺ 😐

2. ☺ 😐

3. ☺ 😐

4. ☺ 😐

5. ☺ 😐

6. ☺ 😐

7. ☺ 😐

8. ☺ 😐

____ / 8

Total

DAY
138

NAME: ____________________________

DIRECTIONS Solve each problem.

SCORE

1. ☺ 😐
2. ☺ 😐
3. ☺ 😐
4. ☺ 😐
5. ☺ 😐
6. ☺ 😐
7. ☺ 😐
8. ☺ 😐

____ / 8
Total

1. Circle $\frac{1}{4}$.

2. 45 plus 31 equals

____________________.

3.

$$\begin{array}{r} 63 \\ -\ 30 \\ \hline \end{array}$$

4. $4 + 7 = \square - 5$

5. Circle the object that can roll.

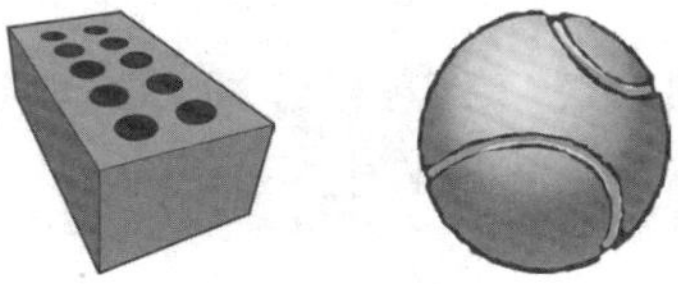

6. Circle the object that would be taller than 1 meter.

7.

Miles Run

Max	
Cheryl	
Brandon	

Key
 = 10 miles

How many fewer miles did Cheryl run than Brandon?

____

8. Julia's family is going out to dinner tonight. Will they go to dinner at 11:00 P.M. or 5:00 P.M.?

____

DAY 139

NAME: ____________________

DIRECTIONS Solve each problem.

1. Write the numeral for four hundred eighty-five.

____

2.
$$\begin{array}{r} 72 \\ +\ 12 \\ \hline \end{array}$$

3. 97 minus 70 equals

____

4. ☐ + 73 = 73 + 55

5. Color the correct cross-section.

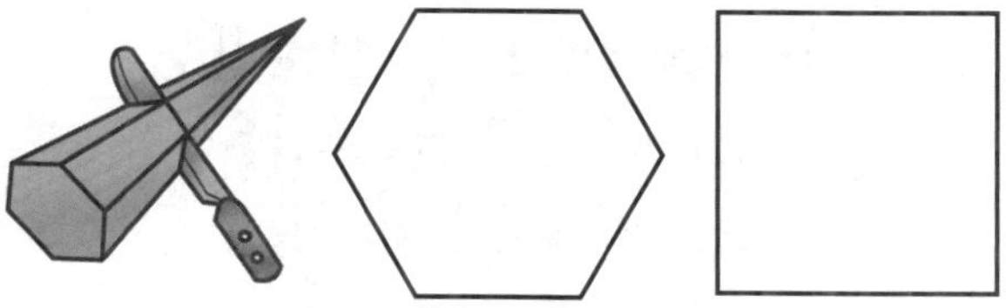

6. Is an elephant taller or shorter than a yard?

____

7. Pets

	Hamster	Dog	Fish	Cat
Mary	X		X	X
Julia	X	X		X
Evan	X	X		X

Which pets do all three children own?

____

8. I am 15 less than 59. What number am I?

____

SCORE

1. ☺ 😐
2. ☺ 😐
3. ☺ 😐
4. ☺ 😐
5. ☺ 😐
6. ☺ 😐
7. ☺ 😐
8. ☺ 😐

____ / 8 Total

DAY

140

NAME: ____________________

DIRECTIONS Solve each problem.

SCORE

1. ☺ 😐
2. ☺ 😐
3. ☺ 😐
4. ☺ 😐
5. ☺ 😐
6. ☺ 😐
7. ☺ 😐
8. ☺ 😐

____ / 8

Total

1. Write the ordinal number for three.

____

2. $37 + 51 =$ ______

3.

$$\begin{array}{r} 77 \\ -\ 36 \\ \hline \end{array}$$

4. There are 50 books on Yui's bookshelf. If she buys 10 new books every year, how many books will she have on her shelf after 4 years?

____

Start	1 Year	2 Years	3 Years	4 Years
50				

5. Circle the plane figure.

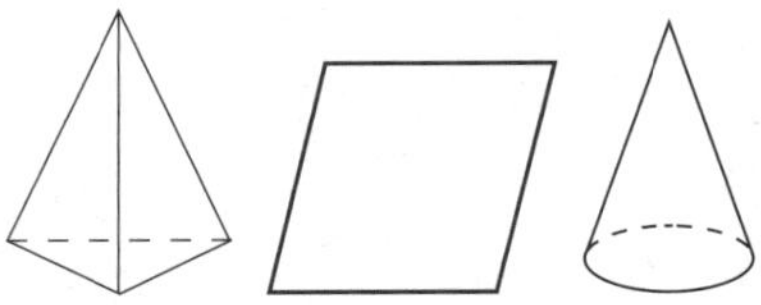

6. Circle the object that weighs more.

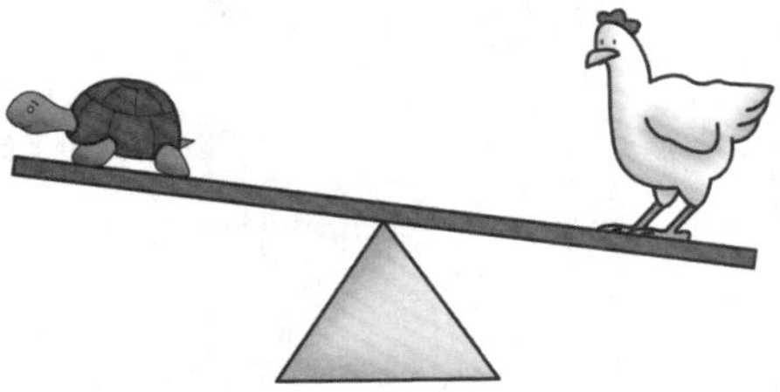

7.

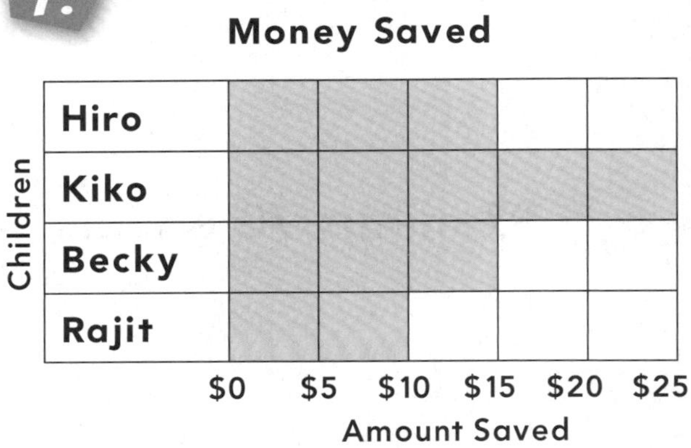

If Kiko saves $15 more, how much will she have?

____

8. Cami has 23 shells in her collection. How many shells will she have if she doubles her collection?

____

NAME: ____________________

DIRECTIONS Solve each problem.

1. Write the numeral.

4	Hundreds	5	Tens	2	Ones

____

2.

$$\begin{array}{r} 5 \\ 3 \\ +\ 4 \\ \hline \end{array}$$

3. What is 50 less than 67?

____

4. Write the missing number.

90	88	86		82

5. Name the shape.

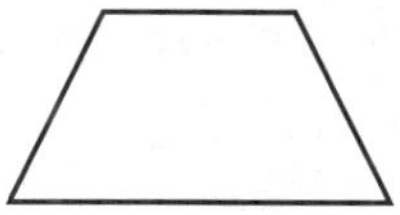

____

6. Ray goes to a friend's house to play at 3:00 P.M. and comes home at 5:00 P.M. How long was he gone?

____

7. Teeth Lost

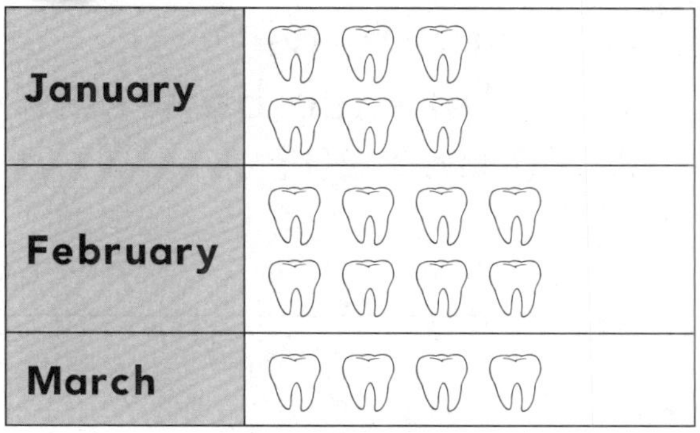

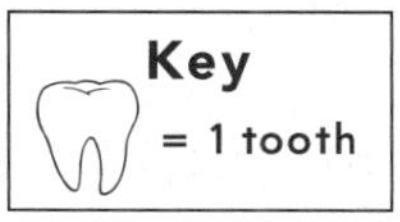

How many more teeth were lost in February than in March?

____

8. Write the number that has 7 in the hundreds place, 3 in the tens place, and 5 in the ones place.

____

SCORE

1. ☺ 😐
2. ☺ 😐
3. ☺ 😐
4. ☺ 😐
5. ☺ 😐
6. ☺ 😐
7. ☺ 😐
8. ☺ 😐

___ / 8 Total

DAY 142

NAME: ____________________

DIRECTIONS Solve each problem.

SCORE

1. ☺ 😐
2. ☺ 😐
3. ☺ 😐
4. ☺ 😐
5. ☺ 😐
6. ☺ 😐
7. ☺ 😐
8. ☺ 😐

____ / 8 Total

1. Round 91 to the nearest ten.

____

2. 83 + 45 = ______

3. What is the difference between 45 and 20?

____

4. ☐ + 10 = 19

5. Name the shape.

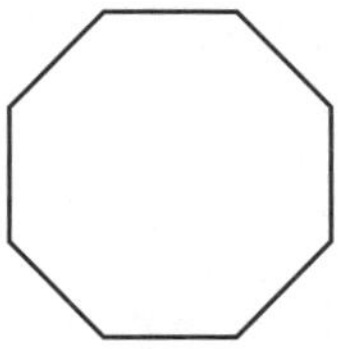

____

6. Circle the smaller container.

7.

School Bags in Class

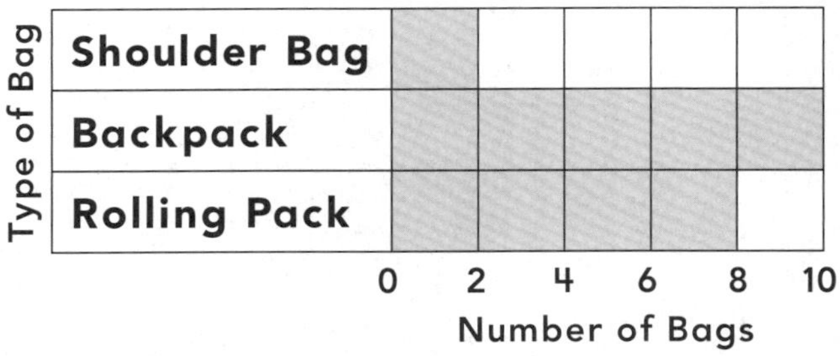

If half of the kids with rolling packs decide to get shoulder bags instead, what will be the new total of kids with shoulder bags?

____

8. Would you wear a jacket or a bathing suit when it is 90°F outside?

____

NAME: ______________________

DIRECTIONS Solve each problem.

1. Name the shaded fraction.

____

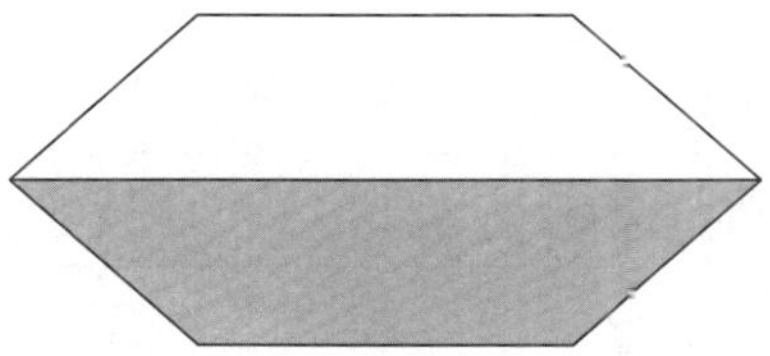

2. What is 52 more than 27?

____

3.

$$\begin{array}{r} 74 \\ -\ 30 \\ \hline \end{array}$$

4. 9 – 7 = 1 + ☐

5. True or false? This shape is a prism.

____

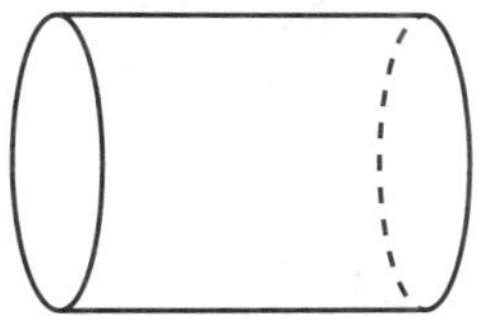

6. Circle the season to match the months below.

winter spring

summer fall

September
October
November

7.

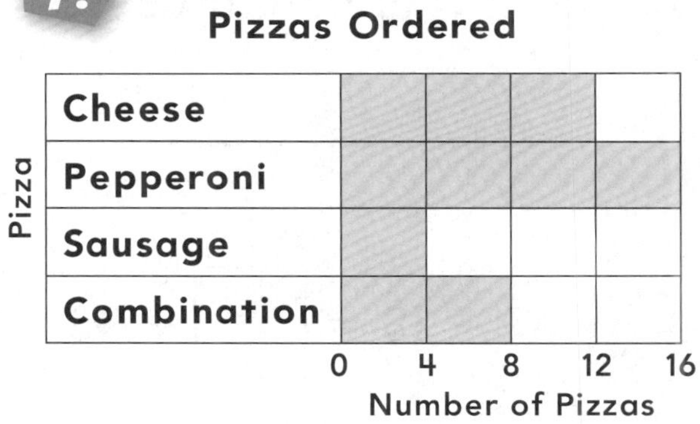

How many fewer sausage pizzas than combination pizzas were ordered?

____

8. How many different 3-digit numbers can you make with the numbers 7, 4, and 3?

____

SCORE

1. ☺ ☹
2. ☺ ☹
3. ☺ ☹
4. ☺ ☹
5. ☺ ☹
6. ☺ ☹
7. ☺ ☹
8. ☺ ☹

___ / 8 Total

NAME: ____________________

DIRECTIONS Solve each problem.

SCORE

1. ☺ ☹
2. ☺ ☹
3. ☺ ☹
4. ☺ ☹
5. ☺ ☹
6. ☺ ☹
7. ☺ ☹
8. ☺ ☹

____ / 8
Total

1. Circle groups of 3.

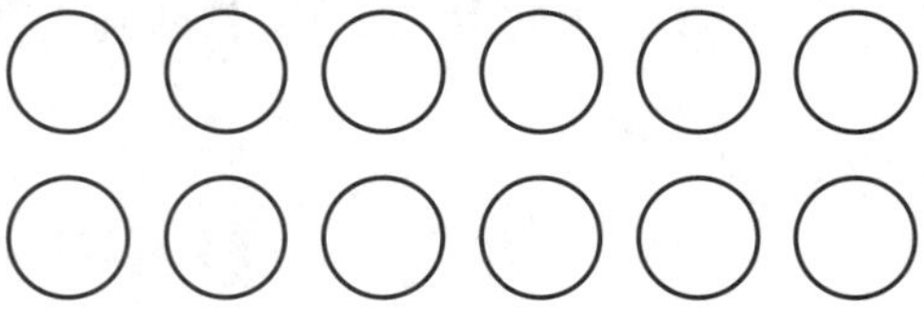

______ groups

2. 67 + 32 = ______

3. What is 97 minus 62?

____

4. 43 + 18 = ☐ + 43

5. Draw a line of symmetry.

6. Record the area.

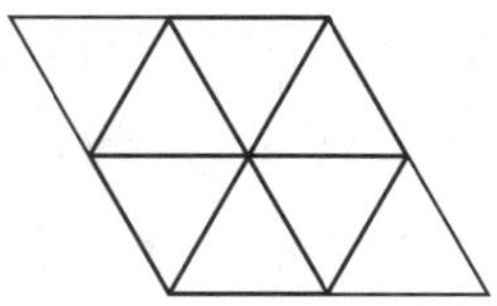

area = ______ triangles

7. Library Books Checked Out

	Week 1	Week 2	Week 3
Jody	4	5	5
Emily	4	4	4
Brenda	5	7	6
Alison	6	3	6

How many more library books did Jody check out in Week 2 than in Week 1?

____

8. Sixty-seven kids like the beach. Ninety-nine kids like the aquarium. Forty-six kids like the zoo. How many more kids like to go to the beach than the zoo?

____

NAME: ____________________

DIRECTIONS Solve each problem.

1. Write the even number that follows 13.

____

2. 6 + 2 + 4 = ______

3. What is the difference between 59 and 42?

____

4. Continue the pattern.

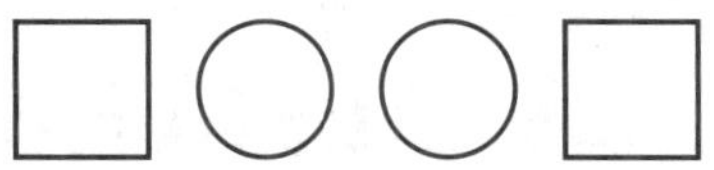 ______

5. Circle the cylinder.

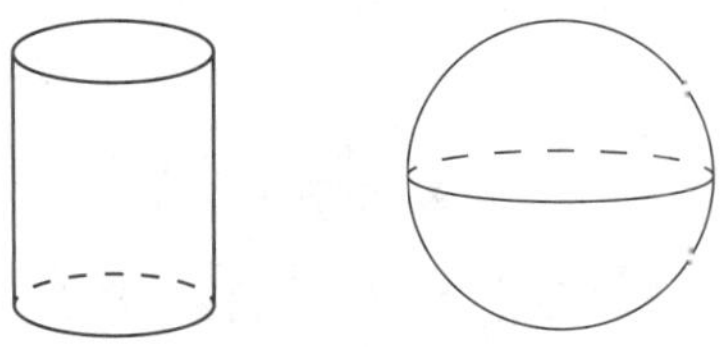

6. Show half past 10:00.

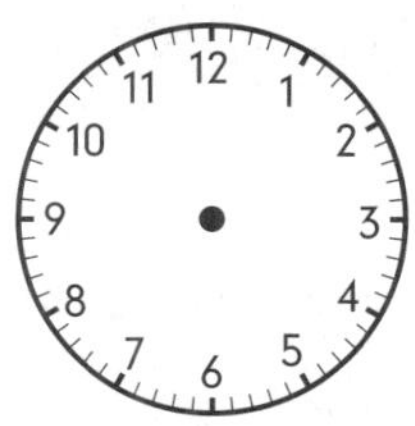

7. Record the data. Complete the chart.

Favorite Game

	Jan	Ben	Tori
Jump rope	X		
Kickball			

- Jan likes jump rope.
- Ben likes jump rope and kickball.
- Tori likes the same games as Ben.

8. Mark is building a tree house. He needs to use 63 nails. Nails come in bags of 20. How many bags of nails should he buy?

____

SCORE

1. ☺ 😐
2. ☺ 😐
3. ☺ 😐
4. ☺ 😐
5. ☺ 😐
6. ☺ 😐
7. ☺ 😐
8. ☺ 😐

____ / 8 Total

DAY
146

NAME: ____________________

DIRECTIONS Solve each problem.

SCORE

1. ☺ ☹
2. ☺ ☹
3. ☺ ☹
4. ☺ ☹
5. ☺ ☹
6. ☺ ☹
7. ☺ ☹
8. ☺ ☹

____ / 8
Total

1.

57	=		Tens		Ones

2.

$$\begin{array}{r} 48 \\ +\ 41 \\ \hline \end{array}$$

3. 36 – 24 = ______

4. ☐ – 8 = 3

5. Does an octagon have 8 vertices?

Circle: yes no

6. Write the month that comes after August.

____

7.

Ages

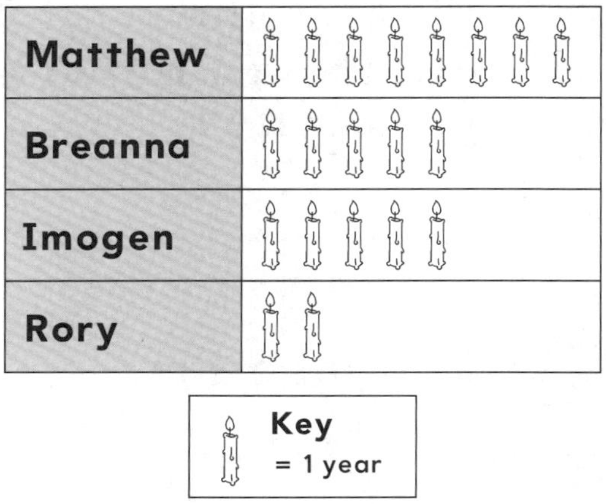

How old is Breanna?

____

8. Write the number that is 3 more hundreds, 5 more tens, and 6 more ones than the number 342.

____

NAME: ______________________________

DIRECTIONS Solve each problem.

1. Order the numbers from largest to smallest.

672 827 439 281

____

2. 25 + 73 = ______

3.

$$\begin{array}{r} 57 \\ -\ 8 \\ \hline \end{array}$$

4. 6 + ☐ = 8

5. Color the shape with 3 sides.

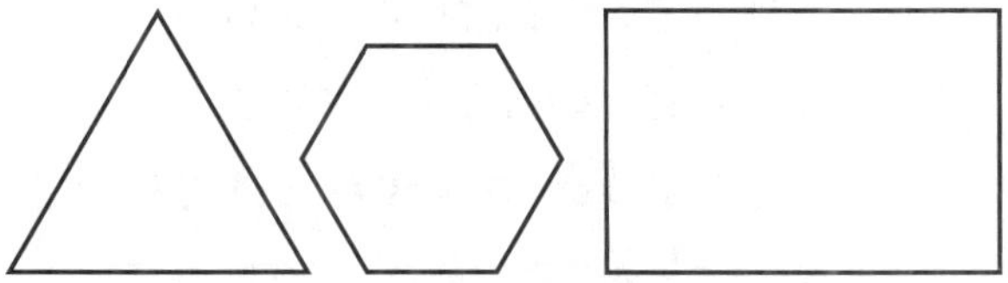

6. Circle the solid that takes up less space.

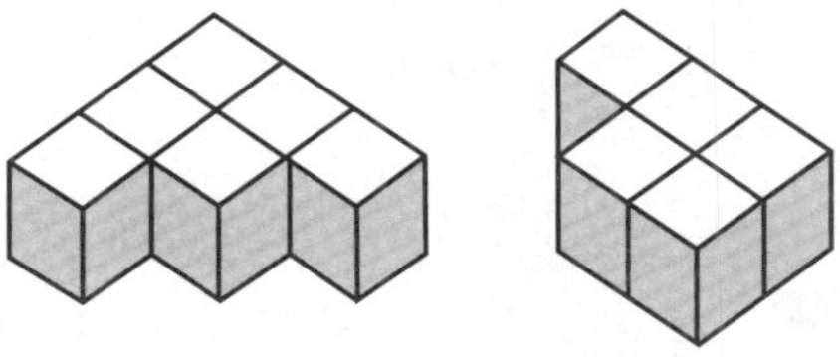

7.

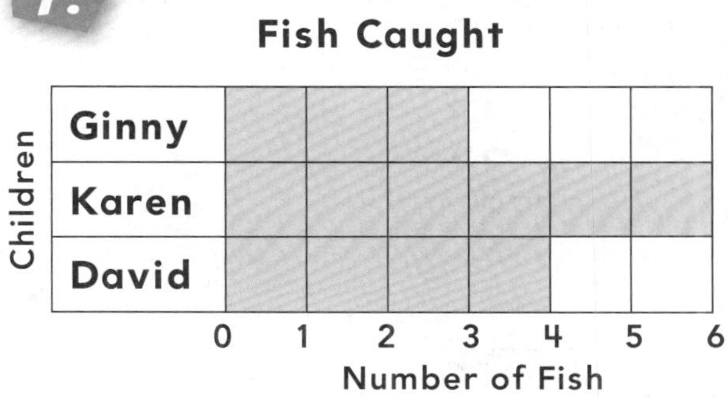

Who caught more fish than David?

____

8. Circle the number sentence that matches the picture.

2 + 6 = 8

8 – 6 = 2

6 + 6 = 12

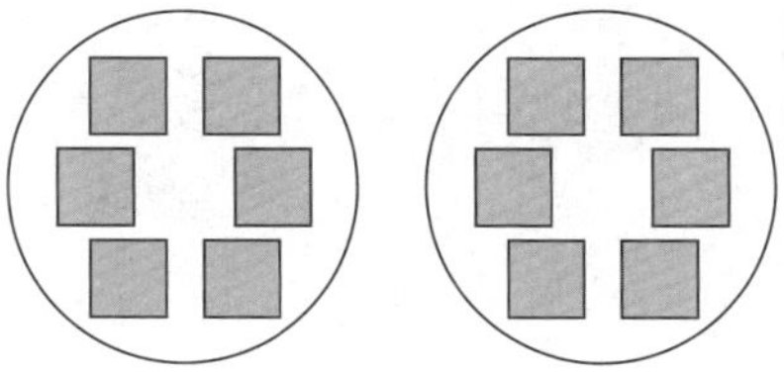

SCORE

1.

2.

3.

4.

5.

6.

7.

8.

____ / 8

Total

DAY
148

NAME: ____________________

DIRECTIONS Solve each problem.

SCORE

1.
2.
3.
4.
5.
6.
7.
8.

____ / 8
Total

1. Circle $\frac{1}{2}$.

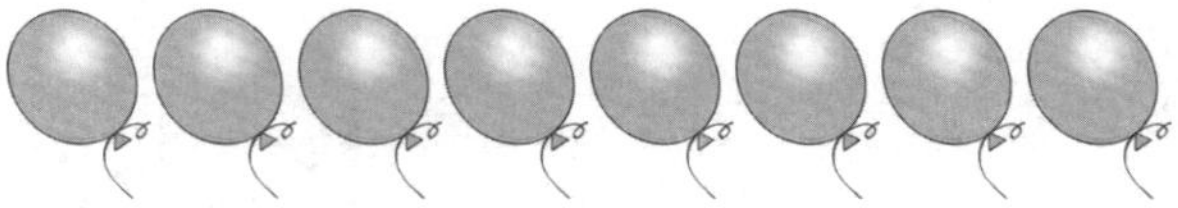

2. 43 plus 55 equals

____________________.

3.
$$\begin{array}{r} 44 \\ -\ 23 \\ \hline \end{array}$$

4. $\square + 0 = 15 - 0$

5. Can the object stack?

____

6. Circle the object that is shorter than 1 meter in height.

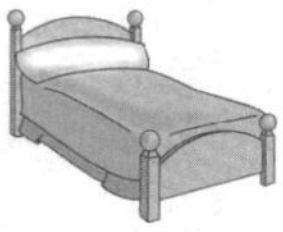 

7. **Toy Train Sales Last Week**

Mon.	
Tues.	
Wed.	
Thurs.	
Fri.	
Sat.	
Sun.	

Key
 = 1 train

The store owner would like to sell 15 trains every week. Did he meet his goal for last week?

____

8. Kristy has a sticker collection with 23 glitter stickers, 56 puffy stickers, and 14 scratch-n-sniff stickers. If she gets 16 more glitter stickers, how many glitter stickers will she have in all?

____

NAME: ______________________

DIRECTIONS Solve each problem.

1. Write the number word for 17.

____

2.
$$\begin{array}{r} 75 \\ +\ 12 \\ \hline \end{array}$$

3. 62 minus 31 equals ______________________.

4. 81 + ☐ = 46 + 81

5. Draw the top view of the solid.

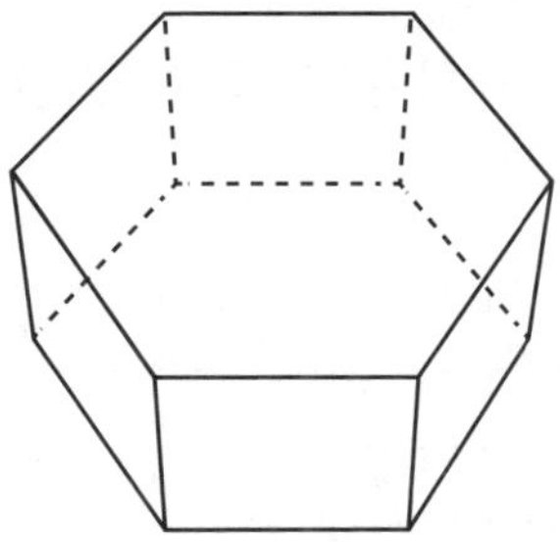

6. Show 1:00.

7. Count the tally marks.

____

8. Name two solids that cannot be stacked.

____

____

SCORE

1. ☺ 😐
2. ☺ 😐
3. ☺ 😐
4. ☺ 😐
5. ☺ 😐
6. ☺ 😐
7. ☺ 😐
8. ☺ 😐

____ / 8

Total

DAY
150

NAME: ____________________

DIRECTIONS Solve each problem.

SCORE

1. ☺ 😐
2. ☺ 😐
3. ☺ 😐
4. ☺ 😐
5. ☺ 😐
6. ☺ 😐
7. ☺ 😐
8. ☺ 😐

____ / 8
Total

1. Write the ordinal number for 16.

____

2. 64 + 23 = ______

3. What is 18 less than 29?

____

4. Count by fours and color each number counted.

1	2	3	4	5	6	7	8	9	10
11	12	13	14	15	16	17	18	19	20
21	22	23	24	25	26	27	28	29	30
31	32	33	34	35	36	37	38	39	40
41	42	43	44	45	46	47	48	49	50

5. Color the hexagons.

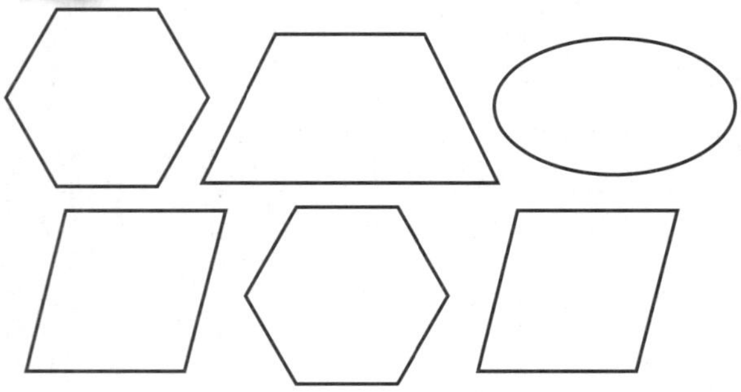

6. Circle the object that weighs less.

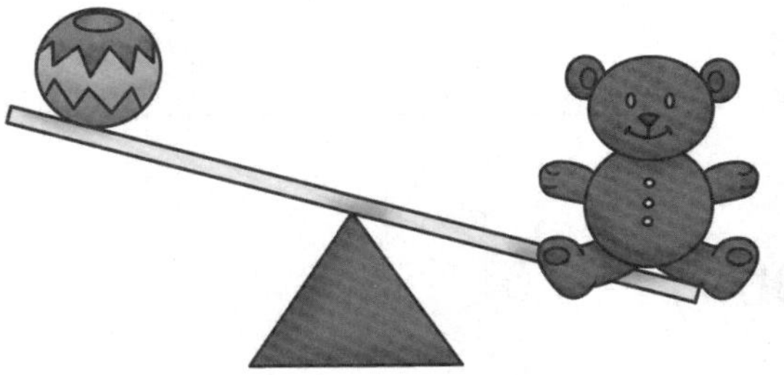

7.

Favorite Pets

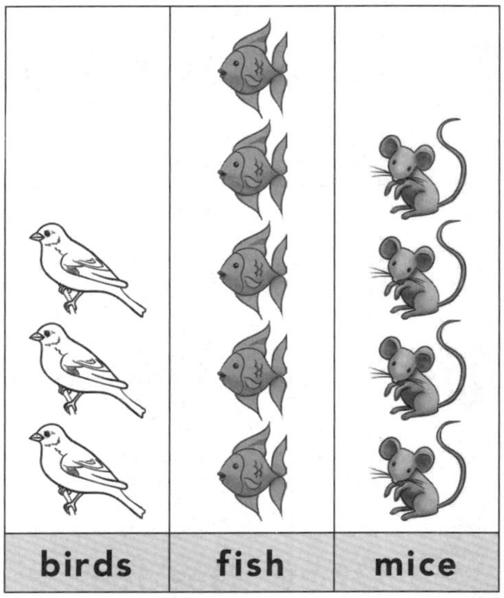

How many votes for birds and fish are there?

____

8. How many hours are there in 2 days?

____

NAME: ____________________

DIRECTIONS Solve each problem.

1. Write the numeral.

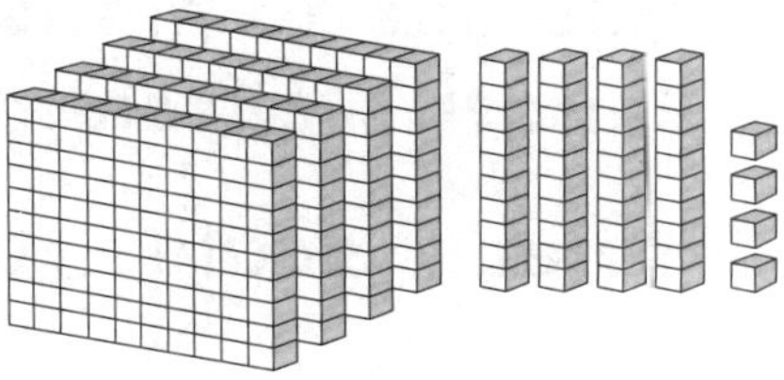

____

2. 8 plus 2 plus 3 is

____________________.

3.

$$\begin{array}{r} 97 \\ -\ 73 \\ \hline \end{array}$$

4. Write the missing number.

43	45	47		51

5. Color one face on the solid.

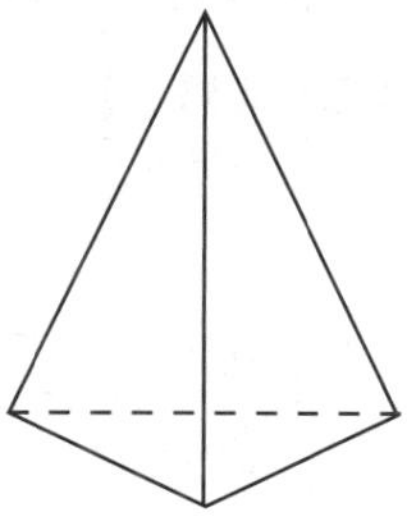

6. How many days are in January?

____

7. Car Colors

Red	𝍸 𝍸 |||
Blue	𝍸 𝍸 𝍸 𝍸 |
Yellow	𝍸 ||||
Green	𝍸 𝍸 𝍸 ||

Are there more green cars than yellow cars?

Circle: yes no

8. Will has a collection of 46 marbles. He saves his money and buys 2 packs of marbles. Each pack has 10 marbles in it. How many marbles does Will have now?

____

SCORE

1.
2.
3.
4.
5.
6.
7.
8.

____ / 8
Total

NAME: ____________________

DIRECTIONS Solve each problem.

SCORE

1. ☺ 😐
2. ☺ 😐
3. ☺ 😐
4. ☺ 😐
5. ☺ 😐
6. ☺ 😐
7. ☺ 😐
8. ☺ 😐

____ / 8
Total

1. Round 47 to the nearest ten.

____

2. 81 + 18 = ______

3. 78 minus 54 equals

____________________.

4. ☐ + 8 = 14

5. Circle the triangle.

6. What tool would you use to measure length? Circle one.

ruler   scale   clock

7. Sports Played

	Soccer	Swimming	Baseball
Mark	X		X
Tracy		X	
Mike		X	X

If Tracy starts playing soccer, how many sports will she play?

____

8. Pearl scored 23 points in the game she was playing. She scored 42 more points. How many points did she score altogether?

____

NAME: ______________________

DIRECTIONS Solve each problem.

1. Name the shaded fraction.

____

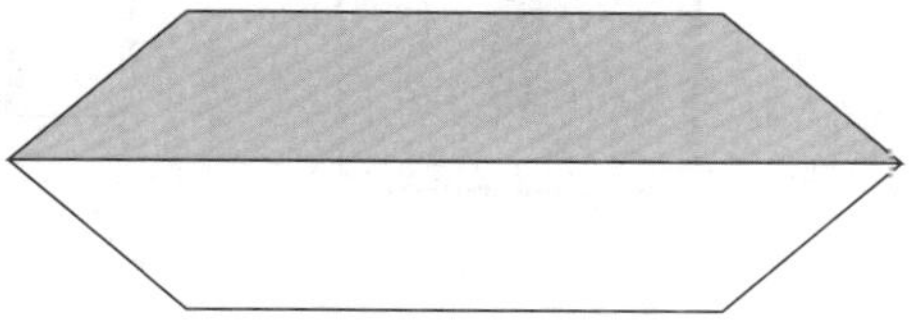

2. 53 + 36 = ______

3. What is the difference between 32 and 21?

____

4. 18 – 9 = ☐ + 2

5. True or false? Shapes with three sides have three angles.

____

6. Write the length.

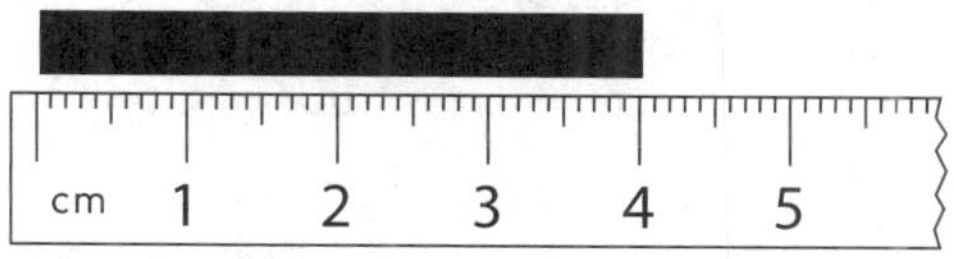

______ centimeters

7. **Flower Shop Orders**

Rose	16
Daisy	23
Tulip	15
Iris	25

Which flower had an even number of orders?

____

8. Write 2 addition and 2 subtraction number sentences using the numbers 33, 56, and 89.

____

____

____

SCORE

1.

2.

3.

4.

5.

6.

7.

8.

___ / 8

Total

DAY
154

NAME: ____________________

DIRECTIONS Solve each problem.

SCORE

1. ☺ 😐
2. ☺ 😐
3. ☺ 😐
4. ☺ 😐
5. ☺ 😐
6. ☺ 😐
7. ☺ 😐
8. ☺ 😐

____ / 8
Total

1. Circle groups of 2.

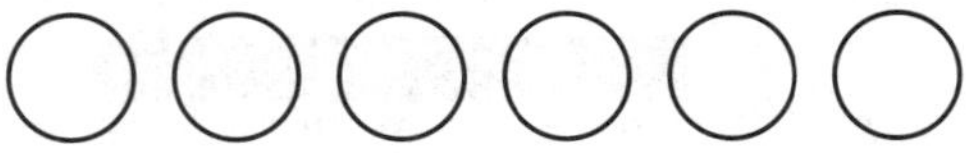

________ groups

2.

$$\begin{array}{r} 47 \\ +\ 12 \\ \hline \end{array}$$

3. 56 – 34 = ________

4. 37 + 61 = 61 + ☐

5. What is above the bed?

____

6. Color the sign with the larger area.

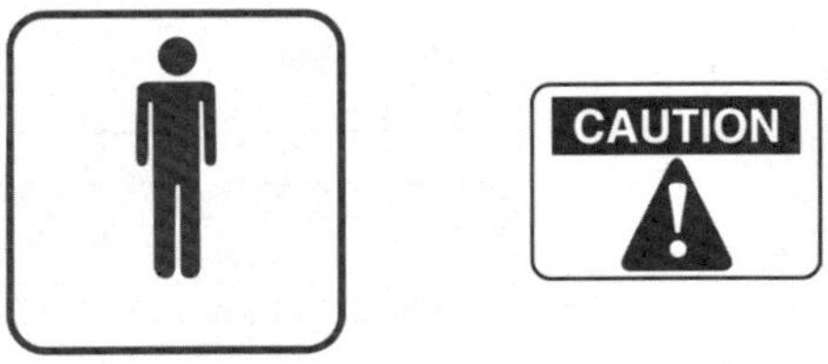

7. Make 25 tally marks.

8. How many hands are on 23 people?

____

DAY 155

NAME: ______________________________

DIRECTIONS Solve each problem.

1. Write the even number that follows 26.

____

2. 7 + 1 + 3 = ______

3.

$$\begin{array}{r} 85 \\ -\ 35 \\ \hline \end{array}$$

4. Continue the pattern.

X, Y, Y, X, Y, Y,

______, ______

5. Color the base of the solid.

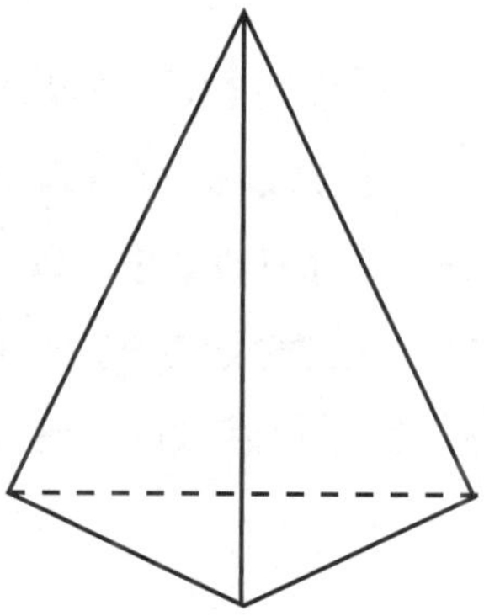

6. Write the time.

half past ______

7. Favorite Activity

Movies	𝍸 𝍸 |||
Restaurant	𝍸 ||||
Park	𝍸 𝍸 ||
Stay Home	𝍸 |||

What is the total number of people surveyed?

____

8. It takes Sharon one hour to get ready in the morning. If she wants to leave for school at 7:30 A.M., what time does she have to get up?

____

SCORE

1. ☺ 😐
2. ☺ 😐
3. ☺ 😐
4. ☺ 😐
5. ☺ 😐
6. ☺ 😐
7. ☺ 😐
8. ☺ 😐

____ / 8 Total

DAY 156

NAME: ____________________

DIRECTIONS Solve each problem.

SCORE

1. ☺ 😐
2. ☺ 😐
3. ☺ 😐
4. ☺ 😐
5. ☺ 😐
6. ☺ 😐
7. ☺ 😐
8. ☺ 😐

____ / 8 Total

1. Write 95 in expanded notation.

____

2. Ninety-one plus eight equals

____________________.

3.

$$\begin{array}{r} 67 \\ -\ 43 \\ \hline \end{array}$$

4. 6 + ☐ = 13

5. How many angles?

____

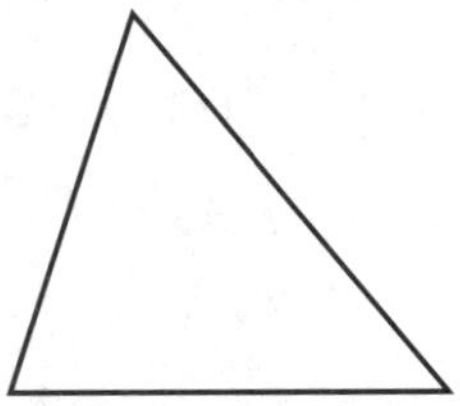

6. Write the day of the week that comes before Sunday.

____

7.

If Brandon runs 10 more miles, how many miles will he have run?

____

8. Write the number that has 2 in the tens place, 6 in the hundreds place, and 0 in the ones place.

____

NAME: ______________________________

DIRECTIONS Solve each problem.

1. Use >, <, or =.

364 ◯ 264

2. 72 + 26 = ______

3. 28 less than 49 is

______________________.

4. 5 ☐ 4 = 9

5. Color the shapes that do not have vertices.

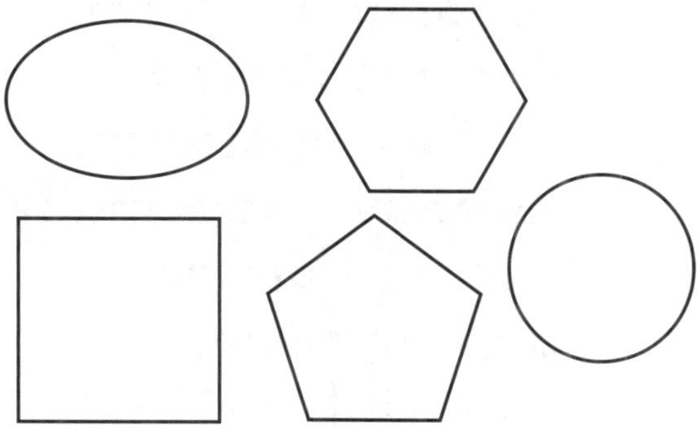

6. What is the volume?

______ cubes

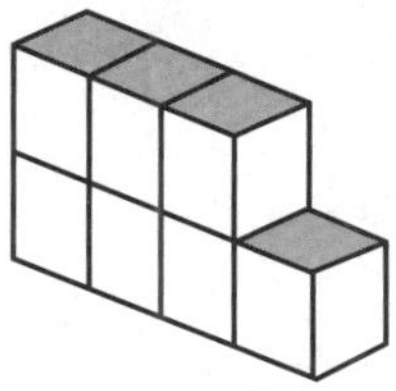

7.

Pets

	Hamster	Dog	Fish	Cat
Mary	X		X	
Julia	X	X		X
Evan	X	X		X

Which pet does Julia need to get to have all the animals?

____

8. There are 7 wheels in all. There is 1 tricycle. The rest are bicycles. How many bicycles are there?

____

SCORE

1. ☺ 😐

2. ☺ 😐

3. ☺ 😐

4. ☺ 😐

5. ☺ 😐

6. ☺ 😐

7. ☺ 😐

8. ☺ 😐

____ / 8

Total

NAME: ____________________

DIRECTIONS Solve each problem.

SCORE

1.

2.

3.

4.

5.

6.

7.

8.

____ / 8

Total

1. Circle $\frac{1}{4}$.

2.
$$\begin{array}{r} 64 \\ +\ 22 \\ \hline \end{array}$$

3. 27 − 16 = ______

4. 5 + ☐ = 14 − 7

5. Circle the object that can roll.

6. Is the object less than 1 meter or more than 1 meter?

____

7.

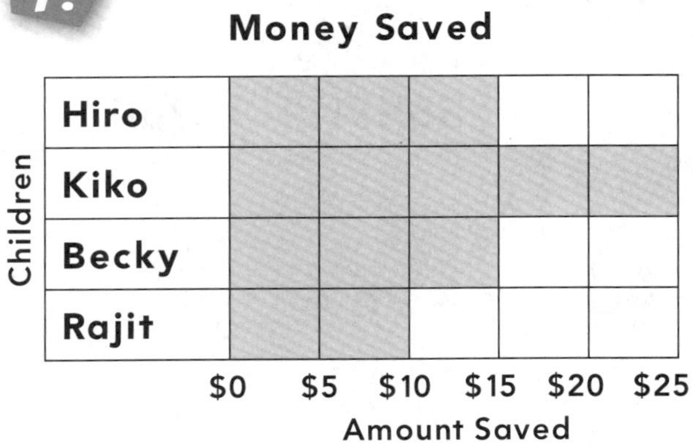

Becky wants to buy a CD player that costs $35. How much more money does she have to save?

____

8. 53 children signed up for a summer reading program. 47 have picked up their materials already. How many children did not pick up their materials yet?

____

NAME: ____________________

DIRECTIONS Solve each problem.

1. Write the number word for the number 85.

____

2.

$$\begin{array}{r} 45 \\ +\ 73 \\ \hline \end{array}$$

3. 95 minus 73 is

____________________.

4. ☐ + 43 = 43 + 80

5. Draw the top view of the solid.

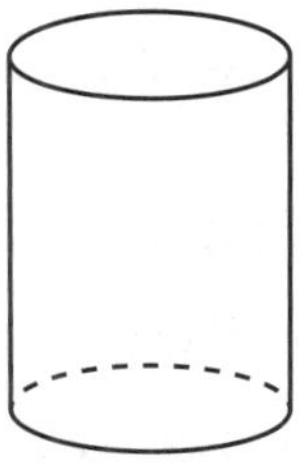

6. True or false? You can jump 5 times in less than 1 minute.

____

7. Teeth Lost

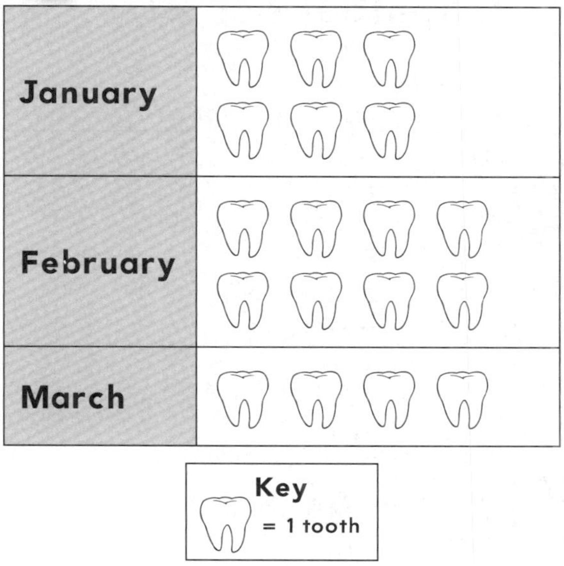

What was the total number of teeth lost during January, February, and March?

____

8. Write the number that is 2 more tens, and 4 more ones than the number 531.

____

SCORE

1. ☺ 😐

2. ☺ 😐

3. ☺ 😐

4. ☺ 😐

5. ☺ 😐

6. ☺ 😐

7. ☺ 😐

8. ☺ 😐

____ / 8 Total

DAY **160**

NAME: ____________________

DIRECTIONS Solve each problem.

SCORE

1. ☺ 😐
2. ☺ 😐
3. ☺ 😐
4. ☺ 😐
5. ☺ 😐
6. ☺ 😐
7. ☺ 😐
8. ☺ 😐

____ / 8 Total

1. Write the ordinal number for 21.

____

2.

$$\begin{array}{r} 7 \\ 6 \\ +\ 3 \\ \hline \end{array}$$

3. 78 – 63 = ______

4. Kaylee has $15.00 in her piggy bank. She gets $5.00 a week for allowance. How long will it take for her to save $30.00?

____

Start	1 Week	2 Weeks	3 Weeks	4 Weeks
$15.00				

5. Circle the prism.

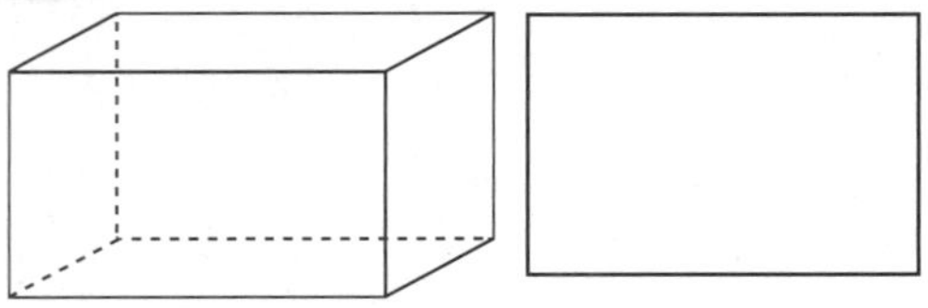

6. Circle the object that weighs less.

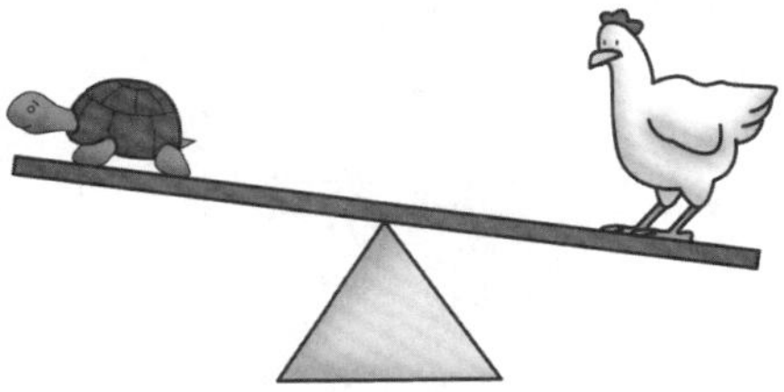

7.

School Bags in Class

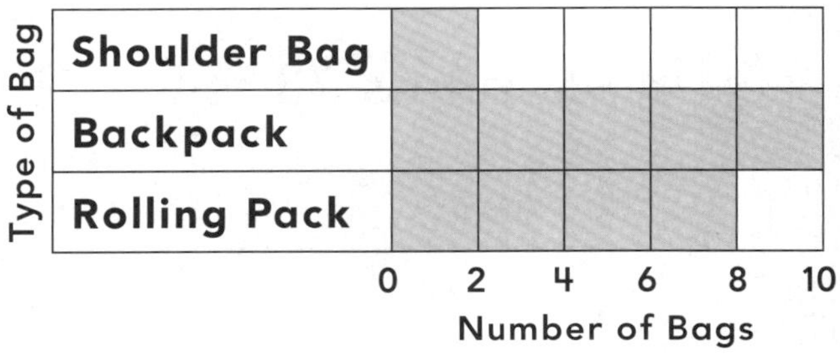

How many more rolling packs are there than shoulder bags?

____

8. Cory has 2 quarters and 3 dimes. He wants to buy a birthday card for a friend that costs 75¢. Does he have enough money?

Circle: yes no

NAME: ____________________

DIRECTIONS Solve each problem.

SCORE

1. Write the numeral.

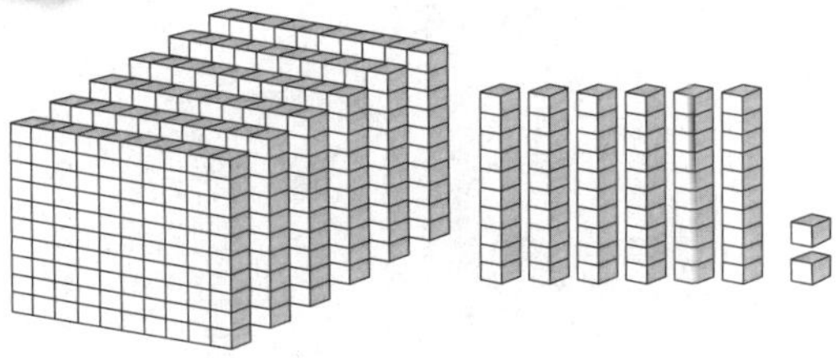

____

2. 76 plus 27 equals

____________________.

3. $\begin{array}{r} 53 \\ -\ 25 \\ \hline \end{array}$

4. Write the missing number.

75		65	60	55

5. Name the solid.

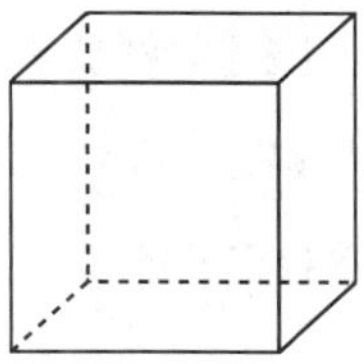

____

6. Write the time.

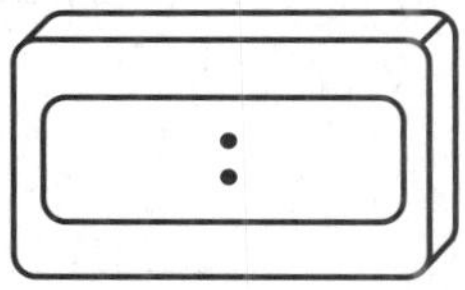

7.

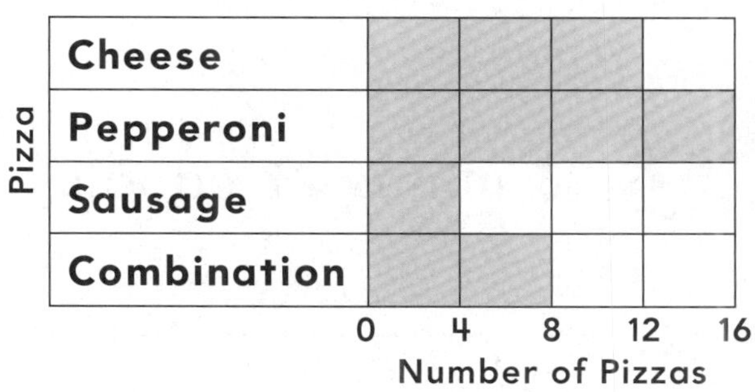

If a pizza costs $20, how much money was spent on the sausage pizzas?

____

8. Paula wants a new bracelet that costs 65¢. She has two quarters. How much more money does she need in order to buy a bracelet?

____

1. ☺ 😐
2. ☺ 😐
3. ☺ 😐
4. ☺ 😐
5. ☺ 😐
6. ☺ 😐
7. ☺ 😐
8. ☺ 😐

___ / 8
Total

DAY
162

NAME: ____________________

DIRECTIONS Solve each problem.

SCORE

1. ☺ 😐
2. ☺ 😐
3. ☺ 😐
4. ☺ 😐
5. ☺ 😐
6. ☺ 😐
7. ☺ 😐
8. ☺ 😐

____ / 8
Total

1. Round 83 to the nearest ten.

____

2. 27 + 46 = ______

3. 36 minus 27 equals

____________________.

4. ☐ + 7 = 14

5. Name the shape.

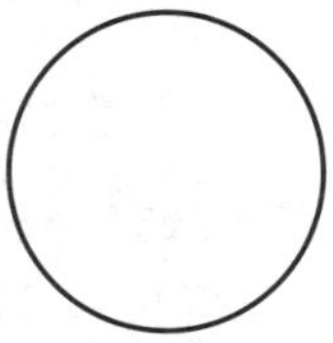

____

6. Circle the larger container.

7. Library Books Checked Out

	Week 1	Week 2	Week 3
Jody	4	5	5
Emily	4	4	4
Brenda	5	7	6
Alison	6	3	6

What was the total number of library books checked out in the first week?

____

8. There are 25 starfish arms. Each starfish has 5 arms. How many starfish are there?

____

NAME: ____________________

DIRECTIONS Solve each problem.

1. Name the shaded fraction.

____

2.

$$\begin{array}{r} 19 \\ +\ 72 \\ \hline \end{array}$$

3. 91 – 43 = ______

4. 16 – ☐ = 6 + 3

5. Complete the chart.

Shape	Number of Sides	Number of Angles
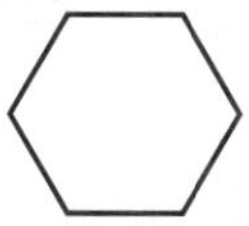		

6. Write the length.

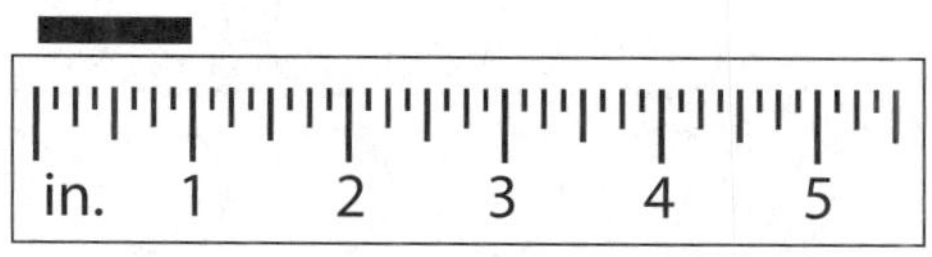

______ inches

7. Draw a key symbol for flowers. Record the data in the chart.

Flowers Bought

Mrs. Chu	
Mrs. Diggs	

☐ = 5 flowers

- Mrs. Chu's bouquet has 25 flowers in it.
- Mrs. Diggs' bouquet has 30 flowers in it.

8. I am 26 less than 88. What number am I?

____

SCORE

1.

2.

3.

4.

5.

6.

7.

8.

___ / 8 Total

NAME: ______________________

DIRECTIONS Solve each problem.

SCORE

1. ☺ 😐
2. ☺ 😐
3. ☺ 😐
4. ☺ 😐
5. ☺ 😐
6. ☺ 😐
7. ☺ 😐
8. ☺ 😐

____ / 8 Total

1. Circle groups of 3.

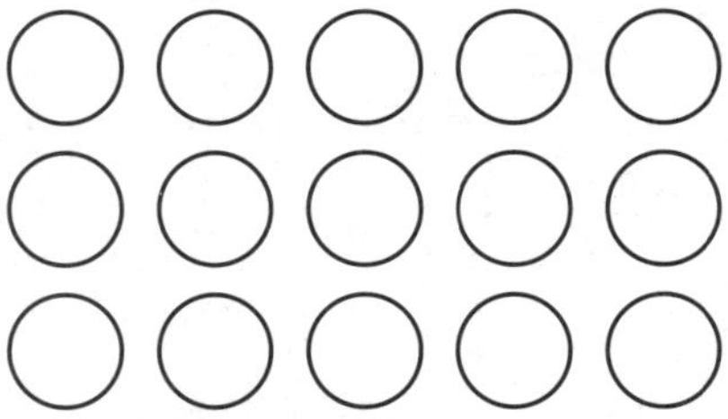

_______ groups

2. 47 + 46 = _______

3.

$$\begin{array}{r} 82 \\ -\ 67 \\ \hline \end{array}$$

4. 76 + 47 = ☐ + 76

5. Draw all lines of symmetry.

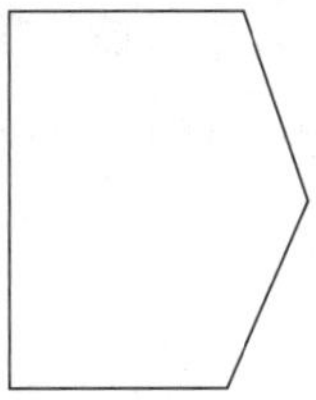

6. Record the area.

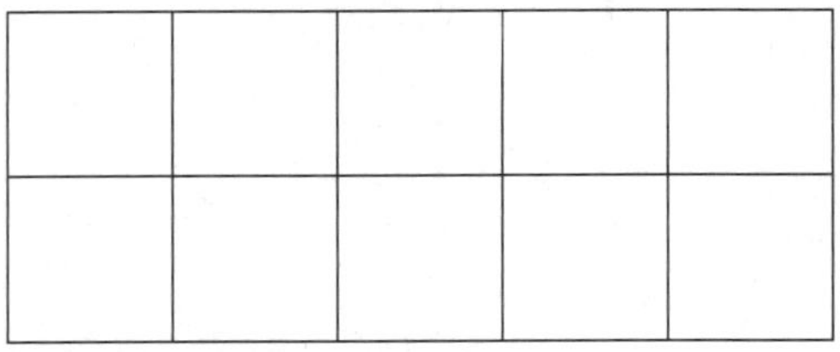

area = _____ squares

7. Ages

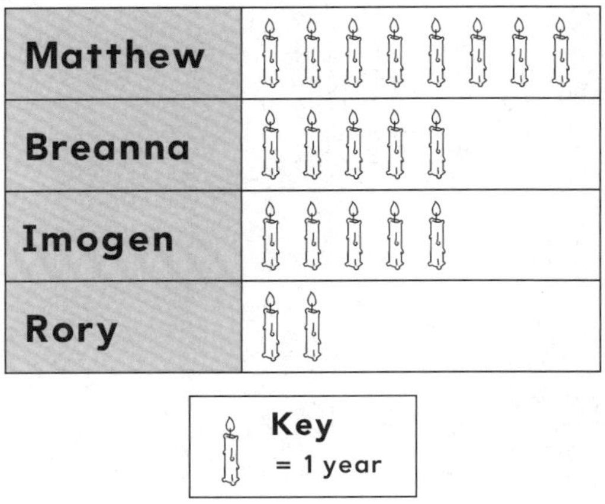

Is Imogen older than Breanna?

Circle: yes no

8. What is the largest 3-digit number you can make with the numbers 5, 7, and 9?

____

DAY 165

NAME: ____________________

DIRECTIONS Solve each problem.

1. Write the even number that follows 35.

____

2. 9 + 2 + 8 = ______

3.

$$\begin{array}{r} 65 \\ -\ 39 \\ \hline \end{array}$$

4. Continue the pattern.

← ← → ← ← → ______

5. Circle the cone.

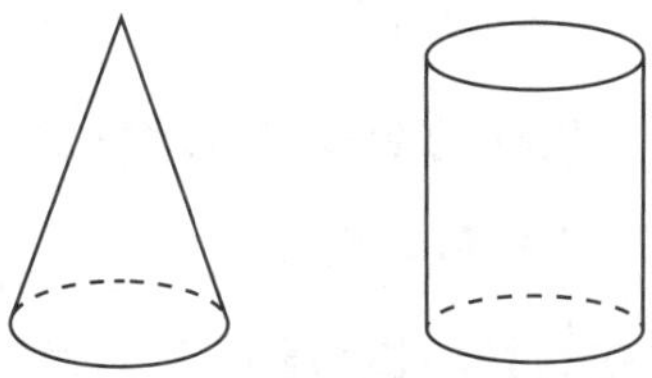

6. Show half past 12:00.

7.

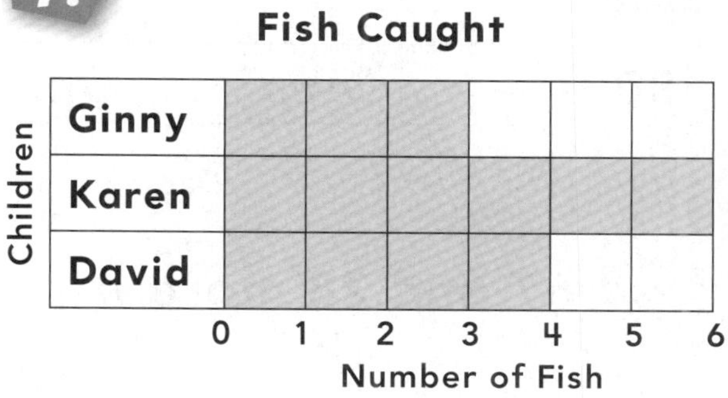

How many more fish does David need to catch to have the same number as Karen?

____

8. Mr. Martin wants to give each of his 25 students 2 pencils. Pencils come in packs of 12. How many packs of pencils should he buy?

____

SCORE

1. ☺ 😐

2. ☺ 😐

3. ☺ 😐

4. ☺ 😐

5. ☺ 😐

6. ☺ 😐

7. ☺ 😐

8. ☺ 😐

___ / 8 Total

DAY
166

NAME: ______________________________

DIRECTIONS Solve each problem.

SCORE

1. ☺ 😐
2. ☺ 😐
3. ☺ 😐
4. ☺ 😐
5. ☺ 😐
6. ☺ 😐
7. ☺ 😐
8. ☺ 😐

____ / 8 Total

1.

80	=		Tens		Ones

2. 67 and 28 more is

______________________.

3.

$$\begin{array}{r} 74 \\ -\ 18 \\ \hline \end{array}$$

4. 15 – ☐ = 6

5. Count the angles.

____

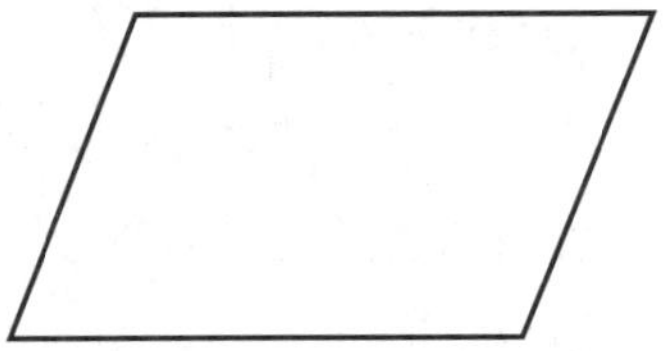

6. Write the month that comes after December.

____

7. Toy Train Sales Last Week

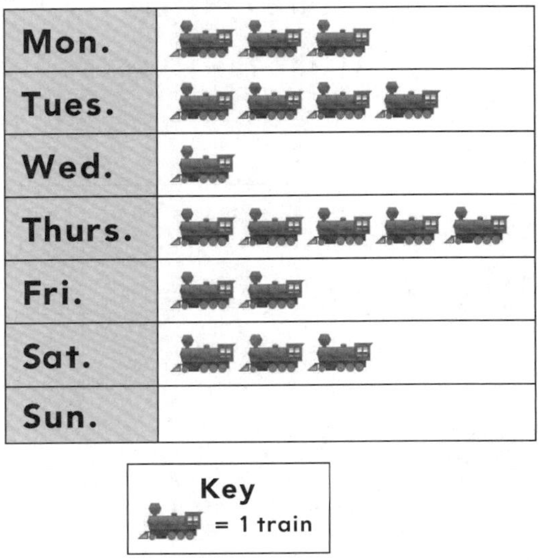

If a train costs $30, how much money did the store make in train sales on Friday?

____

8. Write the number sentence.

Eighty-nine minus forty-seven equals forty-two.

____

NAME: ______________________________

DIRECTIONS Solve each problem.

SCORE

1. Order the numbers from smallest to largest.

   173 673 73 473

   ____, ____, ____, ____

2. 25 + 46 = ______

3. What is the difference between 48 and 29?

   ____

4. 4 + ☐ = 12

5. How many sides does the shape have?

   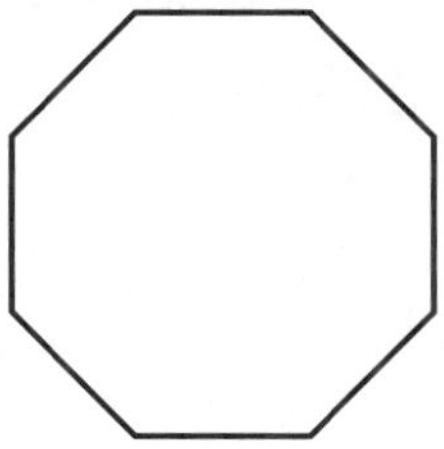

   ______ sides

6. What is the volume?

   ______ cubes

   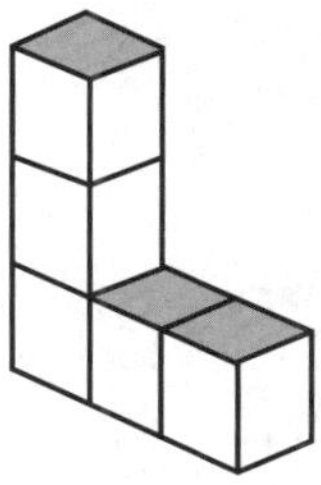

7. Count the tally marks.

   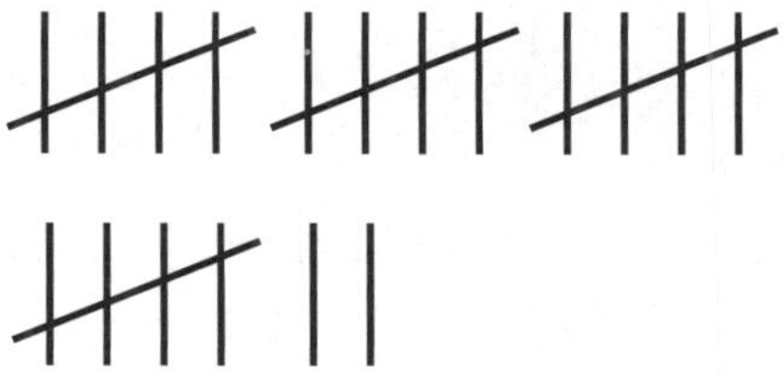

   ____

8. How many edges do two cubes have?

   ____

1. ☺ 😐
2. ☺ 😐
3. ☺ 😐
4. ☺ 😐
5. ☺ 😐
6. ☺ 😐
7. ☺ 😐
8. ☺ 😐

___ / 8 Total

DAY 168

NAME: ____________________

DIRECTIONS Solve each problem.

SCORE

1.
2.
3.
4.
5.
6.
7.
8.

___ / 8 Total

1. Circle $\frac{1}{2}$.

2.

$$\begin{array}{r} 29 \\ +\ 52 \\ \hline \end{array}$$

3. $57 - 39 =$ ______

4. $1 + 7 = 18 - \square$

5. Circle the object that can stack.

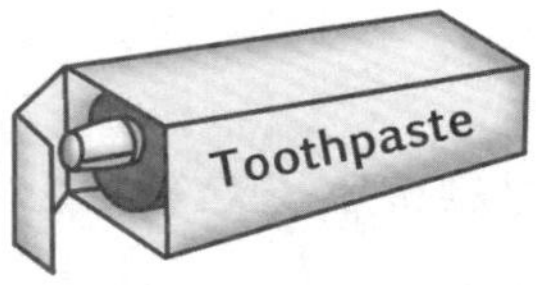

6. Circle the best estimate.

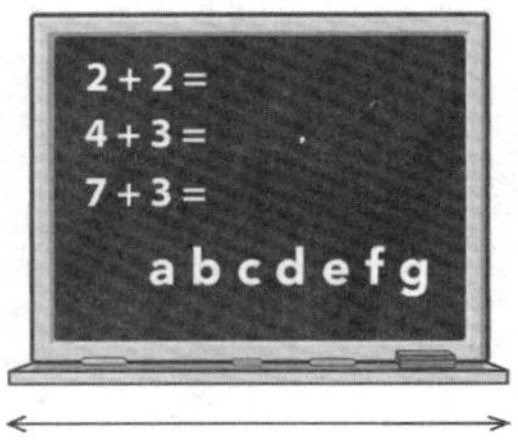

2 m   12 m

7.

Favorite Pets

How many votes for the pets are there altogether?

____

8. It takes Joey $\frac{1}{2}$ hour to ride his bike from his friend's house to his house. If Joey has to be home for dinner at 5:30 P.M., what time should he leave his friend's house?

____

NAME: ______________________________

DIRECTIONS Solve each problem.

1. Write the number word for the number 29.

____

2. 37 + 48 = ______

3.

$$\begin{array}{r} 38 \\ -\ 29 \\ \hline \end{array}$$

4. 73 + ☐ = 52 + 73

5. True or false? A solid shape is a two-dimensional object.

____

6. Show 7:30 on the clock.

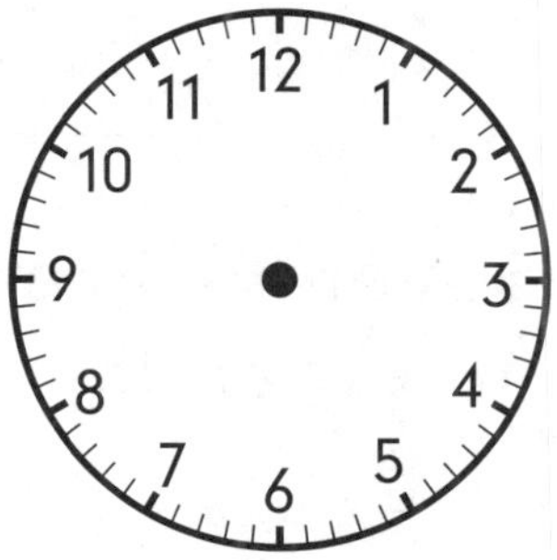

7.

Car Colors

Red	𝍸 𝍸 |||
Blue	𝍸 𝍸 𝍸 𝍸 |
Yellow	𝍸 ||||
Green	𝍸 𝍸 𝍸 ||

How many more red cars are there than yellow cars?

____

8. How many ears are on 36 babies?

____

SCORE

1. ☺ 😐
2. ☺ 😐
3. ☺ 😐
4. ☺ 😐
5. ☺ 😐
6. ☺ 😐
7. ☺ 😐
8. ☺ 😐

____ / 8 Total

DAY
170

NAME: ______________________

DIRECTIONS Solve each problem.

SCORE

1. ☺ ☹
2. ☺ ☹
3. ☺ ☹
4. ☺ ☹
5. ☺ ☹
6. ☺ ☹
7. ☺ ☹
8. ☺ ☹

____ / 8
Total

1. Write the ordinal number for 11.

____

2. Seventy-three plus nineteen is

______________________.

3.

$$\begin{array}{r} 97 \\ -\ 78 \\ \hline \end{array}$$

4. Daniel has 9 trading cards. He gets 3 more every week. How many trading cards will he have in 4 weeks?

____

Start	1 Week	2 Weeks	3 Weeks	4 Weeks
9				

5. Color the trapezoid.

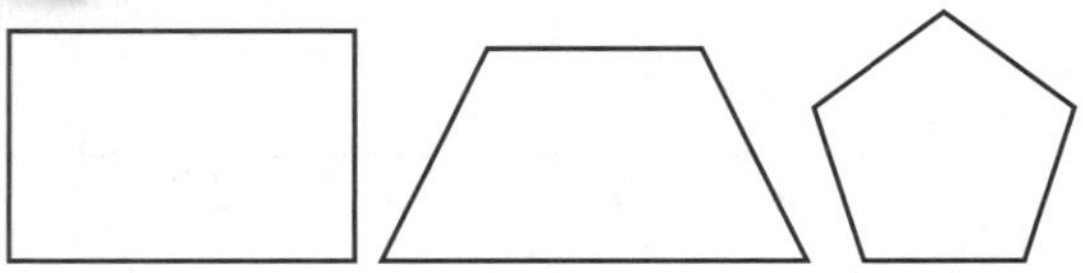

6. Circle the object that weighs less.

7. Sports Played

	Soccer	Swimming	Baseball
Mark	X		X
Tracy		X	
Mike		X	X

Mike stops playing baseball. What other sport will he still play?

____

8. Write the number that is 5 more hundreds and 4 more ones than the number 493.

____

NAME: ____________________

DIRECTIONS Solve each problem.

1. Write the numeral.

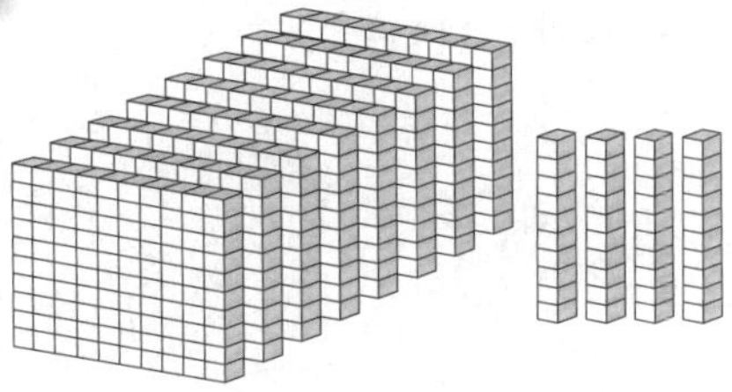

____

2. 8 + 4 + 3 = ______

3. 86 minus 27 equals

____________________.

4. Write the missing number.

78	76		72	70

5. Color one face on the solid.

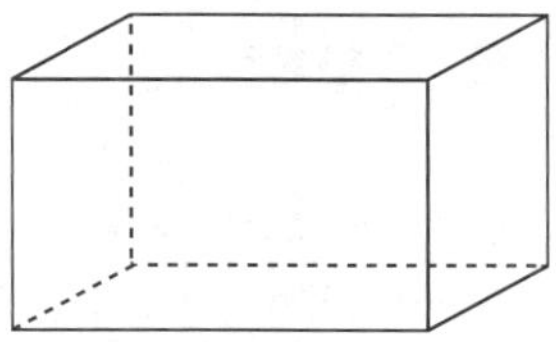

6. A movie starts at 7:00 P.M. and ends at 9:00 P.M. How long is the movie?

____

7. Flower Shop Orders

Rose	16
Daisy	23
Tulip	15
Iris	25

If all the tulips are split evenly into 3 vases, how many flowers will go in each vase?

____

8. Chris scores 26 points in the first quarter. He scores 23 points in the second quarter. He hopes to score 82 points in a game. How many points does he still need to score in order to meet his goal?

____

SCORE

1. ☺ 😐
2. ☺ 😐
3. ☺ 😐
4. ☺ 😐
5. ☺ 😐
6. ☺ 😐
7. ☺ 😐
8. ☺ 😐

____ / 8

Total

DAY
172

NAME: ______________________________

DIRECTIONS Solve each problem.

SCORE

1. ☺😐
2. ☺😐
3. ☺😐
4. ☺😐
5. ☺😐
6. ☺😐
7. ☺😐
8. ☺😐

____ / 8
Total

1. Round 29 to the nearest ten.

____

2. 13 + 58 = ______

3.

$$\begin{array}{r} 64 \\ -\ 56 \\ \hline \end{array}$$

4. 7 ☐ 0 = 7

5. Name the shape.

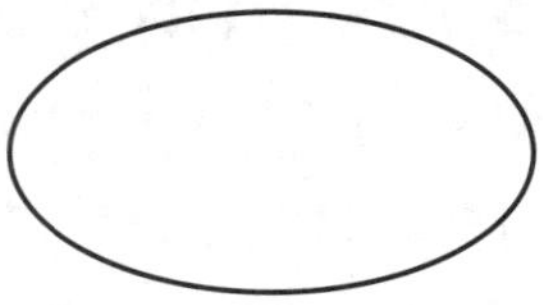

____

6. Circle the smaller container.

7. Make 12 tally marks.

8. Cheryl baked 5 loaves of bread each day for 3 days in a row. How many loaves of bread did she bake?

____

NAME: ____________________

DIRECTIONS Solve each problem.

1. Name the shaded fraction.

____

2.

$$\begin{array}{r} 67 \\ +\ 37 \\ \hline \end{array}$$

3. 42 – 27 = ______

4. ☐ – 7 = 2 + 5

5. True or false? This shape is a prism.

____

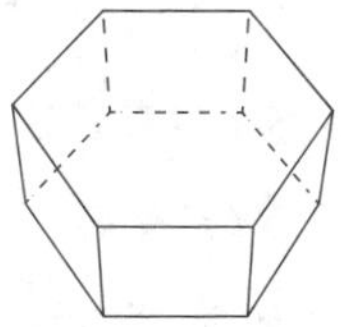

6. Circle the season to match the months in the box below.

winter spring
summer fall

March April May

7.

Miles Run

Cheryl wants to double the number of miles she ran. How many miles does Cheryl want to run?

____

8. Morgan watches $\frac{1}{2}$ hour of TV every weekday and 1 hour of TV each day of the weekend. How much TV does Morgan watch in one week?

____

SCORE

1. ☺ 😐
2. ☺ 😐
3. ☺ 😐
4. ☺ 😐
5. ☺ 😐
6. ☺ 😐
7. ☺ 😐
8. ☺ 😐

___ /8 Total

DAY 174

NAME: ____________________

DIRECTIONS Solve each problem.

SCORE

1. ☺ 😐
2. ☺ 😐
3. ☺ 😐
4. ☺ 😐
5. ☺ 😐
6. ☺ 😐
7. ☺ 😐
8. ☺ 😐

____ / 8

Total

1. Circle groups of 3.

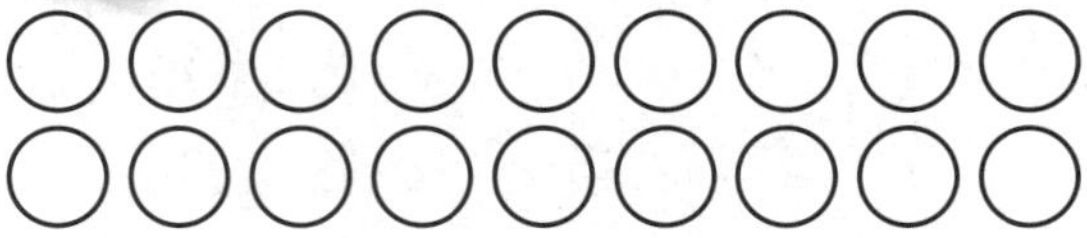

______ groups

2. 82 plus 18 is ______.

3.

$$\begin{array}{r} 56 \\ -\ 48 \\ \hline \end{array}$$

4. 97 + 37 = 37 + ☐

5. Draw all lines of symmetry.

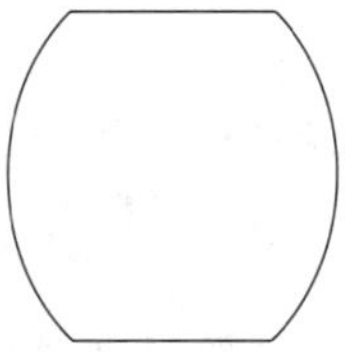

6. Record the area.

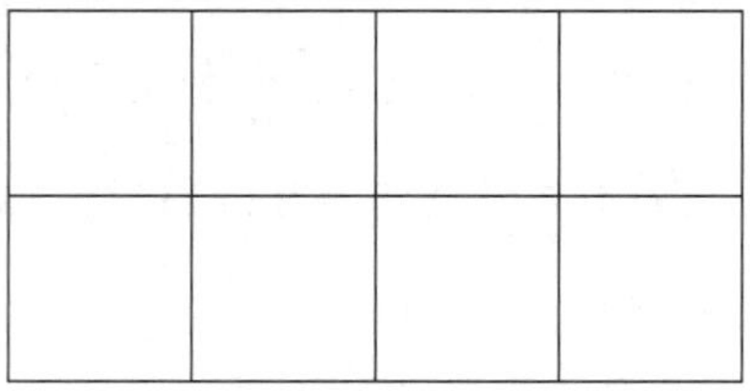

area = ____ squares

7.

Pets

	Hamster	Dog	Fish	Cat
Mary	X		X	X
Julia	X	X		X
Evan	X	X		X

It costs about $5 per week to care for a pet. How much money does Mary pay each week to care for her pets?

____

8. Olivia stacks some blocks on top of each other. Then she stacks 14 more. Her tower is 36 blocks tall. How many blocks did she start with?

____

NAME: ____________________

DIRECTIONS Solve each problem.

1. Write the even number that follows 21.

____

2. 6 + 6 + 7 = ______

3. What is 38 less than 56?

____

4. Continue the pattern.

______

5. Color the base of the solid.

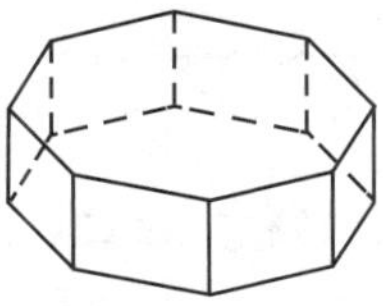

6. Write the time.

half past ______

7.

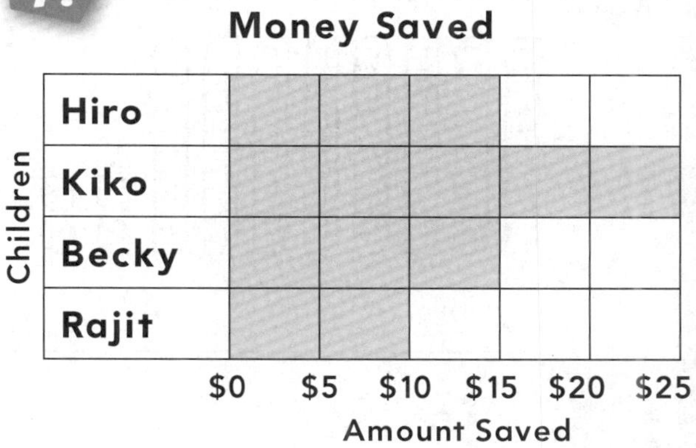

What was the total amount of money that all the children saved?

____

8. Melissa has a doctor's appointment at 3:00 P.M. It takes 30 minutes to get from Melissa's school to the doctor's office. School gets out at 2:15 P.M. Does Melissa have enough time to get to the doctor's office?

Circle: yes no

SCORE

1. ☺ 😐
2. ☺ 😐
3. ☺ 😐
4. ☺ 😐
5. ☺ 😐
6. ☺ 😐
7. ☺ 😐
8. ☺ 😐

____ / 8 Total

DAY

176

NAME: ____________________

DIRECTIONS Solve each problem.

SCORE

1. ☺ 😐
2. ☺ 😐
3. ☺ 😐
4. ☺ 😐
5. ☺ 😐
6. ☺ 😐
7. ☺ 😐
8. ☺ 😐

____ /8

Total

1. Write the numeral.

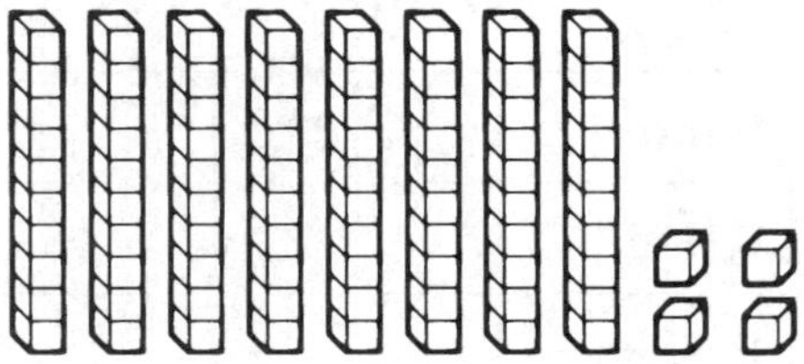

____

2.

$$\begin{array}{r} 69 \\ +\ 32 \\ \hline \end{array}$$

3. 67 – 34 = ______

4. ☐ + 9 = 16

5. Is this a right angle?

Circle: yes no

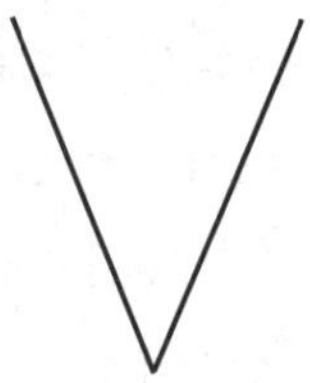

6. Write the day of the week that comes before Thursday.

____

7. **Teeth Lost**

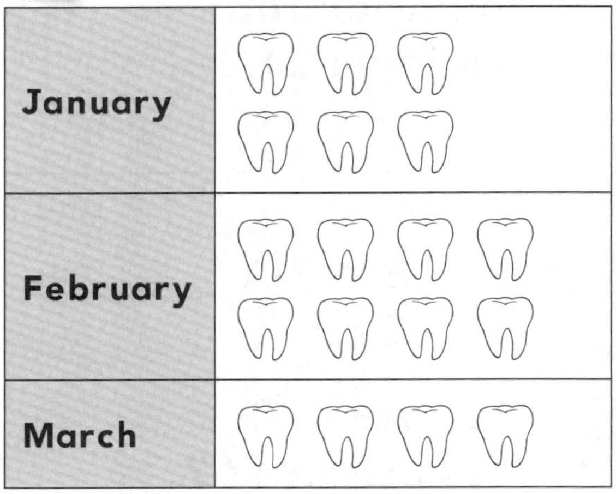

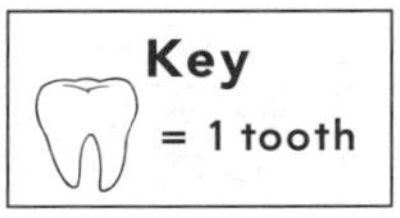

Janie lost half of all the teeth lost in March. How many teeth were lost by other people in March?

____

8. Jeremy earns $4.00 per lawn that he mows. He mows 5 lawns every week. How much money does Jeremy earn each week?

____

DAY 177

NAME: ______________________

DIRECTIONS Solve each problem.

1. Use >, <, or =.

403 ◯ 403

2. 37 + 28 = ______

3.

$$\begin{array}{r} 86 \\ -\ 59 \\ \hline \end{array}$$

4. 5 + ☐ = 8

5. Color the polygon with 3 sides.

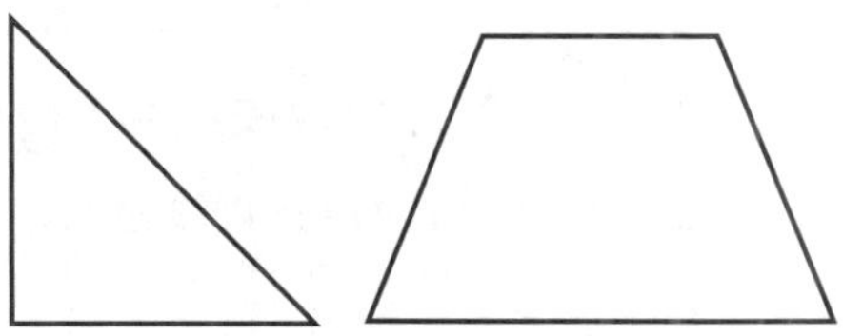

6. What is the volume?

______ cubes

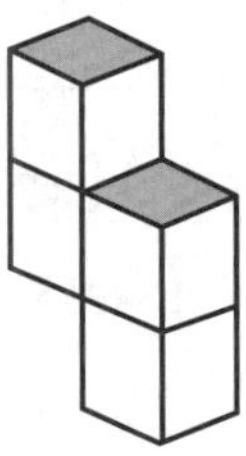

7.

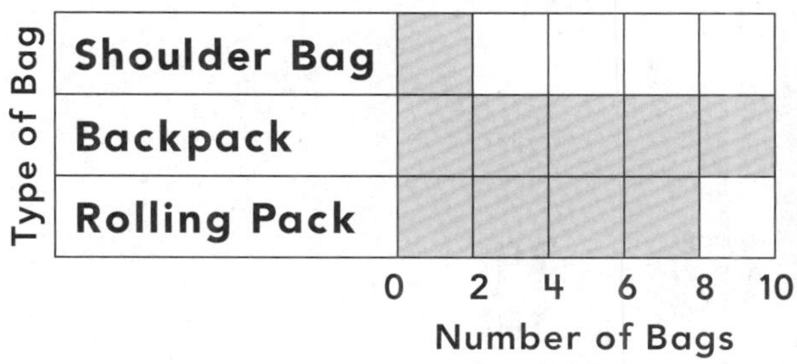

A shoulder bag costs $12. How much money was spent on shoulder bags?

____

8. Mrs. Radis needs ribbon for a project. She needs 7 pieces of ribbon that are each 3 feet long. How many feet of ribbon does she need to buy?

____

SCORE

1.
2.
3.
4.
5.
6.
7.
8.

___ / 8
Total

DAY 178

NAME: ____________________

DIRECTIONS Solve each problem.

SCORE

1. ☺ ☹
2. ☺ ☹
3. ☺ ☹
4. ☺ ☹
5. ☺ ☹
6. ☺ ☹
7. ☺ ☹
8. ☺ ☹

____ /8 Total

1. Color $\frac{1}{4}$.

2.

$$\begin{array}{r} 79 \\ +\ 19 \\ \hline \end{array}$$

3. 91 minus 67 equals

____________________.

4. 7 + 6 = $\square$ – 2

5. Can the object stack?

Circle: yes no

6. How many seconds are in one minute?

____

7.

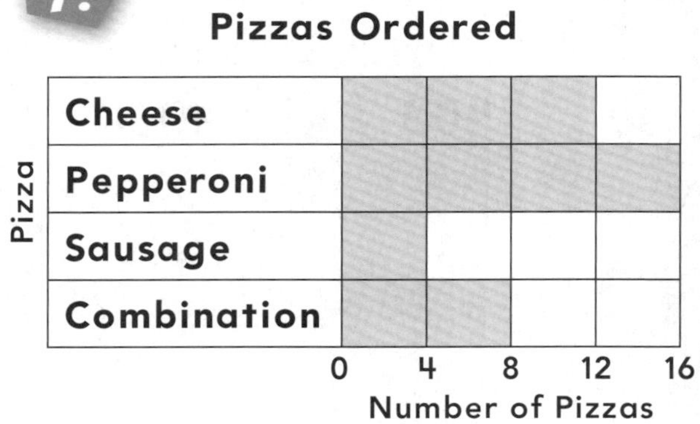

There are 10 pepperonis on each pepperoni pizza. How many total pepperonis were used?

____

8. What is the largest 2-digit number?

____

What is the largest 3-digit number?

____

What is the smallest 2-digit number?

____

What is the smallest 3-digit number?

____

NAME: ____________________

DIRECTIONS Solve each problem.

1. Write the number word for 31.

____

2. 62 and 39 more is

____________________.

3.

$$\begin{array}{r} 67 \\ -\ 18 \\ \hline \end{array}$$

4. ☐ + 61 = 61 + 68

5. Circle the prism.

____

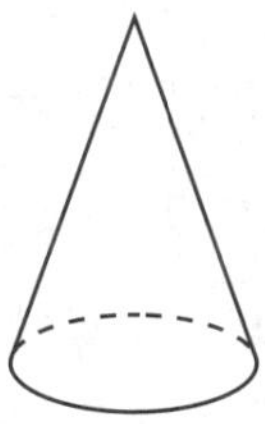

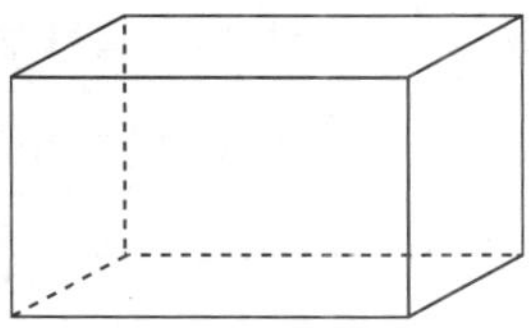

6. Circle the object with more mass.

7. Library Books Checked Out

	Week 1	Week 2	Week 3
Jody	4	5	5
Emily	4	4	4
Brenda	5	7	6
Alison	6	3	6

In which week were the most number of library books checked out?

____

8. A pizza restaurant wants to offer a mini pizza that costs $\frac{1}{2}$ the price of a small pizza. A small pizza costs $8.00. How much should they charge for the mini pizza?

____

SCORE

1. ☺ ☹
2. ☺ ☹
3. ☺ ☹
4. ☺ ☹
5. ☺ ☹
6. ☺ ☹
7. ☺ ☹
8. ☺ ☹

____ / 8 Total

DAY
180

NAME: ______________________

DIRECTIONS Solve each problem.

SCORE

1. ☺ 😐
2. ☺ 😐
3. ☺ 😐
4. ☺ 😐
5. ☺ 😐
6. ☺ 😐
7. ☺ 😐
8. ☺ 😐

____ / 8
Total

1. Write the ordinal number for 23.

____

2.
$$\begin{array}{r} 45 \\ +\ 28 \\ \hline \end{array}$$

3. 45 – 36 = ______

4. Count by sixes and color each number counted.

1	2	3	4	5	6	7	8	9	10
11	12	13	14	15	16	17	18	19	20
21	22	23	24	25	26	27	28	29	30
31	32	33	34	35	36	37	38	39	40
41	42	43	44	45	46	47	48	49	50

5. True or false? A vertex is formed when two sides of a plane shape meet.

____

6. Circle the item that holds the least water.

7. School Bags in Class

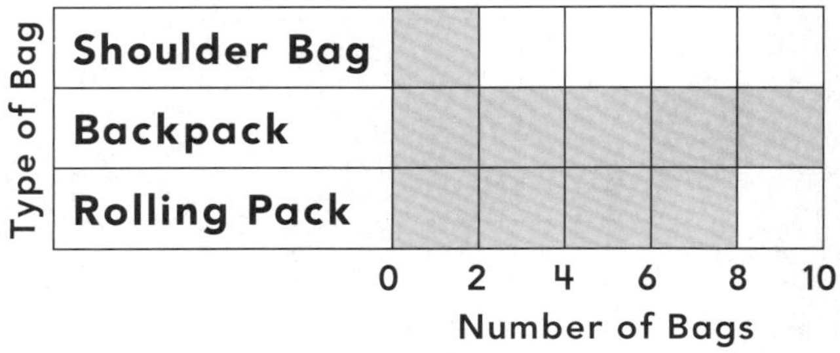

A rolling pack has 2 wheels. How many rolling pack wheels are in the classroom?

____

8. Brittany gets $4.00 in allowance each week. She saves $\frac{1}{4}$ of it and spends the rest of it. How much money does she spend each week?

____

ANSWER KEY

Day 1

1. 50
2. 4 + 3 = 7
3. 5 – 3 = 2
4. 18
5. sphere
6. 7
7. Gail: corn
   Tammy: peas
   Marcia: carrots
   Trish: broccoli
   Terri: corn
8. 11

Day 2

1. 100
2. 9
3. 3
4. 10
5. square
6. clock
7. 6
8. 17 – 9 = 8 or 17 – 8 = 9

Day 3

1. $\frac{1}{2}$
2. 4 + 2 = 6
3. 2
4. 0
5. 4; 4
6. true
7. yes
8. December

Day 4

1. no
2. 8
3. 6 – 3 = 3
4. 7
5. One triangular face should be colored.
6. 8
7. 3
8. 16

Day 5

1. 27
2. 4 + 4 = 8
3. 5
4. B
5. 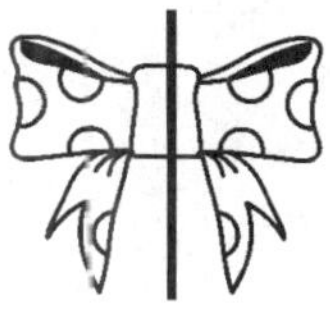
6. 3
7. 6
8. 14

Day 6

1. 67
2. 9
3. 1
4. 6
5. 4
6. February
7. fish
8. yardstick

Day 7

1. 9, 17, 22, 34
2. 2 + 5 = 7
3. 1
4. –
5. rectangle
6. the solid on the left
7. 9
8. 24

Day 8

1. 3 of the cups should be circled.
2. 14
3. 4 – 1 = 3
4. 8
5. can of juice
6. 2 m
7. 2
8. 10 + 8 = 18

Day 9

1. 39
2. 3 + 5 = 8
3. 1
4. 3
5. true
6. ice cream cone
7. iris
8. 468

Day 10

1. 25
2. 11
3. 4
4. The following numbers should be colored: 10, 20, 30, 40, and 50
5. 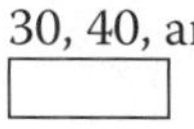
6. the middle sphere
7. 
8. 2

Day 11

1. 70
2. 4 + 1 = 5
3. 3
4. 60
5. One face of the solid should be colored.
6. 3:00
7. Movies: 13
   Restaurant: 9
   Park: 12
8. 2

Day 12

1. tens
2. 12
3. 5 – 4 = 1
4. 5
5. hexagon (left image)
6. bottom row
7. Max
8. 87

ANSWER KEY *(cont.)*

Day 13

1. $\frac{1}{4}$
2. 3 + 4 = 7
3. 5
4. 3
5. true
6. 3
7.

	Hamster	Dog	Fish	Cat
Mary	x		x	
Julia	x	x		x
Evan	x	x		x

8. 1 quarter and 1 penny

Day 14

1. yes
2. 11
3. 0
4. 7
5. cylinder (left image)
6. 4
7. $25
8. banana and apple or two bananas

Day 15

1. 41
2. 2 + 6 = 8
3. 9
4. 2; 1
5. 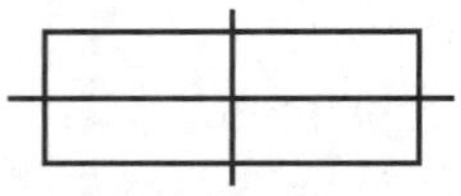
   Two lines of symmetry should be drawn.
6. 5:00 should be shown on the clock.
7. February
8. cylinder

Day 16

1. 39
2. 16
3. 4 – 2 = 2
4. 8
5. 3
6. Wednesday
7. 8
8. 3 feet

Day 17

1. <
2. 5 + 2 = 7
3. 1
4. 8
5. all but the circle and oval
6. 4
7. pepperoni
8. 11 inches

Day 18

1. 4 frogs
2. 8
3. 3
4. 8
5. the jar
6. the camel
7. 6
8. 16

Day 19

1. 67
2. 6
3. 0
4. 0
5. The square should be colored.
6. false
7.

	April	May
Sue	13	16
Toni	14	12

8. 6 + 4 = 10 or 4 + 6 = 10

Day 20

1. 10
2. nine
3. 5 – 2 = 3
4. 8
5. rectangular prism (left image)
6. the book
7. 8 years
8. 11:00

Day 21

1. 80
2. 17
3. 10
4. 32
5. the ball
6. 30
7. Karen
8. 9

Day 22

1. 87
2. 15
3. 4
4. –
5. rectangle
6. more than 1 hour
7. 1
8. 9

Day 23

1. $\frac{1}{4}$
2. 8
3. 1
4. 8
5. true
6. 5
7. 17
8. 3: car
   2: shoe
   1: paperclip

Day 24

1. no
2. 9
3. 6 – 4 = 2
4. 7
5. cone (left image)
6. larger square (right image)
7. 5
8. 5

ANSWER KEY *(cont.)*

Day 25
1. 64
2. 6
3. 3
4. blue
5. 
6. 10
7. blue cars
8. 89

Day 26
1. 42
2. 14
3. 2
4. 16
5. 4
6. October
7. swimming and baseball
8. 976

Day 27
1. 19, 36, 61, 75
2. 5
3. 2
4. 7
5. 4
6. 3
7. 16
8. 6 minutes

Day 28
1. 5 screws
2. 15
3. 7 – 5 = 2
4. 9
5. yes
6. the doll
7. 
8. 3

Day 29
1. 93
2. 12
3. 3
4. 5
5. A square should be drawn.
6. The clock should show 8:30.
7. movies
8. 84

Day 30
1. 5
2. 15
3. 6
4. The 5 and 10 columns should be colored.
5. The rectangle should be colored.
6. The mouse should be circled.
7. 40
8. Kayla: apples
   Tim: oranges
   Rachel: bananas

Day 31
1. 60
2. 18
3. 4
4. 70
5. cone (right image)
6. 1:30
7. hamster, dog, cat
8. 68¢

Day 32
1. ones
2. 13
3. 6 – 1 = 5
4. 9
5. true
6. bottom snake
7. Kiko
8. 20¢

Day 33
1. $\frac{1}{2}$
2. 16
3. 0
4. 6
5. true
6. 2
7. 6
8. 13

Day 34
1. no
2. 10
3. 2
4. 6
5. The circular base of the cone should be colored.
6. 5
7. shoulder bag
8. 5

Day 35
1. 70
2. 12
3. 2
4. A, B, B
5. 
6. The clock should show 10:00.
7. 16
8. 4 frogs

Day 36
1. 76
2. 13
3. 7 – 3 = 4
4. 8
5. 6
6. Monday
7. week 2
8. 8 + 15 = 23 or 15 + 8 = 23

ANSWER KEY *(cont.)*

Day 37

1. >
2. 8
3. 6
4. –
5. The square should be colored.
6. 3
7. 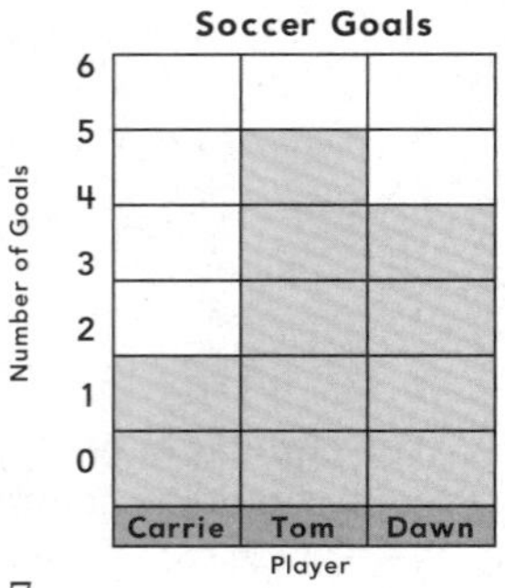

8. 7

Day 38

1. 6 baseballs should be colored.
2. 6
3. 3
4. 8
5. the ball
6. 2 m
7. yes
8. 19

Day 39

1. 86
2. 11
3. 2
4. 6
5. A pentagon should be drawn.
6. taller
7. 4
8. 6

Day 40

1. 7
2. 16
3. 7 – 4 = 3
4. 20
5. cylinder (left image)
6. cup (left image)
7. Thursday
8. 12 inches

Day 41

1. 40
2. 12
3. 6
4. 35
5. the jar
6. 1 hour
7. 12
8. 89°F

Day 42

1. 139
2. 12
3. 2
4. 2
5. triangle (left image)
6. less than one hour
7. 3
8. 20

Day 43

1. $\frac{1}{2}$
2. 15
3. 4
4. 6
5. false
6. winter
7. green cars
8. 73

Day 44

1. yes
2. 7
3. 6 – 5 = 1
4. 6
5. 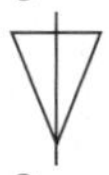
6. 8
7. Mark and Mike
8. 4, 6, 46, 64

Day 45

1. 90
2. 10
3. 4
4. A stack of 4 blocks and a stack of 5 blocks should be drawn
5. cylinder (right image)
6. 7:00
7. 38
8. 3

Day 46

1. 84
2. 14
3. 2
4. 6
5. 4
6. Saturday
7. 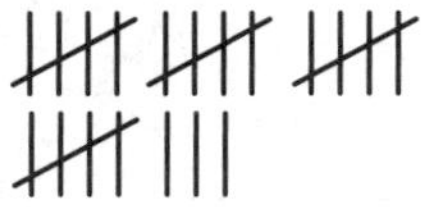
8. 3

Day 47

1. 39, 43, 82, 99
2. 10
3. 4
4. 5
5. 3
6. 6
7. 13
8. 89

Day 48

1. 8 teapots should be colored.
2. nine
3. 5 – 1 = 4
4. 10
5. the brick
6. about 1 meter
7. Cheryl
8. 38¢

ANSWER KEY *(cont.)*

Day 49
1. 74
2. 12
3. 0
4. 7
5. All 4 ovals should be colored.
6. true
7. Mary
8. $1.75

Day 50
1. 5
2. 6
3. 7
4. 15
5. rectangle (left image)
6. the can of peaches
7. $10
8. Answers will vary; cube, cylinder, prism

Day 51
1. 51
2. 13
3. 5
4. 70
5. triangular prism
6. 31
7. March
8. 3

Day 52
1. tens
2. 7
3. 8 – 5 = 3
4. –
5. hexagon
6. The longer fish should be circled.
7. 10
8. 12

Day 53
1. $\frac{1}{4}$
2. 11
3. 7
4. 6
5. false
6. 4
7. sausage
8. 15

Day 54
1. yes
2. 13
3. 7
4. 10
5. The doghouse on the right
6. quarter (right image)
7. 4
8. 13 – 7 = 6 or 13 – 6 = 7

Day 55
1. 61
2. 18
3. 2
4. 
5. cone (right image)
6. 5
7.

	Farm Animal	Zoo Animal
Tyrone	goats	zebras
Emile	sheep	lions
Peter	cows	tigers

8. $2\frac{1}{2}$ hours

Day 56
1. 58
2. 11
3. 7 – 2 = 5
4. 6
5. no
6. December
7. Matthew
8. 18

Day 57
1. =
2. 10
3. 10
4. 7
5. The triangle should be colored.
6. 5
7. Ginny
8. 10

Day 58
1. 1 rectangle should be colored.
2. 8
3. 11
4. 5
5. yes
6. The door should be circled.
7. Sunday
8. 35

Day 59
1. 452
2. 10
3. 8
4. 3
5. A circle should be drawn.
6. pig
7. 29
8. 369

Day 60
1. 5
2. 6
3. 7
4. 6 inches
5. hexagonal prism (left image)
6. baby
7. birds
8. 7

ANSWER KEY *(cont.)*

Day 61

1. 63
2. 4
3. 10
4. 50
5. Any face on the cube may be colored.
6. 9:00
7. 13
8. 7 weeks

Day 62

1. 72
2. 16
3. 8
4. 5
5. hexagon (left image)
6. more than 1 hour
7. swimming
8. 53

Day 63

1. $\frac{4}{8}$ or $\frac{1}{2}$
2. 9
3. 12
4. 8
5. rhombus (left image)
6. 2
7. 23
8. 15

Day 64

1. yes
2. 11
3. 11
4. 9
5.  Any one line should be drawn.
6. 8
7. 
8. cone, sphere, cylinder

Day 65

1. 36
2. 10
3. 6
4. C
5. One of the pentagon faces should be colored.
6. 1:00
7. 5
8. 9

Day 66

1. 92
2. 12
3. 6
4. 18
5. zero
6. Tuesday
7. 20
8. cube

Day 67

1. 86, 49, 22, 17
2. 13
3. 5
4. –
5. parallelogram (left image)
6. 5
7. fish
8. 31

Day 68

1. Two triangles should be colored.
2. 7
3. 6
4. 9
5. yo-yo
6. pencil
7. Rajit
8. 30

Day 69

1. seventy-one
2. 13
3. 16
4. 8
5. A triangle should be drawn.
6. The clock should show 5:00.
7. 8
8. 4

Day 70

1. 1st
2. 17
3. 9
4. All even numbers should be colored.
5. 
6. apple
7. a backpack
8. 78

Day 71

1. 38
2. 14
3. 9
4. 19
5. brick
6. 1 hour
7. 4
8. 99 – 56 = 43 or 99 – 43 = 56

Day 72

1. tens
2. 14
3. 12
4. – or +
5. rhombus or parallelogram
6. The longer stick should be circled.
7. Brenda
8. July 16th

ANSWER KEY *(cont.)*

Day 73

1. $\frac{2}{8}$ or $\frac{1}{4}$
2. 11
3. 5
4. 5
5. true
6. 2
7. Marshall: 58
   Jose: 46
   Mitch: 52
   Esteban: 31
   Amar: 79
8. 24

Day 74

1. no
2. 9
3. 6
4. 8
5.  2 lines of symmetry should be drawn.
6. 7
7. 2 years old
8. 15 books

Day 75

1. 77
2. 5
3. 10
4. 2, 3
5. false
6. 8
7. Ginny
8. swimming pool

Day 76

1. 235
2. 18
3. 9
4. 7
5. 5
6. April
7. 15
8. 4

Day 77

1. <
2. 13
3. 8
4. 9
5. 4
6. 5
7. 13
8. 48 – 32 = 16

Day 78

1. 1 part should be colored.
2. 12
3. 8
4. 8
5. block
6. more than 1 meter
7. 1
8. 940

Day 79

1. 643
2. 4
3. 3
4. 0
5. The square should be colored.
6. shorter
7. 17
8. 34

Day 80

1. 60
2. 9
3. 4
4. 9
   Month 1: 3
   Month 2: 6
   Month 3: 9
5. The rectangular prism should be circled.
6. 2; 1; 3
7. Tracy and Mike
8. 3

Day 81

1. 46
2. 13
3. 12
4. 36
5. Any face of the solid may be colored.
6. 31
7. tulip
8. 4 + 4 + 4 = 12

Day 82

1. 148
2. 6
3. 10
4. 1
5. false
6. scale
7. 16
8. 7

Day 83

1. $\frac{5}{10}$ or $\frac{1}{2}$
2. 17
3. 11
4. 5
5. 3; 3
6. 5
7. 
8. 70¢

Day 84

1. no
2. 14
3. 9
4. 8
5. second/middle fan
6. larger hexagon (left image)
7. 30
8. 20¢

ANSWER KEY *(cont.)*

Day 85

1. 90
2. 8
3. 9
4. 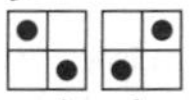
5. cylinder (right image)
6. The clock should show 2:30.
7. 3
8. 37

Day 86

1. 417
2. 14
3. 9
4. 5
5. yes
6. Thursday
7. Hiro and Becky
8. 21

Day 87

1. 39, 43, 82, 99
2. 7
3. 14
4. 4
5. The triangle should be colored.
6. 5
7. 2
8. 15 + 23 = 38 or 23 + 15 = 38

Day 88

1. 2 rectangles should be colored.
2. 15
3. 8
4. 10
5. yes
6. 2 m
7. shoulder bag
8. Wednesday

Day 89

1. forty-seven
2. 10
3. 10
4. 25
5. A square should be drawn.
6. The clock should show 10:30.
7. 28
8. 39

Day 90

1. 6th
2. 19
3. 4
4. $8.00;
   1 Week: $2.00
   2 Weeks: $4.00
   3 Weeks: $6.00
   4 Weeks: $8.00
5. Both circles should be colored.
6. butterfly
7. 6
8. 8

Day 91

1. 43
2. 4 + 4 = 8
3. 5
4. 80
5. box of chocolate
6. 11:30
7. Tanya: 5
   Daniel: 4
   Lauren: 7
8. 15 feet

Day 92

1. tens
2. 17
3. 7
4. +
5. 2 triangles should be circled.
6. less than 1 hour
7. 3 years older
8. 61

Day 93

1. $\frac{1}{4}$
2. 22
3. 11
4. 0
5. true
6. 3
7. 1 more fish
8. 3, 4, 6, 34, 36, 43, 46, 63, 64

Day 94

1. 9 groups of 2 circles should be circled.
2. 17
3. 13
4. 25
5. 
6. 6
7. 3
8. 16

Day 95

1. 45
2. 20
3. 1
4. boy, girl
5. cone (left image)
6. 2
7. 24 tally marks
8. 4

Day 96

1. 356
2. 4 + 4 + 4 = 12
3. 7
4. 6
5. 4
6. August
7. 4
8. 98

ANSWER KEY *(cont.)*

Day 97

1. >
2. 24
3. 59
4. 5
5. parallelogram (center image)
6. the solid on the left
7. 21
8. 18 inches

Day 98

1. 1 triangle should be colored.
2. 22
3. 11
4. 14
5. the jar
6. the hot air balloon
7. baseball
8. 5

Day 99

1. 272
2. 8
3. 6
4. 28
5. A triangle should be drawn.
6. longer
7. 79
8. a circle and an oval

Day 100

1. 3
2. 22
3. 6
4. $32.00
5. rhombus (right image)
6. pineapple
7. 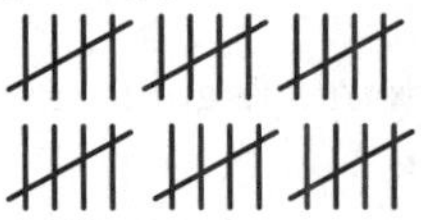
8. 8:00 P.M.

Day 101

1. 64
2. 3 + 3 + 3 = 9
3. 7
4. 62
5. triangular pyramid
6. 1 hour
7. staying home
8. 78

Day 102

1. 92
2. 23
3. 14
4. 7
5. oval
6. The pencil
7. 20
8. 8

Day 103

1. $\frac{6}{12}$ or $\frac{1}{2}$
2. 24
3. 12
4. 7
5. false
6. summer
7. hamsters and cats
8. 24 + 58 = 82, or 58 + 24 = 82

Day 104

1. 3 groups of 3 circles should be circled.
2. 23
3. 21
4. 73
5.  2 lines of symmetry
6. 8
7. $10
8. 30

Day 105

1. 84
2. 7
3. 13
4. B, B
5. 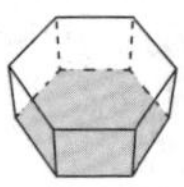 Either base may be colored.
6. The clock should show 8:30.
7. February
8. 33

Day 106

1. 582
2. 23
3. 23
4. 9
5. 6
6. Sunday
7. 2
8. 35

Day 107

1. 176, 149, 73, 43
2. 31
3. 9
4. +
5. 5
6. 5
7. 40
8. 19°F

Day 108

1. 1 rectangle should be colored.
2. 33
3. 2
4. 3
5. the plate
6. the stool
7. Alison
8. 36

ANSWER KEY *(cont.)*

Day 109

1. ninety-six
2. 18
3. 8
4. 82
5. Any 1 face of the prism should be colored.
6. false
7. The Tigers: 7 smiley faces
   The Jets: 6 smiley faces
   The Troopers: 5 smiley faces
8. 50

Day 110

1. 2nd
2. 33
3. 52
4. 3, 6, 9, 12, 15, 18, 21, 24, 27, 30, 33, 36, 39, 42, 45, and 48
5. square (top left image)
6. sock (center image)
7. Rory
8. 347

Day 111

1. 83
2. 9
3. 8
4. 91
5. no
6. 6 hours
7. 13
8. 43

Day 112

1. 60
2. 32
3. 19
4. 9
5. hexagon (left image)
6. less than 1 hour
7. Sunday
8. 4

Day 113

1. $\frac{4}{12}$ or $\frac{1}{3}$
2. 94
3. 16
4. 4
5. triangular prism (right image)
6. 2
7. 16
8. 47

Day 114

1. 3 groups of 4 should be circled.
2. 78
3. 4
4. 2
5. a fork
6. 5
7. no
8. 75¢

Day 115

1. 14
2. 8
3. 16
4. 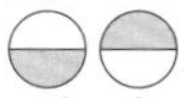
5. cylinder (right image)
6. 8
7. yes
8. 19

Day 116

1. 194
2. 70
3. 10
4. 8
5. no
6. November
7. swimming
8. 36

Day 117

1. $>$
2. 56
3. 16
4. 7
5. The triangle should be colored.
6. 4
7. 9
8. 12

Day 118

1. 2 rectangles should be colored.
2. 43
3. 5
4. 8
5. yes
6. less than 1 meter
7. 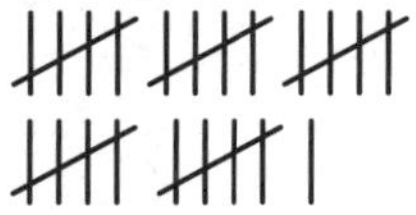
8. 4

Day 119

1. fifty-three
2. 12
3. 24
4. 37
5. A rectangle should be drawn.
6. the fox
7. 3
8. 18

Day 120

1. 20
2. 81
3. 11
4. 60
5. pyramid (right image)
6. cup
7. 20
8. 49 – 23 = 26 or
   49 – 26 = 23

ANSWER KEY *(cont.)*

Day 121
1. 73
2. 6
3. 24
4. 45
5. the ball
6. 30
7. 1
8. 3:30 P.M.

Day 122
1. 150
2. 73
3. 10
4. – or +
5. true
6. The longer bar should be circled.
7. $5.00
8. 75

Day 123
1. $\frac{1}{2}$ or one-half
2. 12
3. 43
4. 5
5. false
6. 3
7. $8.00
8. 84

Day 124
1. 2 groups of 3 should be circled.
2. 82
3. 4
4. 28
5.  A vertical line of symmetry should be drawn the center of the bear.
6. The larger rectangle should be colored.
7. 20
8. 30 feet

Day 125
1. 20
2. 10
3. 25
4. 
5. cone (right image)
6. The clock should read 4:30.
7. 4
8. 5

Day 126
1. 6; 6
2. 52
3. 26
4. 8
5. none or zero
6. May
7. 14
8. 73 + 17 = 90

Day 127
1. 473, 552, 791, 827
2. 96
3. 10
4. 5
5. The quadrilateral should be colored.
6. 5
7. 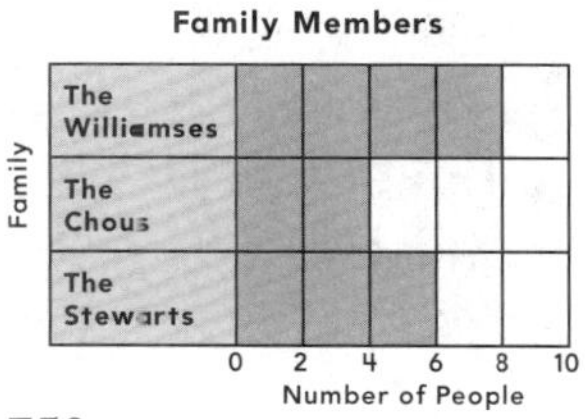

8. 750

Day 128
1. 3 cups should be circled.
2. thirty-eight
3. 17
4. 1
5. the basket
6. 1 m
7. no
8. 26

Day 129
1. sixty-two
2. 74
3. 8
4. 43
5. A square should be drawn.
6. The clock should read 2:00.
7. 3
8. 60

Day 130
1. 4th
2. 33
3. 13
4. 20
5. 2 triangles (first and last images)
6. cup
7. 18
8. 258

Day 131
1. 217
2. 12
3. 3
4. 49
5. Any one surface may be colored.
6. 2:00
7. 8
8. Ralph: scooter
   Ian: skateboard
   Darren: bike

Day 132
1. 80
2. 85
3. 5
4. 8
5. octagon
6. the trash
7. 7
8. no

ANSWER KEY *(cont.)*

Day 133
1. $\frac{1}{4}$
2. 61
3. 13
4. 2
5. false
6. 1.5 or $1\frac{1}{2}$
7. 30
8. cone, sphere, cylinder

Day 134
1. 1 group of 5; 2 left over
2. 50
3. 2
4. 91
5. 
6. 16
7. 2
8. 50¢

Day 135
1. 12
2. 13
3. 39
4. → ↓
5. Any face (triangular side) of the solid may be colored.
6. 4
7. 16
8. 62¢

Day 136
1. 3 tens; 1 one
2. 37
3. 46
4. 5
5. 4
6. Friday
7. 
8. 8

Day 137
1. 40
2. 130
3. 11
4. +
5. 6
6. 4
7. 16
8. 35 + 21 = 56 or 21 + 35 = 56

Day 138
1. 2 hats should be circled.
2. 76
3. 33
4. 16
5. the ball
6. the dinosaur
7. 10
8. 5:00 P.M.

Day 139
1. 485
2. 84
3. 27
4. 55
5. hexagon (left image)
6. taller
7. hamster and cat
8. 44

Day 140
1. third
2. 88
3. 41
4. 90 books
5. rhombus (center image)
6. the chicken
7. $40.00
8. 46

Day 141
1. 452
2. 12
3. 17
4. 84
5. quadrilateral or trapezoid
6. 2 hours
7. 4
8. 735

Day 142
1. 90
2. 128
3. 25
4. 9
5. octagon
6. the mug
7. 6
8. bathing suit

Day 143
1. $\frac{1}{2}$
2. 79
3. 44
4. 1
5. false
6. fall
7. 4
8. 6 (The different combinations are 347, 374, 473, 743, 734, and 437.)

Day 144
1. 4 groups of 3 circles should be circled.
2. 99
3. 35
4. 18
5. vertical line
6. 8
7. 1
8. 21

ANSWER KEY *(cont.)*

Day 145

1. 14
2. 12
3. 17
4. A circle should be drawn.
5. cylinder (left image)
6. The clock should read 10:30.
7. Favorite Game

	Jan	Ben	Tori
Jump rope	X	X	X
Kickball		X	X

8. 4

Day 146

1. 5 tens; 7 ones
2. 89
3. 12
4. 11
5. yes
6. September
7. 5
8. 698

Day 147

1. 827, 672, 439, 281
2. 98
3. 49
4. 2
5. The triangle should be colored.
6. the 5-cube solid (right image)
7. Karen
8. 6 + 6 = 12

Day 148

1. 4 balloons should be circled.
2. 98
3. 21
4. 15
5. yes
6. the drum
7. yes
8. 39

Day 149

1. seventeen
2. 87
3. 31
4. 46
5. A hexagon should be drawn.
6. The clock should read 1:00.
7. 20
8. sphere and cone

Day 150

1. 16th
2. 87
3. 11
4. The following squares should be colored: 4, 8, 12, 16, 20, 24, 28, 32, 36, 40, 48
5. 2 hexagons (top left and bottom center)
6. The ball should be circled.
7. 8
8. 48

Day 151

1. 444
2. 13
3. 24
4. 49
5. Any 1 surface should be colored.
6. 31
7. yes
8. 66

Day 152

1. 50
2. 99
3. 24
4. 6
5. The triangle should be circled.
6. ruler
7. 2
8. 65

Day 153

1. $\frac{1}{2}$
2. 89
3. 11
4. 7
5. true
6. 4
7. rose
8. 33 + 56 = 89
   56 + 33 = 89
   89 – 33 = 56
   89 – 56 = 33

Day 154

1. 3 groups of 2 circles should be circled.
2. 59
3. 22
4. 37
5. curtain or window
6. The boys' room sign (left image)
7. 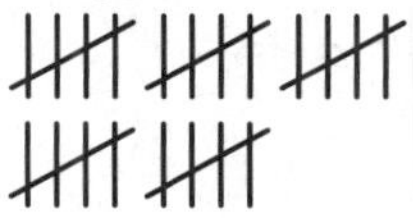
8. 46

Day 155

1. 28
2. 11
3. 50
4. X, Y
5. 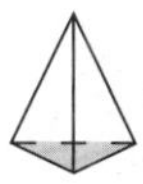 The triangular base should be colored.
6. 10
7. 42
8. 6:30 A.M.

Day 156

1. 90 + 5
2. 99
3. 24
4. 7
5. 3
6. Saturday
7. 40
8. 620

ANSWER KEY *(cont.)*

Day 157

1. >
2. 98
3. 21
4. +
5. The circle and the oval should be colored.
6. 7
7. fish
8. 2

Day 158

1. 1 fox should be circled.
2. 86
3. 11
4. 2
5. the ball
6. more than 1 meter
7. $20
8. 6

Day 159

1. eighty-five
2. 118
3. 22
4. 80
5. A circle should be drawn.
6. true
7. 18
8. 555

Day 160

1. 21st
2. 16
3. 15
4. 3 weeks
5. The rectangular prism should be circled.
6. the turtle
7. 6
8. yes

Day 161

1. 662
2. 103
3. 28
4. 70
5. cube or rectangular prism
6. 8:30
7. $80
8. 15¢

Day 162

1. 80
2. 73
3. 9
4. 7
5. circle
6. the can of peaches
7. 19
8. 5

Day 163

1. $\frac{3}{6}$ or $\frac{1}{2}$
2. 91
3. 48
4. 7
5. 6; 6
6. 1
7. Chu: 5 flowers
   Diggs: 6 flowers
8. 62

Day 164

1. 5
2. 93
3. 15
4. 47
5. 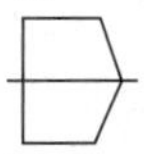 1 horizontal line should be drawn.
6. 10
7. no
8. 975

Day 165

1. 36
2. 19
3. 26
4. ←
5. cone (left image)
6. The clock should read 12:30.
7. 2
8. 5

Day 166

1. 8 tens, 0 ones
2. 95
3. 56
4. 9
5. 4
6. January
7. $60
8. 89 – 47 = 42

Day 167

1. 73, 173, 473, 673
2. 71
3. 19
4. 8
5. 8
6. 5
7. 22
8. 24 edges

Day 168

1. 5 lions should be circled.
2. 81
3. 18
4. 10
5. the toothpaste box
6. 2 m
7. 12
8. 5:00

Day 169

1. twenty-nine
2. 85
3. 9
4. 52
5. false
6. The clock should read 7:30.
7. 4
8. 72

ANSWER KEY *(cont.)*

Day 170
1. 11th
2. ninety-two
3. 19
4. 21
5. trapezoid (center image)
6. The cupcake should be circled.
7. swimming
8. 997

Day 171
1. 840
2. 15
3. 59
4. 74
5. Any 1 rectangular surface should be colored.
6. 2 hours
7. 5
8. 33

Day 172
1. 30
2. 71
3. 8
4. + or –
5. oval
6. smaller cup (left image)
7. 
8. 15

Day 173
1. $\frac{4}{8}$ or $\frac{1}{2}$
2. 104
3. 15
4. 14
5. true
6. spring
7. 40
8. $4\frac{1}{2}$ hours

Day 174
1. 6 groups of 3 circles should be circled.
2. 100
3. 8
4. 97
5.  2 lines of symmetry should be drawn.
6. 8
7. $15.00
8. 22

Day 175
1. 22
2. 19
3. 18
4. 
5. 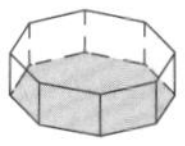 One of the octagonal bases should be colored.
6. 1
7. $65
8. yes

Day 176
1. 84
2. 101
3. 33
4. 7
5. no
6. Wednesday
7. 2
8. $20.00

Day 177
1. =
2. 65
3. 27
4. 3
5. The triangle should be colored.
6. 4
7. $24
8. 21 feet

Day 178
1. 3 baseballs should be colored.
2. 98
3. 24
4. 15
5. yes
6. 60
7. 160
8. 99; 999; 10; 100

Day 179
1. thirty-one
2. 101
3. 49
4. 68
5. rectangular prism (right image)
6. the boat
7. week 3
8. $4.00

Day 180
1. 23rd
2. 73
3. 9
4. 6, 12, 18, 24, 30, 36, 42, 48
5. true
6. cup
7. 16
8. $3.00

REFERENCES CITED

Kilpatrick, J., J. Swafford, and B. Findell, eds. 2001. *Adding it up: Helping children learn mathematics.* Washington, DC: National Academies Press.

Marzano, R. 2010. When practice makes perfect…sense. *Educational Leadership* 68 (3): 81–83.

McIntosh, M. E. 1997. Formative assessment in mathematics. *Clearing House* 71 (2): 92–96.

DIGITAL RESOURCES

Accessing the Digital Resources

The digital resources can be downloaded by following these steps:

1. Go to www.tcmpub.com/digital
2. Use the ISBN number to redeem the digital resources.
3. Respond to the question using the book.
4. Follow the prompts on the Content Cloud website to sign in or create a new account.
5. The content redeemed will now be on your My Content screen. Click on the product to look through the digital resources. All resources are available for download. Select files can be previewed, opened, and shared. For questions and assistance with your license key card, or to report a lost card, please contact Shell Education.

   mail: customerservice@tcmpub.com
   phone: 800-858-7339

CONTENTS OF THE DIGITAL RESOURCES

Teacher Resources

- Practice Page Item Analysis Chart
- Student Item Analysis Chart

Student Resources

- Practice Pages

NOTES